FAKING IT

FAKING IT

The Quest
for Authenticity
in Popular Music

HUGH BARKER
and YUVAL TAYLOR

 W. W. NORTON & COMPANY ✦ NEW YORK LONDON

Manufacturing by The Haddon Craftsmen, Inc.
Book design by Lovedog Studio
Production manager: Anna Oler

Library of Congress Cataloging-in-Publication Data

Barker, Hugh.
Faking it : the quest for authenticity in popular music /
Hugh Barker and Yuval Taylor.
p. cm.
Includes bibliographical references and index.
ISBN-13: 978-0-393-06078-2 (hardcover)
ISBN-10: 0-393-06078-0 (hardcover)
1. Popular musc—United States—20th century—History and criticism. 2.
Music—Performance—United States. 3. Authenticity (Philosophy) 4.
Popular music—Social aspects. I. Taylor, Yuval. II. Title.
ML3477.B33 2007
781.6409—dc22   2006039754

W. W Norton & Company, Inc.
500 Fifth Avenue, New York, N.Y. 10110
www.wwnorton.com

W. W. Norton & Company Ltd.
Castle House, 75/76 Wells Street, London W1T 3QT

1 2 3 4 5 6 7 8 9 0

CONTENTS

INTRODUCTION

WHEN WE LISTEN TO popular music, some songs strike us as "real" and others as "fake." This book explores that distinction, and how, especially in the last fifty years, the quest for authenticity, for the "real," has become a dominant factor in musical taste. Whether it be the folklorist's search for forgotten bluesmen, the rock critic's elevation of raw power over sophistication, or the importance of bullet wounds to the careers of hip-hop artists, the aesthetic of the "authentic musical experience," with its rejection of music that is labeled contrived, pretentious, artificial, or overly commercial, has played a major role in forming musical tastes and canons, with wide-ranging consequences.

What do we mean when we call something authentic? A lot of things, as it turns out, but the word seems to be defined primarily in opposition to "faking it." In a KISS concert, the band wears makeup and plays songs about people they pretend to be, all with the explicit aim of making money rather than telling the truth about themselves or the world they live in. Such a performance can be wildly entertaining, but it's not considered authentic.

When people say a musical performance or recording is authentic, they might refer to representational authenticity, or music that is exactly what it says it is—unlike, say, Milli Vanilli posing as singers, which they weren't. They might refer to cultural authenticity, or music that reflects a cultural tradition—the traditional black guitarist and singer Mississippi John Hurt's version of "Stagger Lee," an old African American song about an outlaw, is more culturally authentic than the Grateful Dead's. They might refer to personal authenticity, or music that reflects the person or people who are making it—when Ozzy Osbourne sings "Iron Man," he tells us nothing about his own life, but when Loretta Lynn sings "Coal Miner's Daughter," she tells us a lot.

Every performance is to some degree "faked"—nobody goes out on stage and sings about exactly what they did and felt that day. Authenticity is an absolute, a goal that can never be fully attained, a quest. Sincerity and autobiography are techniques one can employ in the service of personal authenticity, just as using traditional instruments and singing old songs are techniques one can use in the service of cultural authenticity. But it's important to distinguish the means from the end.

This quest for authenticity has inspired countless musicians to make heartfelt and often groundbreaking music, from Jimmie Rodgers, a pioneer of country music, to Kurt Cobain, a pioneer of alternative rock. On the other hand, some great music—including entire genres such as rockabilly, Bubblegum, and disco—has been scorned as inauthentic. At times, the need to "keep it real" has limited the kinds of music that musicians aspire to make and that critics and listeners appreciate.

White blues fans, for example, redefined the genre in the name of authenticity to exclude anything too jazzy or upbeat, thus enforcing a snobbish and racist exclusion of certain blues artists from the canon because they were too sophisticated. Instead, they lauded the most primitive blues artists they could find, such as John Lee Hooker, from whom blacks turned away. In this way, the quest for authenticity did tremendous damage to the blues by codifying certain traditions and limiting innovation.

Now, after punk, house, grunge, garage, and hip-hop, ideas of authenticity have seeped into even such transparently "inauthentic" genres as heavy metal (Metallica), techno (Moby), and showtunes (*Rent*). Especially in the music aimed at white teenage males, authenticity is seen as the sine qua non of artistic success. It is rare to come across a songwriter, rock singer, or rapper these days who does not aim to "keep it real" for his audience, or who doesn't talk about the difference between making it and selling out. Listeners too are acutely conscious of how much the artists they admire are faking it. It seems that one of the job requirements for a popular musician these days is convincing your audience that you're not the phony celebrity you appear to be. Case in point: Jennifer Lopez's biggest hit ran, "Don't be fooled by the rocks that I got—I'm just Jenny from the block." Even Donna Summer, the queen of disco and a brilliant musical innovator, castigates her former self as "fake" in her autobiography, *Ordinary Girl*.

Of course, for many there is no distinction between real and fake: witness Courtney Love's statement, "I fake it so real that I'm beyond fake." In certain subcultures, being "natural" is either suspect or out of the question, and being theatrical is the only real possibility. For many academics as well, everything is more or less "constructed," and, as the Beatles said, "Nothing is real."

But while we don't claim that the distinctions we make in this book will apply to everyone, being authentic, or real, has been important to a large number of musicians and their fans, and that's where this book comes in. A number of other books have praised the virtues of authenticity and damned the fakes and the sellouts, but it's surprising that no single book has ever addressed the subject in all its complexity or shown how the quest for authenticity has shaped the music we listen to. It's as if the concept of realism in art had never been fully addressed—as if the only books on the subject praised verisimilitude. The question of authenticity in popular music is not only fundamental to understanding the music's history but fundamental to thinking about, listening to, and performing it as well.

Faking It tackles this question by examining, in detail, ten turning points in music history, at most of which the musicians were faced with a choice: fake it or keep it real. Why were these choices made and what were the consequences? We start with Kurt Cobain's choice of a Leadbelly song to close his career, and then go in chronological order from early twentieth-century field recordings to Moby's use of them at the turn of the twenty-first century. Along the way, we discuss the birth of modern country music, the moment Elvis reinvented rock'n'roll, the Monkees' decision to actually play their instruments, the defining moment of disco with a seventeen-minute faked orgasm, the "public image" of punk rock, and much more.

ALTHOUGH THIS BOOK is an entirely collaborative effort, in which we read, commented on, and revised each other's chapters, for the sake of clarity we'd like to note that the primary author of chapters 5, 7, and 8 is Hugh Barker, and the primary author of chapters 2, 3, 4, and 6 is Yuval Taylor; this introduction and chapters 1, 9, and 10 were composed in tandem.

The authors would like to thank their wives and children for their patience and generosity. We would also like to thank Jake Austen, Alan Barker, Ken Burke, Stephen Calt, Paul Elie, Andy Newman, Duncan Proudfoot, David Scott, and Elijah Wald, all of whom looked over portions of this book and gave us valuable feedback. Finally, we would like to thank our agent, William Clark, and our editor, Amy Cherry, who have helped to shape this book in significant ways, vastly improving it in the process.

FAKING IT

CHAPTER ONE

WHERE DID YOU SLEEP LAST NIGHT?

Nirvana, Leadbelly, and the Allure of the Primeval

New York, November 18, 1993

It would be a tragedy to spend your whole life
desperately wanting to be something that you
already were all along.

DAVID BERMAN, "Clip-On Tie"

LIT BLACK CANDLES AND hundreds of lilies decorated the
stage. The television lights burned bright.

Nirvana's *MTV Unplugged* special had started tentatively,
with Kurt Cobain clearly nervous, and the band members and
additional musicians looking ill at ease in the funereal stage

décor. But their confidence—and the audience's appreciation—had built steadily, and the performance had turned into a success.

As a finale, Cobain led the musicians through a chilling, passionate, but peculiar dirge in waltz time, first introducing it as a song by "my favorite performer," Leadbelly, a black singer lionized by left-wing white folk-music fans in the 1930s, '40s, and '50s. He then refused to return to the stage for an encore. As a result, "Where Did You Sleep Last Night" was the last song he performed that night. Technically, it may not have been his swan song—there was one more unfinished recording session in Seattle in January—but it was so powerful and emotionally charged it could have been.

Nirvana had always appeared absolutely genuine in everything they did, and this was one of their attractions for an audience jaded with the contemporary music scene. Cobain's songs were often autobiographical in a fragmented, allusive way, but they always seemed highly personal. His words not only reflected his pain, but they were sung with a raw, stripped-down passion. He had gone to tremendous lengths to "keep it real," to rebel against commercial expectations, and to expose his problems to the public.

As Cobain looked out at the *Unplugged* audience who, unusually for a Nirvana gig, were seated, visible, and unnervingly close to the band, he was aware that they knew a great deal about his private life, both from what he had chosen to reveal and from what had been made public without his consent. When he mentioned "warm milk and laxatives, cherry-flavored antacids" and muttered "I have very bad posture" in "Pennyroyal Tea," they knew he was talking about his health and drug problems. If every detail wasn't explicit, they could fill in the gaps because of the gothic soap opera that his life as half of a celebrity couple had become. The normal embarrassment of being exposed on a stage, which Nirvana could cover up in noise and aggression, would have been magnified by the naked circumstances of this performance. Most musicians have had nightmares about finding themselves on a stage alone and unprotected. It's no surprise that Cobain was slightly nervous.

His solo performance of "Pennyroyal Tea" marked the moment the *Unplugged* performance moved into a higher gear. His guitar playing was clumsy in places and he missed a chord or two, but the stark emotion in his voice was inescapable. A couple of songs later, he performed "Polly," the story of a rape. The song is shocking not just because it is sung from the rapist's point of view but because of the boredom the narrator conveys. Cobain was clearly not drawing directly from personal experience, but the song's nihilism and desensitization seemed overpowering. Even this extreme a song was emotionally honest about a disturbing state of mind, and his listeners recognized and acclaimed this.

The truth is always complicated, however, and between Cobain and his public persona were conflicts and contradictions. In his interviews, and even in his autobiographical songs, he was prone to embellishment and self-mythologizing: for example, he claimed to have swapped his mother's exboyfriend's guns for his first guitar, but he'd had a guitar for a long time by then; and he claimed to have lived under a bridge during his homeless days, almost certainly an exaggeration. His anticommercial stance was at odds with his long-standing desire for success, and the tension between these two led him to alternately celebrate and despise his achievement. When he was younger, he had concealed his commercial ambitions and his liking for "uncool" bands from his punk friends in order to retain his perceived integrity—for instance, he didn't mention in those circles that he wanted his own band to be "bigger than REM or U2." Later, in the same spirit, he castigated himself publicly for selling out while continuing to strive for further success: when he appeared on the cover of *Rolling Stone*, it was in a T-shirt reading "Corporate Magazines Still Suck." In the interview inside, he said, "I don't blame the average 17-year-old punk-rock kid for calling me a sellout. I understand that. Maybe when they grow up a little bit, they'll realize there's more things to life than living out your rock & roll identity so righteously." In the same interview, however, he criticized Pearl Jam, who were currently rivaling Nirvana's success, in similar terms: "I would love to be erased from my association with that band and other corporate bands like the Nymphs and a few other felons. I do feel a duty to warn the kids of false music that's claiming to be underground. They're jumping on the alternative bandwagon."

Success in the music business is rarely achieved without minor compromises and adjustments of attitude along the way. Kurt Cobain, like many other artists, wanted the fans to see a particular version of his self—something more like the person he had been before he started to succeed than the person he was now. Even though he was more obdurate and successful at preserving his self-respect than many musicians, he still felt compromised. He defined honesty as not putting on an act, and felt that performing when he no longer felt enthusiastic about it was a shameful lie.

But for all the complications, Cobain's desire for authenticity, real and perceived, was matched by that of his fans, who saw him as the real thing in a fake business. It was only appropriate, then—if somewhat ironic—that his swan song was performed on *MTV Unplugged*. Launched four years earlier and continuing to this day, *Unplugged* was conceived as a response to the public perception that the contemporary music scene was obsessed with image rather than content. MTV had done more than anyone to foster this perception—the advent of twenty-four-hour music programming and the massive influence the station attained in the 1980s had multiplied the power of video to the point where managers spent more time arguing over the video budget for their bands than they did worrying about the music. So for MTV to present itself as the guardian of real music was both unexpected and bizarre.

The idea behind the show was to strip away as much of the technical and studio assistance that protected the artist as possible. The artists would perform their songs, preferably with only acoustic instruments, or at least (as with Nirvana) in a quieter, more stripped-down form; the audience could then judge whether or not these were musicians and singers who could really perform. Nothing was really unplugged—not only were there electric instruments, microphones, and other sound output and recording devices, but there was, of course, all the other electronic video equipment that television can't exist without. But in an age when tracks are created on computers, all instruments and sounds can be sampled and artificially modified, and vocal performances are pasted together from banks of tape using autotuning to correct imperfections, people want to see artists in "real" conditions. Some performers have thrived more than others in the artificially intimate conditions. For instance, Tony Bennett gave an old pro's performance that made full use of his constricted band, while REM, on their first appearance in 1991, looked like buskers merely pretending to be REM.

Nirvana had little to prove in terms of authenticity, although it was fascinating to see how they would respond to an environment that robbed them of the sheer volume of their live gigs. In the end, they succeeded, and their performance became a classic recording, released shortly after Cobain's death. The stage decorations depicted on the cover and the preoccupation with death apparent in his choice of songs made it an eerie record to listen to so soon after the tragedy.

So given the circumstances, what was it about "Where Did You Sleep Last Night" that fascinated Kurt Cobain and led him to play it on this occasion? Why did he choose that song as his closing statement? Why did he call Leadbelly his "favorite performer"? And what echoes of bygone quests for authenticity can we find in all this?

"WHERE DID YOU Sleep Last Night" is Leadbelly's version of a song commonly known as "In the Pines," which probably dates back to the 1870s and has been recorded hundreds of times by performers in almost every genre. As Dolly Parton told Eric Weisbard for the *New York Times*, "The song has been handed down through many generations of my family. I don't ever remember not hearing it and not singing it. Any time there were more than three or four songs to be sung, 'In the Pines' was one of them. It's easy to play, easy to sing, great harmonies and very emotional. The perfect song for simple people."

Kurt Cobain was not such a simple person, although he sometimes liked to pretend he was. He had been performing the song since the late 1980s, and had accompanied Mark Lanegan, the leader of the Seattle rock group Screaming Trees, on guitar for a version on Lanegan's 1990 album *The Winding Sheet.* At one point the two had tried to start an off-shoot band and had recorded three songs, all by Leadbelly, before other projects prevented them from continuing, and only this song was released. Lanegan owned a copy of Leadbelly's original 78-rpm release of the song, recorded in 1944; Lanegan and Cobain probably listened to it many times. Cobain had also performed the song with Courtney Love at Hollywood's Club Lingerie, on the only occasion the two sang together in public.

The song is about a girl who goes into the pines, "where the sun don't ever shine," after her husband's decapitation by a train. This fits well with Cobain's fascination with death and other grisly subjects, and is given an additional, distressing resonance in retrospect by the near-decapitation caused by the gun he used to kill himself. Throughout his last year he made many mentions of suicide and guns, and it is clear that the idea of killing himself was in his mind long before he carried out the plan.

Cobain made a few modifications to Leadbelly's version: he changed the first chord of each verse from major to minor (occasionally adding a fourth), thus imbuing the song with an even more melancholy tone; he slowed the tempo way down, doubling the song's length and also increasing its sadness; he changed the repeated words "black girl" to "my girl," thus erasing Leadbelly's racial perspective (he also made a few other insignificant lyrical changes, such as changing "driver's wheel" to "driving wheel"); after singing all the verses of Leadbelly's version, he repeated some of them, first sotto voce, then raising his voice an octave (a trick one can trace back to Skip James's 1931 "I'm So Glad"), lending the song an air of complete desperation because of his straining to hit the high notes; and he sang the song's last words ("I'll shiver the whole night through") in half-time, his voice completely hoarse and ragged, thus adding an undeniably dramatic flourish to what was, in the original, only plain repetition.

The result is a terribly haunting and emotional performance. Cobain's anguish is unmistakable, yet there's no self-pity, as in, say, the words to "Pennyroyal Tea." His torment takes on a broader meaning because of the strangeness of the lyrics and the vivid imagery: "His head was found in the driving wheel, but his body never was found"; "In the pines, in the pines, where the sun don't ever shine." The combination of Cobain's passion and the rich cultural heritage of "Where Did You Sleep Last Night" made for an unforgettable production.

THE BLACK GUITARIST and singer Huddie Ledbetter, more commonly known as Lead Belly or Leadbelly, became famous in part because his repertoire was so large and varied. He was considered a kind of repository of American folk music, having learned many of his songs from prisoners, both black and white, while serving time for murder. Folklorists John and Alan Lomax helped him when he was released from jail in

1934, and then took him on tour; playing in concert halls and folk-song circles, he was billed as an exemplar of the riches of black song. Never mind that Leadbelly enjoyed no success whatsoever with his African American peers (the few "race" records he cut for ARC sold poorly, and his stint at Harlem's Apollo Theater was a complete flop); he was lionized by white folk singers, collectors, and Communist Party members, with all of whom he had very little in common.

Although Leadbelly had considerable talents—a powerful, dynamic, expressive voice; a resonant, confident, and energetic guitar style; a prodigious musical memory; an astonishingly varied and rich repertoire; a strong sense of rhythm—his songs didn't *swing*. Not at all coincidentally, Leadbelly achieved fame by playing primarily to white audiences. In some ways the scenario of John Lomax bringing his charge on tour was reminiscent of the pre–Civil War career of Blind Tom, the Negro slave and piano prodigy whose owners made of him one of the biggest performing sensations in American history. But crucial to Blind Tom's success was his sophistication, while crucial to Leadbelly's was his lack thereof.

Perhaps another comparison is more apt, the one Nolan Porterfield makes in his biography of John Lomax: Leadbelly was seen as a real-life King Kong. The movie *King Kong* had been a huge hit just two years earlier; as Porterfield writes, "a savage being, primitive and violent, is discovered by a white man, put in bondage, transported to Manhattan, and placed on public display."

Indeed, whites saw in Leadbelly, who had not only been convicted of murder in 1918 but of attempted murder in 1930, the epitome of the "primitive"—the violent, primordial black man who sings old, deep, unfathomable songs directly from his soul. Back in the eighteenth century, Jean-Jacques Rousseau popularized the idea of the "native" as a "noble savage," the embodiment of Western virtues, uncorrupted by civilization; the concept was applied equally to Polynesians (see Melville's *Typee*), American Indians, and Africans, enslaved or not. But by the twentieth century, with the influence of Darwin and Freud, it was primarily the Negro who had become idealized, and this time as the primitive—brute, savage, untamable—pure id, and therefore profound. You can see this idealization in the vogue for African art, in Picasso's *Demoiselles d'Avignon*, in the career of Josephine Baker, and perhaps most vividly in Vachel Lindsay's 1914 "The Congo: A Study of the Negro Race," the poem that made him famous. In its three sections, entitled "Their Basic Savagery," "Their Irrepressible High Spirits," and "The Hope of Their Religion," Lindsay tried to collapse all distinctions between Vaudeville cakewalks, Harlem society, and the Congo. He began:

> Fat black bucks in a wine-barrel room,
> Barrel-house kings, with feet unstable,
> Sagged and reeled and pounded on the table,
> Pounded on the table,
> Beat an empty barrel with the handle of a broom,
> Hard as they were able,
> Boom, boom, BOOM,
> With a silk umbrella and the handle of a broom,
> Boomlay, boomlay, boomlay, BOOM.
> THEN I had religion, THEN I had a vision.
> I could not turn from their revel in derision.
> THEN I SAW THE CONGO, CREEPING THROUGH THE BLACK,

CUTTING THROUGH THE FOREST WITH A GOLDEN TRACK.

Then along that riverbank
A thousand miles
Tattooed cannibals danced in files;
Then I heard the boom of the blood-lust song
And a thigh-bone beating on a tin-pan gong.

. . . .

A roaring, epic, rag-time tune
From the mouth of the Congo
To the Mountains of the Moon.

Lindsay here captured the rock'n'roll aesthetic forty years before its invention. This wasn't the same as the racist slander you found in the mouths of politicians of the time. This was praise, worship—*primitivism*, pure and simple.

In the same vein, the 1935 *New York Herald Tribune* article that made Leadbelly famous was headlined, LOMAX ARRIVES WITH LEADBELLY, NEGRO MINSTREL. SWEET SINGER OF THE SWAMPLANDS HERE TO DO A FEW TUNES BETWEEN HOMICIDES; *Time* magazine's review was headlined MURDEROUS MINSTREL; *Life* magazine's was headlined BAD NIGGER MAKES GOOD MINSTREL; and the *Brooklyn Eagle* referred to him as a VIRTUOSO OF KNIFE AND GUITAR. Upon Leadbelly's return to the New York stage a year later, the *Herald Tribune* trumped itself with the following headline: AIN'T IT A PITY? BUT LEADBELLY JINGLES INTO CITY. EBON SHUFFLIN' ANTHOLOGY OF SWAMPLAND FOLKSONG INHALES GIN, EXHALES RHYME.

It is true, of course, that without Leadbelly, who served as an archive of a long oral tradition in danger of disappearing, our shared musical heritage would be vastly poorer; he helped inspire not only the American folk movement of the '50s (the Weavers' massive hit "Goodnight Irene") but the UK skiffle movement (Lonnie Donegan's "Rock Island Line"). Later songs drawn from his repertoire include Ike and Tina Turner's "Midnight Special," Creedence Clearwater Revival's "Cotton Fields," Led Zeppelin's "Gallows Pole," and Ram Jam's "Black Betty." But when Leadbelly was alive (he died in 1949), African Americans were creating much of the most sophisticated (i.e., complex, nonprimitive) music in the country, from blues to rhythm-and-blues to jazz. Unfortunately, certain whites of the period seem to have been more interested in celebrating what they considered the most primitive, elemental, and backward-looking African American musicians they could find. Apparently Leadbelly fit the bill perfectly.

One of those whites was John Lomax. Leadbelly had deep concerns over his relationship with the man, ranging from financial matters (Lomax and his son took two-thirds of Leadbelly's income, rather than the fifteen percent mandated by New York law, and paid him an "allowance") to being asked to wear prison garb for his performances rather than the suits and sharply creased shirts that he, like most professional musicians of the era, preferred. He even successfully sued Lomax for a greater share of his earnings. The great black American writer Richard Wright, who befriended Leadbelly, relied primarily on the latter's account for a profile he wrote for the *Daily Worker* in 1937, in which he called John Lomax a "southern landlord," and his touring of Leadbelly "one of the great cultural swindles in history." The left-wing paper *New Masses* similarly reproached Lomax at the time of Leadbelly's first performances, saying of him, "He embodies the slavemaster attitude intact."

But Lomax was more of a showman than a slave master: as Robert Cantwell has written, "John Lomax belonged to a tradition of . . . the medicine-show mountebank of the rural south, with his blackface banjo player and miracle cure." He presented Leadbelly as the very picture of authenticity and, in a paternal manner in keeping with that picture, kept Leadbelly away from more lucrative offers from people Lomax thought might exploit him.

Lomax's conceptions of black Americans, however, weren't that far removed from Vachel Lindsay's. And they laid the foundation for the kind of primitivism Kurt Cobain celebrated.

JOHN AND ALAN LOMAX were indisputably the twentieth century's leading collectors of what they called American folk music. As curators of the Library of Congress's Archive of American Folk Song, they contributed immeasurably to this vitally important collection. Without their work, we'd have no "Home on the Range," no "Midnight Special," no Leadbelly, no conception of African American field hollers. Yet the assumptions that informed much of their invaluable work, particularly those of the elder Lomax, are questionable at best, and pernicious at worst.

In 1947, at the age of eighty, John Lomax published an autobiography, *Adventures of a Ballad Hunter*, and opened it with these words: "My family belonged to the upper crust of the 'po' white trash.'" Lomax effectively transformed this contradiction into an ability to get along with the high and low of American society. But his father, a slaveholder who had moved from Mississippi to East Texas in part because, as he said, "I did not want my family raised in contact with the negro [*sic*]," was more "white trash" than "upper crust." And when it came to black Americans, John Lomax ended up sharing the values of both white classes.

In 1933, at the age of fifty-six, having spent much of his life studying cowboy ballads and other traditional white songs, John Lomax turned his attention to black music. His views had undergone few changes since the day, in 1904, when he attended a student concert at a Negro college and wrote disparagingly to his fiancée, "the old time negro [*sic*] trill is gone. These blacks are civilized . . . it is pitiful, pitiful." Now he and his son Alan were to set out to record "the folk songs of the Negro—songs that, in musical phrasing and in poetic content, are most unlike those of the white race, the least contaminated by white influence or by modern Negro jazz."

In order to eliminate this "white influence," Lomax and his son Alan, according to John's autobiography,

> visited groups of Negroes living in remote communities, where the population was entirely black; also plantations where in number the Negroes greatly exceeded the whites, as in the Mississippi Delta. Another source for material was the lumber camp that employed only Negro foremen and Negro laborers.
>
> However, our best field was the Southern penitentiaries. We went to all eleven of them and presented our plan to possibly 25,000 Negro convicts. . . . The Negro convicts do not eat or sleep in the same building with white prisoners. They are kept in entirely separate units; they even work separately in the fields. Thus a longtime

Negro convict, guarded by Negro trusties, may spend many years with practically no chance of hearing the white man speak or sing. Such men slough off the white idiom they may have once employed in their speech and revert more and more to the idiom of the Negro common people.

John Lomax never explains why this "white influence" would be so undesirable. Instead, Lomax wanted to hear, as he wrote of a Houston party in 1932, the "weird, almost uncanny suggestion of turgid, slow-moving rivers in African jungles"; he wanted to feel "carried across to Africa . . . as if I were listening to the tom-toms of savage blacks." In his autobiography, he comes right out and admits, "The simple directness and power of this primitive music, coupled with its descriptions of life where force and other elemental influences are dominating, impress me more deeply every time I hear it." In other words, the music that was, for Lomax, the most authentic, the most black, the most free from "white influence," was the most primitive.

Lomax seems to have been unaware that African music is far from primitive—its rhythmic sophistication is breathtaking—and that, in America, the white influence was necessarily pervasive, impossible to escape. In prison, he found what he wanted, yet it wasn't the untainted music for which he longed. There, performers had been isolated from their sources for many years and inevitably sang garbled (and simplified) versions of songs of black, white, and mixed origin that they remembered from their days of freedom long ago rather than versions that emerged from actual practice in a community setting. Not only that, but these prisoners were almost all male, and thus an entire range of songs sung more often by women was completely overlooked.

The Lomaxes were not looking for the oldest songs—they were completely open to newly created songs in their narrowly construed "folk" tradition. Rather, they were looking for the songs that struck them as most essentially "genuine Negro folk songs." In their application for a grant from the Carnegie Corporation, they wrote, "The Negro in the South is the target for such complex influences that it is hard to find genuine folk singing. . . . We propose to go where these influences are not yet dominant; where Negroes are almost entirely isolated from the whites, dependent upon the resources of their own group for amusement; where they are not only preserving a great body of traditional songs but also creating new songs in the same idiom." Needless to say, they received the grant. And their quest for "the idiom of the Negro common people" resulted in a treasure trove of songs from both races—as performed by African Americans.

When John Lomax originally came up with the idea, back in 1910, of collecting black "folk" songs, he rightly saw it as a tremendously important project: the only people who had gathered them so far were white people who "dressed them up for literary purposes" or blacks who performed them in a far more sophisticated manner than that in which they were ordinarily sung. But by 1933, quite a bit of black music had already been recorded. Why did the Lomaxes completely ignore the recordings of traditional singers such as Henry Thomas and Mississippi John Hurt? For example, only a dozen of Hurt's songs had been released. The Lomaxes could

have tried to track him down and record more, but they preferred to track down their "genuine Negro folk songs" in
places as removed as possible from the recording industry—
Southern prisons. For in prison they literally had a captive
audience, which made it far easier to persuade people to sing
for them without remuneration. In addition, prisoners were
without access to musical instruments, and the Lomaxes
were far more fascinated by a cappella songs than accompanied ones, perhaps because the instruments blacks played
were not African enough.

In this era, black prisoners were made to work, under whip
and chain, from dawn to dusk; they were fed little better than
dogs and were liable to be beaten. In the pages upon pages of
his autobiography that John Lomax devotes to some of the
worst prisons in the country, he expresses not a whit of hor-
ror or pity, not a hint of the degradation of the men he
recorded. Although in 1933 he had written to the governor of
Texas asking him to investigate the convictions of black prisoners and pardon those who "are only victims of misfor-
tune," in his autobiography he says not a word about wrongly
convicted men, but gives examples mostly of murderers who
acknowledged their guilt, quoting lines such as "Boss, I jes'
got to shootin' niggers an' I couldn't stop," as if marveling at
the blacks' propensity to kill. Lomax visited nearly every penal
institution of the South, which could have given him the
unique opportunity to write about the prison conditions
there; but he covered the subject in the most cursory manner.
Instead, he wrote approvingly, "A volume could be written
about the reception given me by wardens of Southern peni-
tentiaries." And in their credulity-straining introduction to

American Ballads and Folk Songs, the Lomaxes wrote, "The men were well fed and their sleeping quarters looked comfortable. . . . The visitors were given every freedom, and no case of cruelty was noted."

Outside of the prisons, the elder Lomax continued to display a condescending attitude toward the black people he recorded, who were usually the more marginal members of society. One chapter of his autobiography, entitled "Alabama Red Land," consists of nothing but droll tales told by and about poor blacks, reminiscent of *Amos 'n' Andy* routines: " 'I heard that you'd been in jail for stealing a ham,' I ventured. 'Yassuh, I wuz in jail for stealin' a ham, but I didn't steal hit. I done told 'em dat if de feller what did steal hit would jes' divide up, I wouldn't mind stayin' in jail a week for ha'f a ham. Jes' so's I can put my teeth in hit!' "

By the time Lomax brought Leadbelly to New York in 1935, Leadbelly had been working as Lomax's servant for months, waking him up in the morning, fixing his coffee, shining his shoes, brushing his suit. Yet in the fall of 1934, Lomax wrote, "Leadbelly is a nigger to the core of his being. In addition he is a killer. He tells the truth only accidentally. . . . He is as sensual as a goat, and when he sings to me my spine tingles and sometimes tears come. Penitentiary wardens all tell me that I set no value on my life in using him as a traveling companion." And when he arrived in New York, he introduced Leadbelly to reporters by telling them he "was a 'natural,' who had no idea of money, law, or ethics and who was possessed of virtually no restraint." Needless to say, there was little truth to these remarks—Leadbelly was usually a soft-spoken, gentle man who was well aware that his drunken, frenzied murder attempts had been wrong; his understanding of money, law, and ethics was solid and strong.

Here's how Lomax introduced Leadbelly to his New York audience: "Northern people hear Negroes playing and singing beautiful spirituals, which are too refined and are unlike the true southern spirituals. Or else they hear men and women on the stage and radio, burlesquing their own songs. Leadbelly doesn't burlesque. He plays and sings with absolute sincerity. Whether or not it sounds foolish to you, he plays with absolute sincerity. I've heard his songs a hundred times, but I always get a thrill. To me his music is real music." In other words, for John Lomax, Leadbelly was authenticity personified. Anything more sophisticated was "burlesque."

■ ■ ■ ■

KURT COBAIN first approached music as a fan. When he discovered a new band he loved he would become obsessive about them, wanting to absorb as much of their music as he could. Many of his attitudes came from observing how his musical heroes saw the world and wanting to emulate them. His relationship with bands like the Melvins and the Vaselines was nothing short of hero worship, and he would often write to members of bands he liked in friendship and admiration. When he became a successful performer himself he knew well how the fans felt about him, the demands they would make, and the emotional connection they had with him. He knew that above all, his fans expected him to keep it real and to not forget where he had come from.

Many of the performers Cobain admired were either deeply

honest about themselves or politically idealistic. While he loved a wide variety of music, a large part of his ethics regarding the music business came from the punk movement, where bands prized sincerity over skill and saw the corporate nature of the business as an enemy. He was a purist in his approach to song-writing and based many songs on his own experiences. The fact that the life he was writing about was such a complex and, at times, disturbed one was what gave his songs their unnerving power. (Much of this can also be applied to Leadbelly, who sang with an unvarnished directness, wrote songs about his own experiences, and rebelled against his handlers.)

Cobain's childhood was characterized by a series of disillusionments: his parents split up when he was seven, his father broke a promise to not get a new girlfriend, and it became impossible to live with his mother's new boyfriend. He was passed around to different family members and friends, never settling anywhere for long; for periods in his teens he was effectively homeless. As he absorbed the ethics of punk from his heroes and contemporaries, a very personal anger infused his outlook. But one can also feel something else behind this: the hollow feeling of the little kid in "Sliver" who is left with his grandparents while his parents go to a show and who wants his grandma to take him home, or the terrible sorrow of the same boy ten years later, in his early teens, who can't be taken home because he doesn't really have one anymore; in other words, the feeling that people just shouldn't let you down.

Many young punk fans found echoes of their personal frustrations in punk's commands to keep it real, make it raw, do it yourself, and be against everything. Cobain wanted to be authentic partially because the seventeen-year-old fan he had once been would have wanted him to be authentic; he didn't want to let himself down, and he didn't want to let the average seventeen-year-old punk rock kid down. But at the same time he also felt that letting everyone down was inevitable.

BY ALMOST ANY standards, Kurt Cobain's version of "In the Pines" seems "authentic." There doesn't appear to be anything "fake" here: the song is traditional, the passion is real. The subject matter fits closely with his preoccupations, and the dark woods of the chorus must have reminded him of the forested landscape of his small-town home in Washington State. But why did he perform Leadbelly's version of "In the Pines" instead of anyone else's? Like Lomax, did Cobain also consider Leadbelly's music "real music"? No doubt. Was he looking for the same thing that John Lomax was looking for? Not exactly.

Lomax had been searching for the most authentic Negro songs he could find, and he believed that Leadbelly had unearthed some of them, in part because of his exposure to prisoners who had been out of circulation for decades. But Leadbelly's repertoire was replete with songs of purely Anglo-American origin. He once recalled, "I learned by listening to other singers once in a while off phonograph records. . . . I used to look at the sheet music and learn the words of a few popular songs." Lomax himself admitted, "For his programs Lead Belly always wished to include [Gene Autry's] 'That Silver-Haired Daddy of Mine' or jazz tunes such as 'I'm in Love with You, Baby.' . . . We held him to the singing of the

music that first attracted us to him." And during his performances, Lomax would direct Leadbelly as to which songs he
should sing.

Lomax's idea was to trace African American musical culture to its source, its roots, on the Darwinian assumption that
those roots were less complicated, less corrupted, more
"pure," than the songs of his day (again, he was wrong). He
was looking for cultural authenticity, a relatively unadulterated
version of a particular musical culture (in this case African
American).

Cobain was also searching for something "authentic" and
pure, but he wasn't necessarily looking for the roots of
American music. He was in quest of personal authenticity,
"keeping it real," singing about his own, personal pain, his
own idiosyncratic vision. Cobain called Leadbelly his favorite
performer because, for one thing, Leadbelly had by now
become as mythical as Paul Bunyan, an ideal representative of
a purer music that somehow predated the introduction of
artifice into popular culture. But Leadbelly also symbolized
something elemental, resonant, and mysterious, something
akin to the mystery and violence Cobain saw in his own soul.
Doubtless, if John Lomax had not presented Leadbelly as the
embodiment of the primitive, savage, black killer who sings
age-old songs in the most sensual manner conceivable,
Leadbelly would have held far less attraction for Cobain.

Much of Leadbelly's appeal, not to mention his fortune
and fame, both when he was alive and after his death, derived
from a racist view that the most authentic black culture was
also the most primitive. Over time, this view lost much of its
racial tinge: now it is commonly accepted by rock fans the
world over that the most authentic music is the most savage

and raw. Of the many varieties of self-expression, it is the most primitive that rock fans associate with the greatest emotional honesty. (Contrast this to Schubert and Mahler, who conveyed emotional intensity in their songs by the interplay of major and minor modes.) So for Cobain, as for most rock stars and fans today, real rock'n'roll must be shackled to the kind of primitivism that accompanied Leadbelly's career, an idealization of "savage" simplicity. If Cobain had broadcast the facts of his own painful life in the wordy, sophisticated tradition of Loudon Wainwright III rather than the bare-bones tradition of Leadbelly, he would have been a role model for next to nobody.

And this bare-bones tradition extends beyond the artist to the medium itself. We have already mentioned representational authenticity, by which we mean simply that something is what it claims to be and not a counterfeit. Clearly, *MTV Unplugged* fails this simple test: for it to be unplugged, we'd have to unplug our TVs. But on a less basic level, by presenting artists in a more-or-less "acoustic" environment, the program pretends to show us the most "authentic" aspects of the performer. Because the recording of music gives such scope for faking of various kinds, it has become a real question whether or not the artists we listen to are really what they claim to be. Are they really playing their instruments? Can they really sing like that? But such questions of authenticity rarely tell the whole story, and they have often been elided with questions of personal and cultural authenticity. For instance, in *MTV Unplugged*, the stripped-down format ensures that we see the artist perform without adulteration. However, this constriction is then used to reinforce the notion that this performance is authentic in some deeper way.

COBAIN'S DEATH created a problem for grunge. The meaning of the term had already shifted from referring to a small number of bands from the Seattle area to embodying the entire fashion and musical scene that developed around the success of Nirvana and their contemporaries. But at all times it was defined by being honest, gritty, and down-to-earth (not to mention loud). Nirvana's guitar-based simplicity and rawness of emotion, combined with Cobain's punk ethics and apparent loathing of the music business, made them the ultimate authentic band of their era.

What individuals understand by the word *authentic* tends to be influenced by what exactly they perceive as fake, in a pejorative sense; seeing something as authentic is thus often a moral judgment as well as an aesthetic one. Johnny Rotten of the Sex Pistols once sang "We mean it, man" about having "no future," but he was still alive; when Cobain killed himself, he proved that he really had meant it. In his suicide note, aimed at his fans, which his wife Courtney Love broadcast in public with her own angry interjections, he said, "The fact is, I can't fool you, any one of you. It simply isn't fair to you or me. The worst crime I can think of would be to rip people off by *faking it* and pretending as if I'm having 100% fun."

The desperately sad and frustrating thing is that the only way he could see of being true to himself was being true to the person that his fans wanted him to be, the person he had once wanted to become. Having spent so long wanting to be that person, it must have been extremely hard to realize that, having succeeded at last, he no longer wanted the same thing. We may think that he would have been equally true to himself if he had made a different decision: giving up playing live, breaking up the band and carrying through with the sessions he had booked with Michael Stipe, taking a break from music altogether, or whatever. But he was suicidally depressed, and all he could see were insurmountable obstacles.

While his self-loathing and personal suffering had given the music an edge of angst that fans, especially adolescents, could identify with, his suicide raised the stakes too high. Rival musicians and peers wallowed in the reflected tragedy of his death. Eddie Vedder's band Pearl Jam had recently overtaken Nirvana as the best-selling rock band in the United States; in an interview soon afterward, Vedder said, "I always thought I'd go first. I don't know why I thought that . . . it just seemed like I would. I mean, I didn't know him on a daily basis—far from it. But, in a way, I don't even feel right being here without him." Vedder made this self-righteous speech in spite of Cobain's well-documented disdain for Pearl Jam. And in the same interview, Vedder attacked the media for doubting his own authenticity, which he linked to that of Cobain: "They don't know what's real and what isn't. And when someone comes along who's trying to be real, they don't know the fuckin' difference."

As one looks back through other interviews given by other rock stars after Cobain's death, it often seems as though they too were feebly saying, "Look at me, look at me, I feel pain too." Perhaps it is unfair to criticize—it was impossible to come up with the words to express the sadness that so many shared, and they were only fumbling for the right thing to say. But no one was willing to match Cobain's final gesture, and all other grunge music was robbed of its essential gravity. Suddenly it looked like the other bands were just playing a part, whereas Cobain had been for real. Grunge started to ebb into the grunge lite of Bush and the Stone Temple

Pilots; bands like Green Day added a dash of angst to their punk-pop and moved into the same territory; and in general, no post-Nirvana guitar-based band, whether post-grunge, mainstream, or even metal, could ignore the pressure to create autobiographical songs about their misery. Nirvana looked more and more like the only "real" band in history—a one-time phenomenon that had grown out of its extraordinary singer.

And as fans of the music, we ended up with the same guilty, voyeuristic unease that was provoked by Richie Edwards of the Manic Street Preachers hacking "4 Real" into his arm for a photo shoot. The guitarist in the original band's line-up, Edwards's punk sensibilities had driven its early puritanical agenda and public manifestos. His public act of cutting himself had done much to gain the band notoriety. The intensity of his desire to live up to the image he had created and to not sell out was in the end unsustainable, and he disappeared in February 1995 as the band was about to leave for an American tour. His abandoned car and credit card transactions gave some faint hope that he had vanished for only a time, but he is generally presumed dead.

Just like the white fans of Leadbelly and the folk fans who rediscovered blues singers in the 1960s, fans demanded that their heros be *real*, something more than mere entertainers. Cobain and Edwards took this demand seriously, so seriously that they laid their deepest personal problems out for all to see. They allowed us to wallow in their misery. They proved to us that they were the genuine article, and, in the act of proving it, they ultimately destroyed themselves. And they did it because we were watching.

We might wish that Kurt Cobain had calmed down and

grown old, made mellow, grown-up records with Michael Stipe, maybe even given up the band and retired to a farm somewhere. We might wish that Richie Edwards had just moved to a beach hut in Australia and left all his problems behind. But it's too late.

It's too simplistic to say that it is our fault, but deep down we wonder: if we had not encouraged them—if we had thought less of "authenticity" and more simply of good music—might they have survived? This weird complicity between audience and performer can create great songs and great rock stars. But it also sometimes kills them.

CHAPTER TWO

NOBODY'S DIRTY BUSINESS

Folk, Blues, and the Segregation of Southern Music

Memphis, February 14, 1928

The story of American music itself: the story of the black stealing from the black, the white from the white, and the one from the other; of Tin Pan Alley songs culled from the air and taken into the pines and the fields, gone feral and misperceived as primitive folk expression; of ancient breezes from those pines and those fields drifting endlessly anew through the rhythms of generations.

NICK TOSCHES, *Where Dead Voices Gather*

THIS IS THE TALE of two songs, "Nobody's Dirty Business" and "Frankie," that appeared on one record, recorded in a makeshift Memphis studio on Valentine's Day, 1928; it's also a tale of their maker, John Smith Hurt, a thirty-five-year-old black tenant farmer. It's a long, labyrinthine tale stretching from the 1890s to the 1960s, a tale that challenges our conventional ideas of the oppositions between black and white, country and blues, folk and pop, authentic and fake. And it's a tale that tries to explain what American music once was a long time ago, and what it became in the twentieth century.

Like many tales, it centers around a mystery: exactly what were these two songs? What race, what genre, did they belong to? What was their purpose, their meaning, their function, their import? The mysteries of American music have been hallowed ground for decades. Perhaps trying to solve a few of them is finally in order.

PART I: THE ROOTS

We'll start with the hard facts.

A few days before the date of this recording, Willie Narmour, a white farmer who had developed a reputation as one of the best fiddlers in northern Mississippi and who had been playing with his neighbor John Hurt at dances for five years, brought OKeh producer Tommy Rockwell over to Hurt's home in a tiny town called Avalon for Rockwell to listen to Hurt. Impressed by Hurt's original song "Monday Morning Blues," Rockwell told him he'd pay him to come to Memphis and record. Narmour had been playing not only with Hurt, the local whiskey maker, but with the local sheriff, a white guitarist named Shel Smith; the county was dry, and their arrangement would have been well known. The three of them traveled to Memphis together, most likely discussing liquor and song en route.

One of the most successful black blues guitarists of the time, Lonnie Johnson, was working as Rockwell's black talent scout and recorded in the same studio on both the day before and the day after Hurt's session. Hurt had heard his records and met him when he got to Memphis, but didn't believe Johnson was really who he said he was. A white quartet called the Arkansas Barefoot Boys also recorded there that day, but we can't be certain whether or not Hurt met them. Many years later, Hurt talked about the session, evoking his naïve wonder at the time: "[I went into] a great big hall with only Mr. Rockwell, one engineer, and myself. I sat on a chair and they pushed the microphone right up close to my mouth, and told me not to move after they found the right position. Oh, I was nervous, and my neck was sore for days after."

The fifth song out of eight that Hurt recorded that day, and one of only two released, was a fast and energetic number entitled "Nobody's Dirty Business." Over his lively ragtime guitar, Hurt sings the words in a quiet, expressionless voice that leaves one wondering whether all his threats of murder, pleas for his baby to come back, and implied complaints about nosy neighbors are meant in jest or earnest. It certainly doesn't sound anything like "the blues" in the form we're familiar with; but it doesn't sound too much like hillbilly music either. There's a calmness, an unflappable geniality in Hurt's delivery that contrasts strongly with the malevolence of the lyrics, making them far more chilling than if he'd sung them as if he meant them. The lack of projection in both his voice and his guitar playing is also puzzling: this is far quieter music than almost anything else recorded during this era. It seems too soft to be dance music, it's far from confessional, and it doesn't appear to be a joke or novelty number. To our ears, accustomed to music with a far more well-defined purpose, "Nobody's Dirty Business" is a puzzling, unsettling thing, neither white nor black, neither good nor evil, just strange. When Hurt sings, "Ain't nobody's business but my own," it's almost as if he were singing about the nature of the song itself.

"'Tain't Nobody's Business If I Do" had originally been composed about six years earlier by Porter Grainger and Everett Robbins, black songwriters for New York musical shows; there was also an earlier song, "It's Nobody's Business But My Own," which had been composed in 1919, also by black songwriters, for the great black comedian Bert Williams. Three female Harlem blues singers had recorded "'Tain't Nobody's Business": Sara Martin in December 1922, Alberta Hunter in February 1923, and Bessie Smith that April. All three stuck quite closely to Grainger and Robbins's original, though Hunter jazzed it up far more than Martin or Smith; Smith's is the version later blues singers commonly emulated. But Hurt's performance sounds nothing like these versions— or, for that matter, Bert Williams's.

Hurt's guitar picking is rhythmic and regular, as if he were playing for a dance—and he had been playing for dances, both black and white, in a professional capacity for many years. His style is essentially an imitation of ragtime piano, not blues. Hurt bends no notes and keeps a steady beat in the bass while syncopating the treble line, just as in almost all ragtime songs. Unlike most black ragtime guitarists, though, Hurt plays in straight rather than swing time, and never takes a break from his steady alternating bass notes. The melody Hurt sings is also completely different from Martin's or Smith's, and the tempo is about double. It's almost as if Hurt had completely reinvented the song: the sole thing Hurt's version has in common with the others is the words of the chorus.

Or that's what you'd think if you hadn't also heard any of the other recordings of the number made in the twenties by whites from all over the South (most of them entitled simply "Nobody's Business"): Charles Nabell, Earl Johnson and His Dixie Entertainers, Ruben Burns and His Short Creek Trio, Warren Caplinger's Cumberland Mountain Entertainers, Emry Arthur, and Uncle Dave Macon (the tail end of "Tennessee Jubilee"), along with unissued recordings by Riley Puckett and Jimmie Davis. Although the lyrics sung on these records are quite different from Hurt's, the rhythm and melody are the same. In other words, Hurt seems to have performed the Southern white string band's version of the song rather than the Northern black classic blues version.

If, that is, it's even the same song. A black musician from Memphis, Frank Stokes, also recorded it in 1928, and the record was given the same title as Bessie Smith's version, though it's clearly the same as Hurt's version, with practically the same guitar part and melody but with different lyrics. What's more, the folk-song collector Howard Odum included in his 1925 collection *The Negro and His Song* a handful of lyrics (but no melody) of two entirely different numbers entitled

" 'Tain't Nobody's Bizness But My Own" and "Nobody's Bizness But Mine," neither of which appears to resemble any of the recorded versions. Of course, none of this clarifies the origins of the song Hurt recorded. Melodically it has none of the musical characteristics that we now call African American (call and response, blue notes, swing time, etc.). At any rate, it seems to have been popular among musicians of both races.

As for the lyrics, those of the white performers are peppered with hillbilly humor—"She runs a weenie stand, way down in no man's land," sings Earl Johnson and his band. But Hurt made them far more menacing. Where Johnson had sung, "Some of these mornings I wake up crazy, kill my wife and save my baby," Hurt sings, "Some of these mornings gonna wake up crazy, gonna grab my gun, gonna kill my baby." Not only that, but he sings the line three times during the course of the song (although once he substitutes "boozy" for "crazy" and "Susie" for "baby"). This isn't out of character: of the eleven released secular songs he recorded that year, nine feature death, for the most part violent. In "Got the Blues, Can't Be Satisfied," for example, he sings,

> Took my gun, broke the barrel down;
> put my baby six feet under the ground.
> I cut that joker so long deep and wide;
> I got the blues and still ain't satisfied.

As a whiskey maker who had played for dances for both races, Hurt was no doubt just as well acquainted with death and violence as any of the legendary Mississippi blues singers; his life as a farmer had by no means isolated him from these daily facts.

But the blues were not Hurt's forte—he never considered himself a blues singer. When Rockwell first met Hurt, he probably asked him to perform some blues, since that was the music thought to sell best to blacks. "Monday Morning Blues," though, with which Hurt began the session (and with which we are familiar only from a much later recording), is hardly a typical blues: it starts on the fourth rather than on the tonic, the rhyme scheme and line length are unusual, and the guitar picking is in a straight ragtime style, with little resemblance to typical blues guitar playing.

He followed this with "Shiverlie Red Blues," an unreleased song we can no longer identify since the masters have been lost. For his third song, Hurt turned to a murder ballad based on a true story, "Frankie and Albert" (labeled simply as "Frankie"), composed in 1899 by a black barroom bard named Bill Dooley; it had already been recorded close to ten times by different performers, almost all of them white. He then performed another ballad, "Casey Jones," composed by a black man in 1900 about a white man killed in a train wreck that year; it too had been featured on over a half-dozen records, but none by black singers.

After completing "Nobody's Dirty Business," Hurt sang two spirituals, "Blessed Be the Name" and "Meeting on the Old Camp Ground," before concluding his session with "Sliding Delta," a ragtime tune.

OKeh initially planned to release these songs in their "old-time music" series—a group of records aimed at an almost exclusively white audience, and also called "hillbilly." (In fact, record collector Richard Nevins has related that when he was hunting for old records, John Hurt's 78s turned up more often in white homes than black homes.) Instead, OKeh released only one record, featuring two of the eight songs, "Frankie" and "Nobody's Dirty Business," in their "race" series, devoted to black music; they were issued under the moniker Mississippi John Hurt, the name of his state being added as a sales gimmick. Hurt was paid about twenty dollars per song.

That November, Rockwell asked Hurt to come up to New York to record some additional songs, explaining that "the first record you made sold fairly well" (which is rather doubtful) and asking him to "get together about eight selections at least four of them to be old time tunes, similar to selections 'Frankie' and 'Nobody's Business.'" As we shall see, most blacks were asked to sing blues numbers rather than "old-time" tunes; perhaps Rockwell thought he was onto something new. At any rate, under Rockwell's and Lonnie Johnson's supervision, Hurt recorded twelve additional numbers, of which ten were released, resulting in a total of six double-sided 78-rpm records, none of which seem to have sold well at all. Then, despite attempts to record again, Hurt slipped back into obscurity (and farming). Although he continued to play locally for a while, the "dirty business" of music passed him by for another thirty-five years.

THE PART-WHITE, part-black nature of Hurt's music may seem like an oddity to us today. It doesn't fit into our clear-cut categories: folk ballads (white), blues (black), country or hillbilly music (white), spirituals (black). As we'll see, these categories owe a great deal to notions of authenticity that have been promulgated since World War I, if not earlier. But if we listen with an open ear to the music made by Hurt and his contemporaries, a very different picture of traditional American music emerges.

It is one of the great American ironies that the region of the United States with the worst history of racism and segregation is also the region that once boasted the most integrated music. Prior to the twentieth century, in the North one could find parlor music, Irish-derived fiddler tunes, marching bands, English and Scottish ballads; in the West one found frontier and cowboy songs such as "Home on the Range." None of these musics prominently featured African elements (though African Americans often performed them). But in the South, where the large majority of America's black population resided, the European and African elements were inextricable.

By the 1920s, the dance music that both blacks and whites performed there had combined the Irish fiddle with the African banjo. The music we now think of as "old-time" or "string-band" music, music that has been played almost exclusively by whites for the last seventy-five years, is of mixed ancestry. In addition, minstrel numbers, which sometimes relied on elements, however caricatured, of African American story and song, had by this time become a solid part of both black and white traditions. The music of New Orleans blended African, Cuban, and French features. Ragtime had mixed the syncopation of African American music with the African rhythms of Cuba and the German marching band tradition. African American spirituals for the most part shared the basic melodic contours of white spirituals, though they usually spiced them up with new lyrics, rhythms, and intonation. Blues were widely sung by both blacks and whites, and arose from a combination of African musical modes and white harmonies and structure.

All in all, Southern music was a hybrid, a product of musical miscegenation, dependent on a combinatorial ingenuity. Of course, some music sounded more African than others, and some music sounded almost purely Irish, Scottish, English, or some combination thereof, but the basic character of Southern music was one of amalgamation.

This wasn't true of all African music in the Americas. In Cuba, the West Indies, and Brazil, in particular, blacks retained a good deal more of their African culture—music, religion, dress, language—than they did in the United States. As David Wondrich points out in his masterful *Stomp and Swerve: American Music Gets Hot*, black music in these countries retains "a loping, lilting sense of rhythm that's very different from the harder-edged, more urgent beat" of North American blacks. For the uninitiated faced with the sometimes tremendously complex percussion ensembles of Africa, Cuba, or Brazil, it can often be hard to tell which is the downbeat and which the upbeat. That's very different from the rhythms one finds in Irish fiddle music, for example—there's a very basic and inescapable beat there. As music scholar Samuel Charters puts it, "African folk styles 'float,' while European folk styles 'march.'"

The reasons Africans managed to retain so much of their culture in places such as Cuba but transformed it into something entirely different in the United States are various. In Cuba, the concentration of blacks was far higher, the slaveowners were far less concerned with slave culture and far more with issues of productivity, the African religions that syncretized with Christianity were far friendlier to dance music than was U.S. Christianity, and the attempts to ban percussion instruments were far less effective than similar attempts in the United States. In addition, U.S. Africans came primarily from northwest Africa, which had been exposed to Islamic culture for centuries, and thus their music already differed substantially from that of the Africans who came to Cuba from the Congo and Angola.

Once they arrived in the United States, African slaves were forbidden to play their drums, effectively limiting their ability to communicate across long distances, so they took up non-African instruments instead. During the colonial era, slaves played drums, fifes, and trumpet in the military, and sang and performed for their masters at balls, assemblies, and special "entertainments" on a wide variety of other instruments, both European and African. Numerous advertisements for runaway slaves mention that they were proficient violinists. Perhaps the only African instrument that survived U.S. slavery in good health was the banjo.

The story of African music in America is thus one of incessant miscegenation. Thomas Creswell, an Englishman who attended a Virginia barbecue in 1774, wrote, "a great number of young people [whites] met together with a Fiddle and a Banjo played by two Negroes. . . . I believe they have danced and drunk till there are few sober people among them." Thomas Jefferson's brother Randolph "used to come out among black people, play the fiddle and dance half the night," according to one Monticello slave's memoirs. In 1806 Thomas Ashe noticed that the band playing a ball in Wheeling (now in West Virginia) was composed of two black banjo players and a white "lutenist" (most likely a guitarist). The modern five-string banjo was created by black and white banjo players together, and during the Civil War mixed-race fiddle and banjo string-bands appeared not only in rural areas, but actually traveled with the Confederate Army. In general, as the music historian Elijah Wald writes, "African Americans played every sort of music in the South, and made up the majority of full-time musicians. When white plantation society fell in love with the waltz, the schottische, or the latest French ballroom fad during the antebellum years, its dance orchestra would typically be made up of black slaves."

Under the watchful eyes of American slaveholders, African religion all but disappeared, and along with it African religious music; the same can be said of African languages. Here and there pockets of African song survived. But by and large, the music of African Americans slowly became far more American than African. After the Civil War, the railroads, coal mines, traveling circuses, and medicine shows all supplied ample opportunity for musical racial interaction, and black and white musicians kept working together, playing the music we now call American—a unique music that no longer bespoke any other continent.

Back in the eighteenth century, Irish servants and black slaves were closer in class than they were in later years, and the mix of their cultures is most evident in the music that became known, in the nineteenth century, as minstrelsy. Minstrelsy took the country by storm. Its melding of African and Irish instruments was, by all accounts, wildly exciting—the nineteenth-century equivalent of rock'n'roll. Some scholars maintain that minstrelsy was a purely white form of music that only pretended to represent blackness, while others point to examples of white borrowings from black tradition. At any rate, minstrelsy, though usually played by white people in blackface, advertised itself as black music, and its immense impact was due in large part to this claim. Daddy Rice, the "Father of American Minstrelsy," is said to have based his infamous "Jim Crow Song" (which in turn became the basis for "Turkey in the Straw") on a Kentucky slave song. E. P. Christy, founder of Christy's Minstrels, the longest lived of the minstrel groups, was said to have learned to play the banjo at Congo Square in New Orleans, the site of perhaps the largest slave auctions in the country, in the 1820s. Billy Whitlock, one of the original Virginia Minstrels (the first minstrel band), would apparently "steal off to some Negro hut to hear the darkies sing and to see them dance, taking a jug of whiskey to make things merrier"; and fellow Virginia Minstrel Dan Emmett, who was later to compose "Dixie," apparently learned the banjo from a circus hand named Ferguson who, according to the circus manager, was " 'nigger all over' except in color." Other minstrel numbers such as "Clare de Kitchen" and "Long Time Ago" were also supposedly based on slave songs.

Moreover, minstrelsy was far from a whites-only phenomenon: hundreds of blacks also put on blackface and formed their own minstrel troupes, and were not only just as successful as their white counterparts, but outlasted them in the South and Midwest. As Eileen Southern, a historian of black music, writes, "Here was a curious kind of interaction. The minstrel songs, originally inspired by genuine slave songs, were altered and adapted by white minstrels to the taste of white America in the nineteenth century, and then were taken back again by black folk for further adaptation to *their* musical taste. Thus the songs passed back into the folk tradition from which they had come."

This is not to say that minstrelsy was racially neutral or that it promoted any kind of racial power-sharing: minstrel musicians were, on the whole, strictly segregated. The minstrel show—at least that of whites—denigrated blacks, ridiculed them, robbed them of dignity and power; it presented them as primitive savages, foolish and weak-willed, easily contented and docile in the face of abuse. The point is that minstrel music—simple Anglo-American tunes, for the most part, but played on African and Irish instruments—quickly passed into both black and white traditions.

By the 1920s, minstrelsy was active largely in the South, where its influence was most enduring. And the recordings made in that region during that decade testify to how remarkably integrated Southern music remained. Even judging by song titles alone, it is astonishing how many were sung by both black and white performers. In his book *Blacks, Whites, and Blues*, music scholar Tony Russell gives examples of over fifty songs played widely by both blacks and whites in the pre-Depression years, among them such familiar numbers as "Casey Jones," "John Henry," "Stack O'Lee," "Frankie and Albert," "Ain't Nobody's Business," and "Make Me a Pallet on the Floor"—all sung by John Hurt in 1928—along with "Salty Dog," "Easy Rider," "I Got Mine," "Poor Boy, Long Way from Home," "Corrine Corrina," "Careless Love," "Turkey in the Straw," "Buffalo Gals," "St. Louis Blues," "Hot Time in the Old Town Tonight," "Old Dan Tucker," and "Give Me That Old-Time Religion." Nick Tosches goes further, naming black versions of such sixteenth-century British ballads as "Barbara Allen," "The Maid Freed from the Gallows," "Lord Lovel," and "Lady Isabel and the Elf-Knight."

The New York record companies uncovered the richness of this dual heritage when they decided to make field recordings in the South rather than in the Midwest or the West in the 1920s, in part because the region was already legendary for its music. And if one listens to these field recordings without looking at the record label, occasionally it can be difficult to place musicians by race. Of course, one can't claim that when it came to music, the racial divide that characterized the rest of Southern culture didn't exist. But it was far less pronounced in music than it was in the educational system, the government, or, for that matter, the music in New York City, which was more strictly segregated. In fact, music may have been the only aspect of Southern life in which blacks and whites were more or less on an equal footing.

IN LIGHT OF this parity, it shouldn't be surprising that OKeh originally filed Hurt's songs as "old-time music," nor that he had been introduced to the record company by a white musician he'd played with, nor that his recordings should have been supervised by both a black and a white person, nor that his repertoire consisted mainly of songs that whites also performed, nor that his guitar style closely resembled the ragtime and hillbilly stylings of the white guitarist Sam McGee (who had, in turn, learned a great deal from black guitarists). What should be surprising, then, is that Hurt ever came to be considered a blues player at all (not to mention a representative of "the Delta blues" simply because he lived on the edge of the Mississippi Delta). How did this happen?

The blues, like ragtime and New Orleans jazz, both

invented around the same time, and like bebop, free jazz, and hip-hop since, is an African American musical form that may have owed its development in part to the fact that it served as a form of racial protection. In other words, this was a music quite different from the typical Anglo-American song and, as Wondrich suggests, its practitioners may have developed its more overtly African characteristics in the knowledge that whites would have difficulty imitating it. But because of the porousness of the boundaries between black and white music in the South, this protection ultimately failed. While few, if any, white blues performers displayed the seemingly unbounded inventiveness or searing emotion of Blind Lemon Jefferson, by the early 1930s the blues had nonetheless become a common heritage, popular among both blacks and whites. And it can't have been simply a matter of whites imitating blacks. Considering how integrated almost all Southern music was, the development of the blues must have been a two-way street.

Contemporary scholarship paints the blues as a purely black form: the magazine *Living Blues* has avoided covering white blues players for thirty-five years now, and even as late as 1993, Alan Lomax could write, with a straight face, "the whites have not yet grasped the body-based African rhythmic scheme." Mississippi blues, in particular, has been painted as so racially isolated that its blackness has become almost pure, holy.

But John Hurt was far from the only black Mississippi musician to play with and for whites, so it's not surprising that some of the music that whites played found its way into his own. The Mississippi Sheiks, including Bo Carter, earned much of their income playing for whites at private dances and parties. Henry Sims, another black Mississippian who recorded with Charlie Patton and Muddy Waters, also played as part of a string band, the Mississippi Corn Shuckers, for a white square dance every Friday night in Clarksdale.

The racial isolation of many black performers is, simply put, a fiction: they were exposed to a wide variety of white and black music, and learned from what they heard. In fact, the roster of black blues musicians who have openly acknowledged the influence of white blues singer Jimmie Rodgers on their music includes Howlin' Wolf and B. B. King; and in 1963 John Hurt and Skip James enjoyed fooling around with a duet of Rodgers's non-blues song "Waiting for a Train."

Hurt, Stokes, a black Texan named Henry Thomas, and a few other black singer-guitarists are commonly labeled "songsters," a term originally applied to Mance Lipscomb by blues researcher Mack McCormack, who seized hold of the prevalent word for "singer" and misconstrued it to mean a black singer whose repertoire consisted mostly of non-blues songs—the same songs rural whites performed. Roy Acuff, Dock Boggs, Fiddling John Carson, Frank Hutchinson, and Uncle Dave Macon, all of whom could be called white "songsters," worked the same medicine shows as the black "songsters," and all of them could have been mistaken for black on the basis of some of their records (for example, the black musician John Jackson thought that Macon was black until informed otherwise during the folk revival). As Elijah Wald cogently argues in *Escaping the Delta*, the distinction between "bluesmen" and "songsters" "is utterly modern and artificial, and has no bearing on the way musicians thought of themselves in the 1920s or 1930s." The word "songster" applied equally to John Hurt and Enrico Caruso.

It has long been assumed that most of the repertoire of those singers now labeled "songsters" predates the blues, particularly since the majority of these singers were older when they started recording than the average blues player; but most of the material Hurt performed was either written by him or was no older than he was. There is no way of telling how greatly white musicians influenced Hurt, if at all, but since both his repertoire and guitar style were shared by white musicians, it seems probable that he gleaned some of it from them, and it's hard to believe that five years of playing at white dances with a white fiddler wouldn't have influenced Hurt in some way. Much the same could be said for Henry Thomas, a.k.a. "Ragtime Texas," who recorded some two dozen songs in the late 1920s. A number of his songs had earlier been recorded by Uncle Dave Macon, and both Tony Russell and Robert Cantwell conclude that Thomas heard Macon's recordings or may even have based some of his own recordings on them.

There's actually a very simple reason why there are so many blues records from this era and so few records of blacks singing songs like those that Hurt and Thomas recorded: most black musicians who preferred older or hillbilly styles simply didn't get recorded unless they could play the blues, and those who could were allowed to record primarily blues. Hurt was lucky that he was recorded by OKeh, not Paramount (which recorded Blind Lemon Jefferson, Skip James, and many others). Paramount's director, Mayo Williams, told Stephen Calt, a blues biographer, that if a black performer came in with a non-blues tune, "I would very quickly say: 'Well, we can't use it. Write me a blues.'" This is probably why the first two numbers Hurt recorded were blues numbers (or at least labeled as such).

And from its very beginnings, the blues had its white performers: the first blues records were recorded by whites, not blacks. There were a host of Southern white blues artists during this era: the Allen Brothers, Dock Boggs, Frank Hutchinson, Darby and Tarlton, Jimmie Rodgers, Jimmie Davis, and Sam McGee were some of the better-known. The Allen Brothers serve as an excellent example: most of their recordings were blues, at least according to their titles, and for the non-specialist it's hard to tell from listening to their first records that the brothers were white—in fact, Columbia accidentally released their second record in their "race" series. (Some people claim that the Allen Brothers turned around and sued Columbia for this mistake, but there is no solid evidence for this story.) In 1979, the music scholar Charles Wolfe asked Lee Allen, "Where did you learn to play the blues?" Allen answered, "That was just kind of natural. We lived in those days when people—that's about all they knew."

Yet the Allen Brothers, like all their white brethren, were labeled old-time or hillbilly musicians in the 1920s and '30s, and today we call them "country," not blues. Black musicians like Hurt and Thomas, who were playing fewer blues tunes than any of the above-mentioned white musicians and who were less blues-oriented in their guitar and vocal stylings, are *never* called country musicians, but simply bluesmen. How did black and white musicians become so segregated?

IT WAS PROBABLY the record companies who were most responsible, for they were all based in New York, where the music was far more segregated than it was in the South. These record companies, in fact, had mostly barred their doors to black musicians (though quite a few exceptions can be found) until Mamie Smith and her Jazz Hounds' groundbreaking "Crazy Blues" was recorded by OKeh in 1920, against the will of those in charge.

The first blues song recorded by a black singer with black accompanists, "Crazy Blues" sold like crazy, allegedly 75,000 copies in Harlem alone in the first month after its release. So in 1921 OKeh started a series of records devoted to black artists, and soon everyone was doing it. A black-owned label, Swan, appeared that year; Paramount started a line in 1922; Columbia followed in 1923 and Vocalion in 1926. As late as the 1930s, the recording companies kept these "race" records in entirely separate catalogs: in 1933, Victor admitted hillbilly records into its general catalog but kept records by black artists out; and by the end of the 1930s Bluebird's separate catalog for non-pop records was divided into the following sections: "Old Familiar Tunes" (hillbilly), "Race Records," "Children's," "Cajun," and "Irish." Even the recording scouts maintained as absolute a separation as they could between the races. This explains why Hurt and Willie Narmour did not record together, although they were in the same studio on the same day and had been playing together for five years.

Ralph Peer was in part responsible for both "Crazy Blues" and the first successful old-time record, Fiddling John Carson's "The Little Old Log Cabin in the Lane." The thinking of Peer, who did more than anyone else to establish the popularity not only of early blues and early country music but of field recordings in general, exemplifies the mentality of the Northern record companies. A polished businessman with sophisticated tastes in art and music, Peer held much of the material he recorded in contempt—he would later boast dis-

dainfully, "I invented the hillbilly and nigger stuff"; he characterized Carson's record as "horrible"; and when asked about
the hillbilly artists he was responsible for, he replied, "Oh, I've
tried so hard to forget them."

He also clearly felt that black and white musics belonged to
two very different spheres. He later recalled his first impression of Jimmie Rodgers, who at the time was a member of a
group called the Tenneva Ramblers, as follows: "The records
would have been no good if Jimmie had sung with this group
because he was singing nigger blues and they were doing old-
time fiddle music. Oil and water . . . they don't mix." (Despite
this fanciful recollection, Jimmie Rodgers may have indeed
played his "nigger blues" at his first session, but Peer did not
record them. Nolan Porterfield points out that "Peer was still
on a determined quest for 'hillbilly music' (or whatever would
pass for it back in New York) and was willing to invent it on
the spot if necessary." And Jimmie Rodgers, after first meeting Peer, wrote to his wife that Peer wanted "these old-
fashioned things . . . love songs and plantation melodies and
the old river ballads.")

Peer did not come to this perception of two musics, one
black and one white, through any evidence he gleaned from
his recording sessions, at which the miscegeneity of American
music was all too apparent; rather, he had inherited a prejudice from his staid Midwestern upbringing that he found difficult to put aside. It was Peer who chose the word "race"
rather than "Negro" to describe the series of black-oriented
records that OKeh released, and it was he who was responsible for heavily promoting the records to the African
American market. Eventually, Peer did arrange some integrated sessions—he may have been the one to come up with

the idea of asking Louis Armstrong to back one of Jimmie Rodgers's records in 1930. But his earlier efforts to segregate American music were far more lasting.

The record companies' attitudes toward white blues are exemplified by their treatment of Jimmie Rodgers. Porterfield is correct in pointing out that Rodgers's performance of "Blue Yodel," "insofar as it is a direct, serious, and authentic rendering of the material, is scarcely distinguishable from that heard on dozens of black blues recordings of the time." (In fact, Rodgers is suspected to have learned much of his repertoire from the black "songster" Frank Stokes.) But Victor records viewed it as a novelty number, sold it as "Popular Song for Comedian with Guitar," and praised Rodgers for his "grotesque style." Edward Abbe Niles, the great critic of folk and popular music, called it "bloodthirsty" when it was first released and wrote condescendingly of Rodgers's "Blue Yodel No. 3" that his "singing and guitaring are as easy and lazy as ever, but [he] needs a gag-writer, for he is running short of verses." Imagine anyone writing such tripe about a black blues player, and you'll see the difference.

Indeed, as Bill Malone points out, Northern stereotypes about Southern music were profoundly segregationist in general, and Peer and Niles were far from alone in their prejudices.

> Stephen Foster, the blackface minstrels, and the song-writers of Tin Pan Alley had fashioned a musical vision of a placid, romantic South filled with banjo-strumming "darkies" that was hard to extricate from the popular mind. The music of the South's plain white folk, on the other hand, was . . . perceived as an archaic form of Elizabethan culture preserved in the Appalachians. Plain

white people, as a whole, were not ignored, but visions of sharecropping, poverty, racism, religious fundamentalism, ignorance, and pellagra prevented a clear or compassionate understanding of their culture. . . . A few musicians bitterly resisted the negative stereotypes, but, like the early African-American entertainers who had to deal with demeaning images, most country entertainers tried to adapt to the various perceptions that clung to their art and profession. Some musicians deliberately played the roles of awkward hillbillies or shy country boys or girls. A few, in fact, projected exaggerated hayseed personas.

It was from an adherence to these stereotypes that modern country music was born, exemplifying an imaginary, purely white traditional or "old-time" music. And, paradoxically enough, "old-time" is what Tommy Rockwell would call the music of Mississippi John Hurt.

THE FIRST "HILLBILLY," or "old-time," record appeared in 1923: Fiddlin' John Carson's "The Little Old Log Cabin in the Lane" (a minstrel song), backed with a fiddle instrumental called "The Old Hen Cackled and the Rooster's Going to Crow," recorded in Atlanta that June, which was also the first commercial field recording in American history. Carson was almost legendary in Atlanta. He had performed before many of the crowds that called for the death of Leo Frank, a Jew who was falsely accused of killing a white girl and was lynched. Carson had participated in a series of Georgia fiddlers' contests, and his defeat in one of them inspired a famous poem by Stephen Vincent Benét, "The Mountain Whippoorwill." Also, Carson was one of the first country performers heard over the radio: he was featured on station WSB in Atlanta.

An Atlanta furniture dealer and OKeh record distributor named Polk Brockman saw a newsreel of Carson performing in a fiddling contest and talked to Peer about recording him. Brockman thought that since Atlanta blacks were buying more record players now that blues and jazz records were being released, whites would be more likely to buy them too if their own kind of music were available. Peer was apparently convinced, and went down to Atlanta to record Carson for OKeh records. When the initial print run of five hundred copies quickly sold out, Peer realized that what he characterized as "hillbilly" music could reach an untapped market of rural record buyers.

By the mid-1920s, the field recordings of real Southern music, both white and black, were proving so successful that artists discovered in the process were brought to New York City to record for the major labels. There was a chauvinist appeal in branding the white music "Songs from Dixie," as Brunswick records did, making a strong argument for its authenticity:

> They are recordings of songs and tunes that were born in the hills of Kentucky, the railroad towns of West Virginia. . . . Most of these songs have been carried down from generation to generation by word of mouth and are closer to what may be called American Folk Music than anything in the United States. They are recorded not by imitators, but by people who have been born and raised in the sections of the country where

they are popular, and the obvious sincerity of their efforts will make them interesting to everyone.

Here, in a nutshell, is the aesthetic behind the music that was labeled old-time, hillbilly, folk, and, later, country: "not by imitators," "obvious sincerity"—the aesthetic of authenticity. Just imagine, if you will, a record company trying to use such language about a New York vaudeville number, and you'll see the difference right away. For these early recordings, as Robert Cantwell points out, "were *already old-fashioned* when they were recorded. . . . When Peer and the rest first sought it out, old-time music was the relic of a generation which swift industrialization, mechanization, migration, and war had virtually buried." A. P. Carter, patriarch of the Carter Family, one of the greatest and most popular of the "hillbilly" groups, was typical in this respect, seeking out songs from old and isolated people in rural communities. Almost all of these "old-time" records were performances of traditional numbers—rarely would a performer bring a song he'd written himself to a session, for that wouldn't be "authentic" enough. And if they were pressured to produce uncopyrighted material, these musicians would either dredge up half-forgotten relics of the past, or compose original songs that sounded just like the old ones.

What did all this have to do with the blues, or with black musicians? Wald states the case succinctly:

Having found that there was a large market for nostalgic "Old Fashioned Tunes" among white rural buyers, but that black consumers tended to prefer newer styles, the recording scouts made their choices accordingly. [Some artists were thus] banned from the hillbilly catalogs because they were black, and from the Race catalogs because they played hillbilly music. . . . By the end of the 1920s the chance to work both sides of the color line had pretty much disappeared.

John Hurt, a black artist who played distinctly "old-time" music, was a true rarity in this world.

IT WAS OUT of the "old-time" milieu that Willie Narmour—who introduced John Hurt to OKeh, and, therefore, to the world—appeared. Narmour had recently entered a fiddling contest in Winona, Mississippi, where he was spotted by a talent scout for OKeh (which had recently been acquired by Columbia). He was by far the most famous musician in Carroll County—in fact, his "Carroll County Blues" is still a fiddler's classic. Narmour and Smith recorded their first session on February 15, 1928, the day after Hurt's first session; all six of their sides were released and sold well.

Fiddling contests were far from new: the first American fiddling contest may have been in 1736, and only a year later came the first printed reference to black fiddlers. These contests soon became an ingrained part of American musical life, and the object of a full-scale revival in the mid-1920s, spearheaded by none other than the great industrialist Henry Ford. Ford harbored an unshakable animosity for jazz and Tin Pan Alley (the popular songs written in New York and broadcast the world over), and in 1925 it occurred to him to champion something more old-fashioned. The ultraconservative *Dearborn Independent*, a hugely influential weekly he published (its circulation was as high as 700,000), ran an editorial titled "The Old American Dance" in its Christmas issue, invoking a nationalist appeal:

> The old music, the neighborly mingling of people in the square dances, the rollicking reels and joyous jigs, together with the vocal harmony of the calls, are all found to impart a pleasure which the more sophisticated of the manufactured dances and the synthetic music of Tin Pan Alley (N.Y.) cannot give. . . . We are learning to play in the large-hearted, social and wholesome way of those whose characters and traditions shaped the nation.

Of course, Ford was far from alone in promulgating such ideas. By 1926 the proliferation of jazz, blues, and Charlestons had reached such a peak that even Irving Berlin, who would write many of the most enduring jazz standards, wrote, "The old fashioned ballads are becoming popular again. The public, I think, are tiring of jazz songs"; and country-music pioneer Jimmie Rodgers, who genuinely liked jazz and would record some excellent jazz numbers himself a year or two later, commented to his wife around the same time, "Folks everywhere are gettin' tired of all this Black Bottom–Charleston–jazz music junk."

But Ford was in a position to do something about it. He started running stories about the benefits of fiddle music and diagrams showing how to dance the Virginia reel; he founded a record company to record fiddle square-dance songs; and he staged a series of fiddling contests at Ford dealerships throughout the South and Midwest, garnering front-page stories in newspapers and newsreel footage in theaters. Old-fashioned dancing became all the rage, and thirty-four colleges and universities added courses in traditional American dance to their curricula.

Clearly, this old-fashioned music was just as quickly becoming the "authentic" American music, and the songs that were emphasized were those most removed from the influences of blacks (jazz) and Jews (almost all of the Tin Pan Alley songwriters were Jewish). The *Dearborn Independent* promoted "those good old songs" that "our grandmothers used to sing," which presumably did not include any blues. Ford was a rabid anti-Semite who not only influenced Hitler (*Mein Kampf* quoted from the *Dearborn Independent*'s editorials) but supported him financially for close to twenty years, and he justified his hatred for jazz by blaming its invention on Jews. He was not anti-black, per se—by hiring African Americans to work in his factories when nobody else would, he helped engineer the growth of the black middle-class. But promoting his Northern idea of traditional American music could not help but whiten the music of the South. And indeed, fiddling contests in the mid-1920s were sponsored not only by Henry Ford but by the Ku Klux Klan.

Ford's idea of what constituted authentic American music was by no means unique to him. Others in the 1920s were also trying to promote a uniquely American aesthetic that was separate from the prevailing European influence. One result was the publication of handbooks like Lamar Stringfield's *America and Her Music* (1931). Stringfield argued that America's national music must come from the "ground emotions of the people," and that those people had to be white. American Indians were out, since their music was "based on the ideas and themes made by a vanishing race." African Americans were out too: the "rhythms and almost monotonal expressions with their voices" were so "primitive" that they had to imitate white people's music instead. "The Negro's lack of originality in music prevents his songs from being carried on from generation to generation," Stringfield laughably asserts. Jazz is "a mathematical and commercially concocted music and, as opposed to sincere music, is artificial." And as for spirituals, "Since the emotions of the Negro race are foreign to the white man, an essentially Anglo-Saxon nation derives its nationalism in music only from its own people." What's left? Old-time music, of course.

AUTHENTICITY HAS COME to define country music more, perhaps, than any other musical genre. When *Billboard* asked the nine leading country record producers in 1953, "What factors do you consider in selecting new talent?" the most common answer was either authenticity or a synonym thereof. This was as true back in the 1920s as it is today. Of course, the implications of the word have changed to some degree, but country-music aficionados have always prided themselves on being able to tell when someone's not *real* country.

Back in the 1920s, the record companies pushed as hard as they could for *genuine* old-fashioned music. Clayton McMichen, the youngest member of the Skillet Lickers, one of the most popular string bands of the era, wanted to play modern rather than traditional music, but was turned down point blank by Frank Walker of Columbia records, who told him he'd brought the recording equipment down to Atlanta to record hillbilly, not pop music. When radio station WSM in Nashville aired its first country music program, the featured performer was a seventy-seven-year-old fiddler, Uncle Jimmy Thompson, who'd learned some of his songs during the Civil War.

It soon became de rigeur to be a "hillbilly" when performing hillbilly music, even if one hailed from the city. Of all the regulars on the Grand Ole Opry in the late 1920s, the majority had been urban tradesmen, and only one came from a poor, rural background. But they all pretended to be pure white trash. The Opry's impresario, George Hay, gave the bands that appeared on the program names like the Gully Jumpers, the Fruit Jar Drinkers, the Possum Hunters, and the Dixie Clod Hoppers (the latter two had originally been Dr. Bate and His Augmented Orchestra and the Binkley Brothers Barn Dance Orchestra). Of course, there was nothing the least bit authentic about all this. But who could tell the difference? Certainly not the nationwide audience—WSM was a "clear channel" station that could be heard over much of the country—that made the Grand Ole Opry one of the most successful shows in the history of radio.

THE AESTHETIC of authenticity dates back at least to the eighteenth century, so in one sense this valorization of "old-time" or traditional songs as "real" and the concommitant denigration of the "fake" songs of Tin Pan Alley was nothing new. But the twentieth century had seen a major shift in emphasis. As scholar Miles Orvell has shown, in the nineteenth century, high culture had been brought down to the masses and the prevailing aesthetic was therefore one of imitation and illusion. With the twentieth-century elevation of the vernacular into the new high culture, authenticity became of supreme value, for calling something "authentic" is the easiest way to add value to low-culture products. The new life characterized by the use of machines to replace manual labor was seen as fake; the more intense varieties of natural experience were contrasted with the humdrum everydayness of this new life, and were called "the real thing."

This was nowhere more true than in the consumer culture of which recordings were so much a part. In that culture, if you wanted to sell something, have it offer more than what it really offered, you differentiated it from similar products by calling it real, genuine: "The Durham-Duplex is a real razor"; Cuban cigars "are real cigars"; Faultless Pajamas will give you "real sleep"; Kaffee Hag coffee is "not a substitute"; Fleischmann's Gin is "The Real American Mixer." As Orvell writes, "It was as if there were some defect in everyday reality that had to be remedied by the more authentic reality of the object to be consumed." Of course, this was in part because of the huge number of frauds and shams that pervaded the marketplace in this era, from patent medicines to shoe-polish liquor. The world of advertising had started to run amok, and the real was getting harder and harder to discern among all the fakes.

So here was one reason why "authentic" American music was now such a hot commodity. Unfortunately, as we have seen, most of what was being labeled as "real" American music was no more "the real thing" than was Coca-Cola.

THE OTHER SIDE of the ten-inch shellac disk of "Nobody's Dirty Business" held "Frankie," a song that Hurt later claimed to have been playing since he was twelve years old.

Apparently, on October 15, 1899, in a black neighborhood of St. Louis, Frankie Baker shot her boyfriend, Albert "Allen" Britt, after he'd been caught fooling around with Alice Pryor; the song, a ragtime tune, was written by a "barroom bard" named Bill Dooley the following night, and spread like wildfire. It was first recorded as "Frankie Baker" by Ernest Thompson, a white man, in April 1924; by 1932, it had been recorded some twenty-five times. In 1933 it was made into a movie starring Mae West (*She Done Him Wrong*), which prompted Frankie Baker, who was alive and well, to sue the studio (she lost, of course).

The song tells a complex moral tale, in which Frankie peeps through a keyhole at the corner saloon to see her man Albert in Alice's arms, shoots him dead, makes friends with the judge, and then buries Albert. Hurt sings it in his usual laconic style, but the guitar playing is something else: blues researcher and guitarist John Fahey called it "the best guitar recording ever," and record collector Dick Spottswood has related that the classical guitarist Andrés Segovia couldn't believe there weren't two guitarists on the record.

John and Alan Lomax highly esteemed "Frankie and Albert," including two very lengthy versions of it in *American Ballads and Folk Songs* (1934), and an even longer one, complete with Leadbelly's explanatory notes, in *Negro Folk Songs as Sung by Lead Belly* (1936). In the former book they wrote, tongue firmly in cheek, "No one has ever heard precisely the same song sung by two individuals, unless they happened to be roommates." They included the song under the heading "Negro Bad Men," along with ballads such as "Stagolee," "Ida Red," and "De Ballit of de Boll Weevil." Of course, they were not alone: folklorists had published the song at least five times prior to the Lomaxes, all in collections of Negro folksong.

Characteristically, though, the Lomaxes didn't pay any attention to any of the twenty-five commercially recorded versions—of which Hurt's was one of the best—when they published their seminal folksong collection. It's a fair bet that they had never heard of John Hurt, and if they had, they almost certainly wouldn't have thought much of him. For at the time, Hurt was altogether too close in contact with whites for their tastes. Perhaps Henry Ford, who hated black music, and John Lomax, who loved it so much he spent years recording it, had something in common. For both, the most authentic American music was that which evidenced a clear and absolute divide between white and black.

FOR LOMAX, Odum, and their fellow folklorists, as for later folklorists, "Nobody's Dirty Business" and "Frankie" were "folk songs." But what exactly is "folk" music? Of course, almost anything can be, and has been, called folk music: that's what Lester Bangs called Lou Reed's *Metal Machine Music*, and by now the label embraces almost any music at all. But let's stay in the prewar period for the moment. What separated "folk" music, the songs of the people, from the contemporaneous songs of Cole Porter and Irving Berlin?

Although this has been disputed ground ever since the coinage of the term "folklore" in 1846, the traditional anthropological definition is, more or less: the orally transmitted expression of a small homogeneous group with a long common tradition, that expression being usually anonymous, unselfconscious, and spontaneous. It's certainly not hard to call the music of the Navajo Indians or the Ba-Benzélé Pygmies folklore according to this definition. But when you begin to apply it to American song in the twentieth century (or, for that matter, almost anything else in the twentieth century), all sorts of problems arise. By the 1920s, there were very few such homogeneous groups with a long common tradition left: cultural integration had all but eliminated them. Many folklorists, including John and Alan Lomax, believed that American blacks still constituted such a group, despite the evidence that their music had undergone countless transformations through relentless mixing with that of whites.

But by the time he reached his twenties, Alan Lomax probably no longer trusted his father's racially insensitive views and was beginning to be bothered by the established definitions of folk music, which did not fit the functional ideas embraced by the folklorists of the late 1930s. Alan Lomax was an idealist, and wanted folk music to encompass more than just the music of racially and culturally homogeneous groups, which were, in any case, becoming almost impossible to find.

In 1940, at the age of twenty-five and probably under the influence of Woody Guthrie (whom he'd met earlier that year), Alan Lomax wrote an obscure and pleasant manifesto called "Music in Your Own Back Yard," which lays out an informal definition of folk music that encompasses not only his own vision, but that of Guthrie, Pete Seeger, and even the later visions of the 1950s and '60s. Precisely because of its utopian simplicity, it may be the most eloquent essay on the subject we have.

It's just a pleasant way of passing the evening, the way of the cowpuncher on the Western plains, of the Kentucky mountaineers gathered around the smoky oil lamp. And when you sing a song about your own lives, you are doing the same thing they do—you are making folk music. . . .

Since the beginning of the world, people have told their feelings in song. And they're still doing it. Doing it mostly in lonely spots where there are no radios and phonographs, no movies and concerts, where people have to entertain themselves. . . .

These songs are our heritage as Americans. Woven in bright strands through the pattern of pioneer life, they are part of the American tradition of which we are so proud. To-day, almost too late, we realize that they are in danger of disappearing.

Yet these folk songs can easily be preserved. You, and all Americans, can find them right in your own back yards. Somewhere in your neighborhood there may be an old man, or woman—or perhaps a young one—who can sing you hundreds of love ballads and work songs. Your own grandmother may remember some.

Here Lomax abandons the traditional view—and that of his father, too. No longer must folk song be specific to a homogeneous group. Now it can be shared by the entire nation. And beneath this gentle and seemingly all-encompassing picture, Lomax is laying out a new, if hidden, criterion for what makes a song "folk": it is sung without expectation of remuneration.

Whether or not Lomax's portrait of America in 1940 is believable, things have changed even further since then. If you look at the songs sung today by grandmothers while knitting, construction workers while riveting, teenagers while serenading their sweethearts, or families around the campfire on their summer vacations, you'll find nothing but the detritus of pop songs.

But is this really so different from what one might have found in prewar America? Let's look at "Nobody's Dirty Business" and "Frankie." These songs may have been sung by African Americans while working or among friends at get-togethers, in which case they would have indeed functioned as "folk" songs, despite the fact that "Frankie" was by no means an anonymous ballad. But they were certainly also performed at more formal dances at which the entertainer was paid. They were certainly also recorded by record companies, who made money from them; the performers on those recordings were also paid. Street singers certainly sang them for the loose change of passersby. They were probably performed by seasoned and professional entertainers at medicine shows and perhaps even on the minstrel stage. In other words, though they may have been performed in folk settings, they were primarily performed as the Southern equivalent of pop songs. As a black American storytelling song, "Frankie" was initially the 1890s equivalent of R. Kelly's "Trapped in the Closet."

Obviously, there are large categories of songs that can only be called "folk," by any definition: sea shanties, camp-meeting songs, playground songs, field hollers, and so on. But outside of these categories, folk music today doesn't exist apart from pop music, and in this sense things haven't changed that much since the 1920s. The majority of folk music is either pop music, its equivalent, or the detritus thereof.

BUT THE IDEA of folk music has had an extremely powerful hold on the imagination, for unlike pop music, it is held up as the authentic voice of the people. If folk music is so much like pop music, must this claim vanish altogether? What exactly *is* the authentic voice of the people?

Music scholar Benjamin Filene, in a fascinating examination of the question of the nature of American folk music entitled *Romancing the Folk*, points out that "as late as 1910, most Americans would have been surprised to hear that America *had* any folk music. . . . Rural musicians had had no reason yet to think of themselves as 'the folk' or of their music as 'folk' music." The ideas of "authentic" or "folk" music were entirely foreign to performers such as John Hurt when he first recorded his songs. For him, "Frankie" was just as much of a pop song as a contemporaneous hit such as "Am I Blue" might have been—in fact, it had been composed only six years before he learned it.

The attention Americans devoted to folk music came shortly thereafter, spurred on by many of the same factors that spurred the desire for authenticity in "old-time" music. It's worth quoting Filene's conclusions on the subject at length:

> The notion held by early folklorists . . . of an unself-conscious, unmediated, and wholly uncommercial mode of musical expression strikes me as fundamentally

flawed: almost all musicians, after all, are influenced by others and make use of their talent in social settings. Given the explosion of mass media, rigid definitions of folk music become especially illusory when applied to the twentieth century. Since the turn of the century, even seemingly isolated musicians have spent their afternoons listening to phonographs and dreaming of recording contracts. What makes the formation of America's folk canon so fascinating, though, is that just as isolated cultures become harder to define and locate in industrialized America, the notions of musical purity and primitivism took on enhanced value, even in avowedly commercial music. Twentieth-century Americans have been consistently searching for the latest incarnation of "old-time" and "authentic" music. . . . One might therefore imagine terms like "folk" and "pure" as ciphers waiting to be filled: people imbue them with meanings that have cultural relevance and power to them.

And those meanings, then, reflect not the nature of the music itself but the nature of those making the cultural decisions as to what is and what is not "folk" music.

Take the case of Cecil Sharp. What could be more "folk" than the ancient ballads he found in the Appalachian mountains? A British authority on British folk song, Sharp came to America to document the survival of the British tradition in isolated mountain communities. He richly succeeded, collecting more than 1,600 versions of 500 songs between 1916 and 1918. Like other song collectors of his era, he believed that, in his own words, "posterity will need the primitive songs and ballads to keep their two arts of music and dance *real, sincere and pure"*—in other words, *authentic*. In Filene's words, Sharp "depicted the mountaineers as still living in a rosy distant past in which plain-speaking farmers with upstanding values occupied quaint log cabins, worked in harmony with nature to feed their families, and entertained themselves by dancing old-time steps to old-time ballads."

Of course, this is strongly reminiscent of the language we've seen used by the record companies to promote "old-time" music—white music, that is. And, it seems, racism goes with the territory. "The reason, I take it," Sharp wrote, "why these mountain people, albeit unlettered, have acquired so many of the essentials of culture is . . . to be attributed . . . chiefly to the fact that they have one and all entered at birth into the full enjoyment of their racial heritage." Their "language, wisdom, manners, and the many graces of life that are theirs, are merely racial attributes which have been gradually handed down generation by generation." African Americans, by contrast, he dubbed "a lower race."

Just as John Lomax had recorded only the most isolated black men he could find and focused on the repertoire he considered most authentically Negro, Sharp and his cohorts deliberately isolated the British ballads they collected from the countless other songs performed by the people of the Appalachians—fiddle tunes, hymns, sentimental songs—and isolated the white "British" folk from the 13.4 percent of the Appalachian population that was black.

THE PRACTICE of "folk music," at least in the prewar period, was logically entwined with the elevation of certain music over other music. And it was always music of a distinct racial cast, music assumed to have existed prior to the race mixing of the modern age. There is no essential difference between the fiddling contests sponsored by Henry Ford to promote nineteenth-century values and the folk music festivals that followed. One can see this most clearly in an example from the 1930s, the White Top Folk Festival in southwest Virginia, which lasted from 1931 to 1939.

The idea of the folk festival in general originated in the late 1920s as an explicit expression of a quest for authenticity: as David Whisnant explains in his study of folk "interventions," *All That Is Native and Fine,*

> A public festival . . . would bring the performers out of their isolated surroundings and place them before an appreciative audience. That approval would heighten the performers' sense of self-worth and pride in their imperiled culture. Confronted by the beauty and authenticity of the "real thing," the audience would be moved to forsake vulgar commercial imitations. If such an event were repeated enough times, the public would be reeducated and its taste refined and elevated.

White Top was one of four large festivals of traditional music inaugurated between 1928 and 1934, all quickly claiming national attention. By 1933, it was drawing more than twenty thousand people to the mountaintop, including the first lady, Eleanor Roosevelt. But one of its organizers, John Powell, was, as Whisnant succinctly puts it, "a thoroughgoing racist who had for many years worked persistently to maintain the racist social and political structure of Virginia. For him, White Top was a tactical instrument to be used in a broader cultural and political strategy." The Festival's "underlying aim was to develop a white national culture expressive of the values and esthetics of a white America."

Powell, like many others of his time, was searching for a "distinctive American music," a music that was authentically American, and in a 1927 article—anticipating the work of Lamar Stringfield—he categorized American music into six branches: American Indian music, Negro music, Stephen Foster–type music, pop music, "ultra modern" music, and, finally, Anglo-Saxon folk music, which he viewed as the one viable branch. "Our only hope for a nation in America," he wrote, "lies in grafting the stock of our culture on the Anglo-Saxon root. . . . [If] we desire a music characteristic of our racial psychology . . . it must be based upon Anglo-Saxon folk-song."

The White Top Festival, Powell and the other organizers concluded, would be a way to reaffirm the supremacy of Anglo-Saxon folk song, and therefore no black contestants were permitted. The only blacks even allowed on the mountain were Eleanor Roosevelt's father's servant and three black cooks to prepare her meals. And this was so despite "a rich banjo playing tradition among blacks at the time of the White Top festival in counties adjacent to the festival site," as Whisnant's research has shown.

The racism of White Top was not the only absurdity the festival indulged in. It also imported Morris dancing, a tradition that had never taken root in America, from England, and told musicians they could not play traditional but black-derived songs such as "Salty Dog." In sum, Whisnant writes, "The White Top festival must finally be seen not as the presentation of a preexisting reality but as a manipulation of it—

indeed at some levels as the *creation* of a 'reality' tautologically certified as authentic by the self-assured promoters who presented it."

The example of White Top is only one among many of how those who ascertain what is "folk" or "real" or "traditional" or "authentic" rarely if ever present a definition that accurately reflects the entirety of the culture they are defining. For, by the very nature of the act, ascertaining what is "authentic" excludes cultural artifacts that are then deemed "inauthentic." The culture that is celebrated, preserved, or revived by folklorists is always at least somewhat different from the culture that they found to begin with, and necessarily reflects the ideas of the folklorists more than the ideas behind the culture itself.

IT MIGHT SEEM that Sharp and Powell, who defended white music as folk, and John Lomax, who defended black music as folk, would have little in common: they took opposite views of the richness of black culture. Yet they shared the common belief that blacks were a "lower" race, and they deliberately ignored the music that resulted from the mixture of the races. Must Sharp's and John Lomax's racist views tarnish the songs that they collected? Of course not. But they tarnish America's folk song heritage, since they helped provide its foundation—just as the U.S. Constitution's embrace and perpetuation of slavery tarnished that document. By defining "folk" music as the most racially pure music, Sharp, Powell, and John Lomax established a heritage of American folk song that was far more racially pure than American music really was.

But there was much more to it than that. The ballad collectors and folk revivalists also ignored the fact that many of the "folk" songs they championed were once the equivalent of pop songs themselves, albeit several hundred years old. Nick Tosches puts it plainly: "Street balladry, the roots of traditional American music, was pop. The purest mountain airs, lustily pursued by sweaty, obsessive folklorists and concerned young things, were once the pop junk of urban Britain."

For several centuries, folklorists had assiduously separated what they thought were older songs from those more recently composed and called the older ones "folk," dismissing the newer ones with terms ranging from "penny dreadfuls" to "hillbilly" to "pop." Yet the people who sang folk songs made no such distinction. One folksong collector, the Texan James Ward Lee, noted that for every "real" folksong a collector found, he'd get six or eight of these "penny dreadfuls." He concluded that "one of the things highbrow collectors do not like to admit, but are forced to, is that their informants have almost no taste whatsoever."

Perhaps the only way to properly separate what we now think of as "folk" songs ("Barbara Allen") from "pop" songs (Stephen Foster's "Camptown Races") is the context of their performance. In other words, "pop" songs often become "folk" songs; and "folk" songs are basically old "pop" songs. It didn't take long for "Puff the Magic Dragon," composed in 1962, to become a "folk song" by Alan Lomax's criteria, and R. Kelly's 1996 "I Believe I Can Fly" and Green Day's 1997 "Good Riddance (Time of Your Life)" are enjoying the same fate. These songs are not just "standards"—they are sung by children and teenagers at camp, on the school bus, and at other informal gatherings.

Actually, the methods of transmitting "folk" material are often quite difficult to distinguish from the methods of transmitting "pop" songs. Even in the middle ages, professional entertainers would absorb music from communities they visited and then share it with other communities; and those communities would learn songs from professional musicians and transform them into new folk songs. Malone persuasively argues, "The pipers, fiddlers, jig dancers, or ballad vendors who entertained on street corners and village greens or at the rural fairs or other social or community functions, or who displayed their talents in taverns and alehouses, were as 'commercial' as their societies would permit them to be. It is now impossible, and irrelevant, to assess properly their varying degrees of 'folkness' or 'professionalism.'"

Perhaps if we can bring ourselves to jettison these old ideas of folk music and accept the inherent democracy of Tosches's "pop junk," we can more quickly overcome the racism to which our "folk" heritage has been linked.

AFTER READING all this, perhaps it's easier now to listen to Mississippi John Hurt's "Nobody's Dirty Business" as simply a good example of Southern popular music in early twentieth-century America.

Yes, the contradictions can seem overwhelming: it's sung by a black man but neither the guitar playing nor the melody seem distinctly black or white; the song appears at first to have been composed by black musicians, but its origins are far more obscure, and it was widely performed by whites; and it combines a jesting good humor with threats of deadly violence and an extraordinarily gentle delivery.

But if you look at Southern American music as a fundamentally integrated venture reflecting the closeness of the lives of blacks and whites, all this begins to make sense. For "Nobody's Business" doesn't function like folk music as we used to conceive it: age-old authentic material limited by race, region, and class, reflective of a well-established social tradition, and handed down from father to son. No, it functions in the same ways that pop music—integrated entertainment for a mass audience—does.

In the context of pop music, the violence of Hurt's lyrics is natural: you get a bigger rise out of your audience if you exaggerate. Pop music, from Elizabethan ballads through blues to metal and hip-hop, has always featured exaggerated violence. A line like "One of these mornings gonna wake up boozy, gonna grab my gun, gonna kill my Susie" is far more appropriate for the 1920s equivalent of a hip-hop song than for a campfire sing-along.

So let's now reimagine John Hurt as a modern-day pop musician—someone who gleaned from a variety of sources in order to create a new and original sound—not as a pure conduit for some age-old authentic black form of expression. Hurt had been playing in a semiprofessional capacity off and on for perhaps fifteen years by the time he made these recordings: he had had ample time to glean influences from a variety of sources, to imagine himself as a record-maker, and to adjust his music accordingly. One can easily explain the intimacy of Hurt's delivery by invoking the probability that he played mainly for small audiences at house frolics and Saturday night suppers. But I think that he also may have known full well how his gentle tone would affect his listeners. These songs sound as if they were designed for a three-and-a-half-minute pop record: they certainly could not have been heard very well at the dances that Hurt so often played. We have ample evidence that many of Hurt's contemporaries, ranging from Skip James to Jimmie Rodgers, considered themselves original artists and consciously crafted their songs for recording purposes. I suspect that Hurt also tailored his performances for Tommy Rockwell's recording horn.

Unfortunately, none of this worked. Hurt's records failed to sell. And the racially integrated world of traditional pop music that he was so much a part of was beginning to vanish. Encouraged by record companies and other cultural authority figures who promoted the authenticity of "old-time" white American music and by folk collectors and blues aficionados who promoted the authenticity of the most isolated forms of black music, the segregation of American "folk" musics—blues versus old-time country—would become enshrined and canonized.

PART II: THE REVIVAL

IN 1952, a twenty-nine-year-old amateur folklorist used John Hurt's "Frankie," among other songs, to try to alter the legacy of traditional Southern music and, in doing so, offer it its greatest chance for reintegration. He wasn't a Southerner, he wasn't a musician, and he wasn't a scholar: he was first and foremost a collector, not just of records but of artwork, ideas, and all sorts of cultural ephemera. His tastes could be called catholic or democratic, but not indiscriminate: he had a knack for unearthing things that were intrinsically interesting in and of themselves, not just indicative of some preconceived idea about culture or race. He is perhaps the most heroic figure in the long story of the segregation of traditional American music. His name was Harry Smith.

Smith had grown up poor in the Pacific Northwest and was, essentially, a beatnik long before the term was in use: he lived in bohemian cultural centers, never earned any money, made abstract films and paintings, did research into American Indian folklore and the Kabbalah, took quite a few drugs, and, mostly because of his desperate financial situation, made such a mess of everything that he abandoned all of his own films, lost or destroyed all his own paintings, and lost a painstaking phonetic transcription he'd made of all the songs in his *Anthology of American Folk Music.*

According to Smith, Moses Asch, the head of Folkways Records and a man of similarly broad-minded vision, approached him with the idea to put together an album of "folk" songs along the lines of Folkways's earlier five-volume anthology of jazz. By this time, Smith, one of the premier record collectors of his day, had amassed several thousand high-quality race and hillbilly records whose record-company owners had shown no interest in reissuing. He went about compiling his selections for his anthology with few hard-and-fast rules, except to steer away from anything that smacked of jazz, classical, Tin Pan Alley, or drawing-room music, and to concentrate on songs of the South; but he did seem to have one other guiding principle—as he later put it, the songs "were selected because they were odd"; "I was looking for exotic records."

Odd and exotic to Smith and his listeners, yet far from odd to those who had originally recorded them. But in this oddness lay these songs' tremendous power. It was what made them so influential to the conception of traditional music that Bob Dylan and others would delineate in the 1960s, a conception far removed from Woody Guthrie's, Alan Lomax's, or Pete Seeger's ideas of folk music (though equally seductive—and equally specious). As Dylan put it in his most eloquent statement, a 1966 *Playboy* interview conducted by Nat Hentoff,

> Folk music is a word I can't use. Folk music is a bunch of fat people. I have to think of all this as traditional music. Traditional music is based on hexagrams. It comes about from legends, Bibles, plagues, and it revolves around vegetables and death. . . . All these songs about roses growing out of people's brains and lovers who are really geese and swans that turn into angels. . . . I mean, you'd think that the traditional-music people could gather from their songs that mystery is a fact, a traditional fact. . . . In that music is the only true, valid death you can feel today off a record player.

What both Smith and Dylan sought, then, was mystery. There was very little mystery in the popular songs of the 1950s and early '60s; by contrast, the commercial cultural musical products of the South a generation or two earlier already sounded as weird to them as traditional Bulgarian, Mongolian, or Central African music might have. And this mysteriousness wasn't just that of songs whose methods of transmission through the ages had resulted in strange corruptions and recombinations, or whose sound was abrasive and harsh in comparison to the music of the 1950s and early '60s, or whose subject matter was the universality of death and the unknown, or whose very existence seemed to betray time's ellipses. It was also the oddness of blacks sounding like whites and whites sounding like blacks, of songs that defied all the categories the folklorists and record companies had put them into for so many years, of songs like John Hurt's. The "mystery" that so many have argued is at the heart of American music is in large part the result of our inability to fully grasp the ease and confidence with which that music was created in spite of and across racial boundaries.

SMITH'S TONGUE-IN-CHEEK headline summary of John Hurt's "Frankie" read: "ALBERT DIES PREFERRING ALICE FRY, BUT JUDGE FINDS FRANKIE CHARMING AT LATTER'S TRIAL." It's easy to see why Smith liked the song and Hurt's version of it: despite the frequency with which it was recorded, Hurt's rendering is clearly one of the most compelling because of his clear enunciation, steady rhythm, and matter-of-fact, genial delivery. Smith was so taken with Hurt's 1928 recordings in general that he included two of them in his 84-song collection, while the large majority of artists were represented by only one.

Although Folkways's title for Smith's *Anthology of American Folk Music* might lead one to think that it represents the entire country (or, indeed, hemisphere), every single song on this six-record collection was performed by a Southerner (with only two curious exceptions: a dance band from Minnesota and a Hollywood cowboy who originally hailed from Indiana). By design, every song was also recorded by a commercial recording company between 1927, the year in which electrical recording began to be used with great frequency, augmenting acoustical fidelity, and 1932, after which the Depression made it financially impractical for the record companies to do many field recordings.

Unlike almost everyone else who was studying American music at the time, Smith recognized the integrated nature of the music in the South and cavalierly placed black and white performers next to each other on each of the album's twelve sides. In his elaborate liner notes, he deliberately omitted any mention of the performers' race or the record companies' classification of the music. As he later said,

> There had been a tendency in which records were lumped into blues catalogues or hillbilly catalogues, and everybody was having blindfold tests to prove they could tell which was which. That's why there's no such indications of that sort (color/racial) in the albums. I wanted to see how well certain jazz critics did on the blindfold test. They all did horribly. It took years before anybody discovered that Mississippi John Hurt wasn't a hillbilly.

This was a radical conception of "folk" music. There were none of the folklorists' "labor songs" or "songs of the Negro" or "songs of the cowboy" here. There were no non-commercial field recordings, and, in an anthology of "folk" music, their absence was pure heresy. Not only that, Smith, who had studied anthropology at the University of Washington, deliberately included songs that most folklorists would have excluded out of hand—songs composed by professional musicians and songs about the politics of the time. Instead he simply presented a fascinating melange of disparate styles and an acoustic manifesto that implicitly equated "folk," "pop," and "classical."

The long-playing record, or LP, was a relatively new medium in 1952, and most LPs of the era contained classical performances and were aimed at highbrows or high-fidelity buffs. To put recordings of the 1920s on an LP was to lend them a cultural authority that otherwise would have eluded them. As Cantwell points out, "What had been, to the people who originally recorded it, essentially the music of the poor, the isolated, and the uneducated, the *Anthology* reframed as a kind of avant-garde art."

But Smith's criteria for choosing the songs on his *Anthology* remain obscure. His fullest attempt to explain them came in telling folk music researcher John Cohen in 1968, "You couldn't get a representative cross-section of music into such a small number of records. Instead, they were selected to be the ones that would be popular among musicologists, or possibly with people who would want to sing them and maybe would improve the version. They were basically picked out from an epistemological, musicological selection of reasons." He might as well have said that he chose these songs simply because he liked them.

Smith's *Anthology* would become, as Cantwell puts it, the "enabling document," the "musical constitution" of the folk music revival of the 1950s and '60s. But it has now become more than that. Upon the 1997 reissue of the *Anthology* on CD, Luc Sante, one of our most perceptive cultural critics, wrote,

The *Anthology* is a work of art, rounded and complete unto itself. Other anthologies are good or not, historical or aesthetic, instructive or inspiring, nicely sequenced or random, but even the best ones are merely collections. The *Anthology* is . . . an essential element of American culture, deserving of a place on the narrow shelf between *Huckleberry Finn* and Walker Evans's *American Pictures.* Every twelve-year-old should have a copy.

There is certainly something to be said for this point of view. But even if Smith's anthology had extended to sixty, rather than six, LPs' worth of songs, I think there would have been little diminution of the experience. For it is the music of this particular time and place that is so timeless and fully rounded, not only the songs Smith happened to choose. You could, if you wanted to back up Dylan's take on traditional music, compile at least three dozen songs that are simply about mysteriousness and the unknown, ranging from the Allen Brothers' "Old Black Crow in the Hickory Nut Tree" to Blind Willie Johnson's "Dark Was the Night, Cold Was the Ground" (neither of which were in the *Anthology*). Here's another example. I tried taking a completely random dip through the 25,000 records in Joe Bussard's peerless collection (see www.vintage78.com for a complete listing), and the thirty-song cassette tape I compiled was almost as compelling as Smith's anthology.

Smith's reissuing of Hurt's songs, then, was not just artistically noteworthy, but terribly bold in its refusal to segregate musicians by race. Unfortunately, though, it had little impact on Hurt or his reputation at the time. It wasn't until the early 1960s that blues researchers, inspired by jazz collectors, began to pay serious attention to Hurt's 1928 recordings.

■　■　■　■

BY THIS TIME, John Hurt, now in his seventies, no longer owned a guitar, and had long since stopped playing music of any kind. He had remained in Avalon, his hometown, oblivious to his renown as a result of the reissue of some of his 1928 recordings. He had never heard of Harry Smith or *The Anthology of American Folk Music*; he had no idea that a group of enthusiasts had found and listened to all his old records, had marveled at how strange and different they were, and had assumed that he was long since dead. Instead, he had abandoned music in favor of more lucrative work—on farms, picking cotton and corn, or on the river, or with the railroad. Now he was working with cattle for $28 a month. And then, one day in 1963, two young white men appeared as if out of nowhere.

Tom Hoskins and Mike Stewart were young blues aficionados who had heard some of Hurt's 78-rpm records in the collection of their friend Dick Spottswood. One of them was "Avalon Blues," a song of homesickness, which Hurt had composed during his trip to New York. Putting two and two together, they figured that Hurt must have hailed from Avalon, Mississippi; the town didn't seem to be on any maps, though. Finally they located it on a nineteenth-century map, and determined to go visit to see if Hurt was still alive.

Stewart recently wrote me:

I remember going with Hoskins to the country store in Avalon, asking if anybody knew where John Hurt lived; they told us it was out near Willie Narmour's, of Narmour and Smith, whom Hurt played with (you might notice that some of the fiddle runs and Hurt's guitar runs are almost identical; when I play Narmour and Smith on the guitar, it sounds a lot like Hurt). I remember driving through some rolling countryside until we came to a very modest, medium-size clapboard house, with chickens and a big iron pot in the front yard. I remember the "Blackdraught" calendar on the wall, and the ambience of the one-room house.

(Hoskins and Hurt both later recalled that Hurt had initially suspected his visitors had been from the FBI. But Stewart calls that story "bunk . . . I think it was made up by Hurt and Hoskins to add some color. Nobody even half as smart as John would have thought two scuzzy, unshaved guys in a beat-up car with beer and a guitar would be from the FBI.")

What Hoskins and Stewart had done was unprecedented. Blues players had been "rediscovered" before by impresarios such as John Hammond, who had first brought Big Bill Broonzy to play for whites. But Broonzy had never stopped being a professional musician. Never before had anyone resuscitated an old black man's completely dead career.

The result was overwhelming. Inspired by Hoskins's success, blues aficionados began making a series of forays into the deep South, bringing back with them musicians such as Skip James, Son House, Booker White, and Robert Wilkins. The blues revival had begun in earnest.

Meanwhile, the friendly welcome Hurt had received from Hoskins and Stewart continued once he accompanied them to Washington, D.C. It seemed that everyone he met was simply in awe of him. He recorded thirty-nine songs in one day for the Library of Congress, made some commercial recordings for the Piedmont and Vanguard labels, and gave his first major concert appearance at the 1963 Newport Folk Festival.

His guitar playing, singing, and choice of material were all virtually unchanged since his 1928 sessions.

The plaudits came fast and furious. *Newsweek* named him one of the three standout musicians of the Festival, along with Joan Baez and Bob Dylan. *Time* magazine called him "the most important rediscovered folk singer to come out of Mississippi's Delta country, the traditional home of Negro country blues singers," even though Hurt lived in predominantly white Carroll County. The *New York Times* wrote that "his performances have [an] introspective quality," despite the fact that they revealed nothing whatsoever about his inner life.

He was soon appearing everywhere from *The Tonight Show* to Carnegie Hall, from university campuses to coffee houses and festivals, with a booking agent handling the overwhelming demand. A musician who had failed to find much of an audience in the 1920s because he was too far behind the times had now become one of the most popular traditional musicians of the 1960s.

TO UNDERSTAND HOW this could happen, let's look at a parallel but very different example.

Lonnie Johnson, who had been present at Hurt's 1928 recording sessions, and whom Hurt had at first held in awe and then worked with closely, was a brilliant guitarist and a mellow, urbane singer who excelled not only at blues, but also jazz and pop. He was one of the most popular guitarists of the 1930s, recorded hundreds of solo records, and played with such greats as Bessie Smith, Louis Armstrong, Duke Ellington, and Eddie Lang. Guitarists including Robert

Johnson, B. B. King, and John Lee Hooker idolized him. Moreover, he virtually invented the guitar solo. In many ways, Lonnie Johnson's music exemplifies the blues.

The blues, that is, as defined by its traditional black audience. For them, the blues had once encompassed not only singer-guitarists such as Charley Patton and Blind Lemon Jefferson and singers such as Bessie Smith and Victoria Spivey, but also a range of performers whom we now think of as jazz musicians, from Jelly Roll Morton to Count Basie to Coleman Hawkins.

But the white blues audiences of the 1960s had remarkably different tastes. Lonnie Johnson was alive and well, but few were interested in seeing him. Johnson had always been one of the most elegant, sophisticated, and suave musicians, rivaling even Duke Ellington in urbanity. The image he consciously cultivated was a powerful counterexample to the prevailing views of black Americans. And after the blues revivalists showed some initial interest, he was virtually ignored. Johnson liked to perform not only blues but pop songs like "How Deep Is the Ocean" and "I Left My Heart in San Francisco," and he liked to play both acoustic and electric guitar. At a folk music concert at Town Hall in New York City, for example, Johnson confounded expectations by performing, instead of a blues song, "This Heart of Mine," an old Fred Astaire number. The audience was, of course, horrified, and he was not invited to perform there again.

LONNIE JOHNSON is a good example of what the blues meant to black audiences. The great black critic Albert Murray may have exaggerated the case somewhat, but his words on the subject indicate a fundamental difference between black and white aesthetics of the blues:

> The blues as such are synonymous with low spirits. Blues music is not. With all its so-called blue notes and overtones of sadness, . . . its preoccupation with the most disturbing aspects of life, it is something contrived specifically to be performed as entertainment. Not only is its express purpose to make people feel good, . . . it is actually expected to generate a disposition that is both elegantly playful and heroic in its nonchalance. . . .
>
> Blues-idiom merriment is not marked either by the sensual abandon of the voodoo orgy or by the ecstatic trance of religious possession. One of its most distinctive features, conversely, is its unique combination of spontaneity, improvisation, and control.

Furthermore, by the 1950s, most blacks regarded traditional acoustic blues performances (as opposed to the then-popular blues of B. B. King and Dinah Washington) with the same disdain that whites might have had for Al Jolson and Eddie Cantor records. This music was dead. It represented everything that blacks did not want to be reminded of: peonage, pimping, and primitivism.

THE NUMBER OF white people interested in the blues has always been very small. But their image of the blues was quite different from Murray's and has had far more influence on popular perceptions. The best example of this contrast, perhaps, is the music of Big Bill Broonzy.

Big Bill was well known to black Americans as an immensely popular Chicago blues singer whose hundreds of 1930s sides, usually featuring a small combo of three or more players, often sound to today's ears like '50s rock'n'roll. In 1938, however, in a career-defining move, he played solo acoustic guitar in John Hammond's "From Spirituals to Swing" concert at Carnegie Hall. Hammond, a music impresario later famous for promoting Billie Holiday, Count Basie, Bob Dylan, and Bruce Springsteen, presented Broonzy as an amateur, writing that he "was prevailed upon to leave his Arkansas farm and mule and make his very first trek to the big city," and though any knowledgable listener could have pegged that for a lie, enough people believed him. Broonzy, who had always worn fashionable suits and had recorded with jazz artists in major cities across the land, now became, whenever he appeared before largely white audiences, an Arkansas farmer, playing up to the stereotype as much as he could. He made dozens of LPs in the 1950s featuring songs like "John Henry" and "Goodnight Irene"—"folk" songs he would have never recorded for a black audience—and the liner notes frequently included lies such as "He spent the first forty years of his life on a farm in Arkansas" or "Big Bill resisted the possibly hazardous temptation of becoming an 'entertainer.'"

WHAT DOES THIS have to do with "authenticity," then? Wasn't Big Bill being more "real" when he played his hits of the '30s than when he recorded his solo records in the '50s? Weren't

Lightnin' Hopkins and John Lee Hooker being more "real" on their fiercely electric, proto-rock '40s and '50s sides than on their post-rediscovery acoustic albums?

Not for the white folkies. With the rediscovery of John Hurt, their new image of the blues—"Playing guitar was a relaxing outlet after a full day's work in the field," to quote the liner notes to a Broonzy record—became enshrined, and it is the one that still commands the popular imagination. Blues artists had primarily played at juke joints, parties, or street corners. But now, the prevailing image of the blues was a poor lone guitar player sitting on his porch playing for nobody in particular, singing just to pass the time away or perhaps to ease his pain.

Yes, many blues singers played on their front porches for white folks like Tommy Rockwell, Tom Hoskins, Peter Guralnick, and myself, who all traveled down to Mississippi to visit them. (By the 1950s, juke joints were a thing of the past, and blues singers were no longer welcome on street corners.) But the rest of the time, they mostly kept their guitars packed away, saving them for more social or lucrative occasions. The myth of the solitary blues performer may be good for gracing album covers and selling coffee, but it paints the blues in an utterly false light. Blues had always been a music directed at a live black audience—there was little reason to sing it on one's own. But now it became reimagined as pure bardic self-expression, and the sex and violence in the lyrics were rendered harmless by the advanced age of the performer.

Hurt, who seemed to fit this myth perfectly, may have done more than anyone else to confirm and cement it in the popular imagination. For here was a man whose songs had been full of violence and who had played in rough environments, now revealed to be the personification of the sweet grandfatherly Negro farmer—Uncle Remus come to life.

One can't blame Hurt here—there can be no doubt that he was one of the gentlest, kindest people to ever gain worldwide fame as a musician. His mild delivery was perfectly suited to the image of someone singing to himself or to a few close friends. And it's more than likely that the violence of his songs—a violence that the '60s blues fans completely ignored—did not reflect his actual personality, reflecting instead his former milieu.

But Hurt was a far cry from his Delta blues contemporaries, who tended to be a much rougher group of men. That this gentle soul, who didn't actually play much blues, denied he was a blues singer, and never enjoyed any real success with a black audience, should become one of the most popular "blues" singers of the early 1960s is thoroughly ironic.

OF COURSE, this benign image of the blues isn't the only one to dominate the popular imagination. Shortly after Hurt's rediscovery, a new audience, powerfully influenced by the Rolling Stones, latched onto a very different image of the blues, one that harked back to John Lomax's portrayal of Leadbelly. This audience went for John Lee Hooker's one-chord boogie drone and spooky lyrics and the unadorned and often brutal sound of the Howlin' Wolf–Willie Dixon–Muddy Waters–Bo Diddley stable at Chess Records. And their new image was the inspired outlaw, personified by Robert Johnson, Wolf, Hooker, and, later, Buddy Guy, with his

"Stone Crazy" shtick. The blues singers were threatening, not mild, and the thrill of hearing them was heightened by a measure of fear—as Wald puts it, in this image the "blues is . . . raw, dirty, violent, wild, passionate, angry, grungy, greasy, frightening outlaw music." Of course, this wasn't entirely a misperception on the part of the audience: male blues singers have always combined machismo with violence and elements of the supernatural derived from their traditions. For most of them, "mojo" is a simple fact, one among many. But the white audiences emphasized this aspect of the blues far more than black audiences had, and soon enough blues musicians like Hooker and Guy were deliberately catering to their tastes, in the process losing the small black audiences they once had.

After World War II, blues had greatly diminished in popularity. Some blues musicians remained popular among the (mostly female) black audience: Louis Jordan, Dinah Washington, T-Bone Walker, Memphis Slim, B. B. King, Bobby Bland, Etta James, Joe Turner, Amos Milburn. But they didn't fit either the down-home back-porch acoustic guitarist image or the wild and violent axe-wielding electric guitarist image in the least. These were all sophisticated, urban musicians who dressed to the nines. As a result, most of them had, at first, far less appeal to the (mostly male) white audience. They were too "jazzy," it seemed.

Both the front-porch and outlaw images of blues musicians were romantic fictions that fit perfectly with John Lomax's conception of authentic black music as uncivilized, "uncontaminated by white influence"—not to mention the conventions of minstrelsy. These images perpetuated stereotypes of blacks as poor sharecroppers to be pitied or untamed savages to be feared, as folks uneducated and isolated in their own peculiar world. In the fictions of the blues, there was little room for hardworking crowd pleasers, sophisticated innovators, or musical miscegenators.

The blues presented a perfect opportunity for the resurrection of a nineteenth-century cultural condescension. While the music was inaccessible, haunting, and violent—a personification of the other, the shadow side—its surviving practitioners were humble old men, as harmless and quiet as a cheap acoustic guitar. The blues fan could thus simultaneously play the roles of voyeur and benefactor. As one record collector told Calt, "It was really a plantation mentality. Everyone wanted to own a nigger."

PROBABLY EVERY FAN of old-fashioned blues has fantasized about doing what Hoskins did—going down to Mississippi to visit a legendary blues player. I've done it myself, and it was an unforgettable experience.

Jack Owens was born in 1905 in Bentonia, Mississippi, where he lived all his life. Bentonia is in the hills above Jackson, just outside the Delta; its present population does not exceed six hundred. Owens's blues style was largely derived from that of his fellow Bentonian Skip James, one of the most brilliant and inventive of blues musicians, with whom he played.

In 1970, blues researcher David Evans recorded Owens for an LP on Testament records, which, like many "folk" recordings, is difficult to listen to—here because of poor editing, poor sound quality, uneven performances, and the muffling effect of the harmonica playing of his partner, Bud Spires. However, when the German label Wolf Records rereleased Skip James's seminal 1931 recordings, they added some 1981 recordings of Jack Owens to the end of the CD, and these five songs are immediately captivating for the clear sound of Owens's guitar, his exceptionally strong and melancholy vocals, and his lyrics, which offer interesting variations on those of Skip James. For example, he added to James's stark and malevolent "Devil Got My Woman" the line, "Devil got religion, joined the Baptist church."

In 1992, on a trip to Mississippi, I decided to visit Jack Owens, accompanied by Edd Hurt, a friend from Memphis. After a catfish lunch at a white establishment in Bentonia, we crossed the railroad tracks upon the advice of the waitress and approached two men who were talking and drinking beer outside a bar. Henry Bussey was a leathery sixty-seven-year-old, apparently drunk; Kenny Burch was his cousin, sober and in his early thirties. (I have changed their names for the sake of anonymity.) Kenny later told me he didn't normally enter the bar because it was a very rough place, but that day he'd come to talk to his cousin; on the other hand, he confessed to using a little cocaine on occasion. They knew Jack well and agreed to show us to his house; they drove in Henry's blue pickup truck, and we followed in my Honda.

After turning down three different dirt roads, we saw Jack's shack, the first in a row of three or four. The yard was occupied by two pickup trucks and an abandoned Buick, and Jack was sitting on his front porch, looking exactly like his pictures. Despite the midsummer heat, he wore black shoes, long johns beneath his stained work pants, a T-shirt beneath his stained work shirt, and a black "Benson & Hedges Blues Festival" cap. His teeth were mostly gold- or silver-capped; his back was hunched; his hands were large but wrinkled. His eyes were remarkable: around a large black pupil, the iris was a thin circle of bright blue. (Coincidentally, Skip James also had blue eyes.) He smelled of dirt and sweat.

He greeted us with little surprise, and he and Henry immediately started joking around. He agreed to play some blues for us after he asked us if we could pay him, and we said we could. He shuffled inside the dark shack and emerged with a twelve-string guitar strung with just six strings, already in perfect tune. He played "Cherry Ball Blues" and "Hard Times," both numbers associated with Skip James. He sounded impressive—his voice high and wailing, his picking sure. But then he said he couldn't play well without some "hog's mouth" (his term for Gordon's gin, after the picture of the boar on the label). Kenny, Edd, and I drove to a nearby liquor store, but couldn't find any Gordon's; when we returned with a fifth of Seagram's, Jack upended it like a bottle of beer and chugged down the equivalent of three shots in as many seconds.

After a few more numbers, we passed around the bottle and talked. Jack told us how Alan Lomax had come down and spent a week there, recording him and paying him $600 for his songs. Lomax had brought him up to Greenville to play on a big stage with a lot of other blues players, and they put something on his collar and something on his guitar and you could hear him clear to Bentonia. He talked about teaching David Evans to play guitar, about playing with "Skippy" James, about learning songs from his parents, about people coming to see him from "'cross the sea," about legal matters, about how he'd bought his pickup truck from money earned playing the blues, about how he'd operated a club with Skippy, about how he'd quit playing the blues when he got married but then felt he couldn't go back to church once he'd started playing the blues again. He asked us inside to see whether we could fix his record player. Inside were three rooms without electric lights; the only furniture in the living room was a fan, a table, and a tape deck. We showed him how to work the tape deck, which wasn't broken, and listened to a recording of him playing a song that ran, "Jack don't want no water, Jack don't want no wine." He told us that all of his records had been stolen (I suspect he meant tapes), and we talked about the thief, who had been caught but released on bail, and who had needed money for his drug habit.

While Jack was playing, Henry stopped joking and started to get serious about the music. Jack let him sing a verse of "The Devil" and pick a few licks on the guitar. It was obvious that he remembered quite a bit, but was ashamed and embarrassed about it—possibly because the music was considered low, possibly because he was only an amateur.

By the end of the day, Kenny, who had apparently never seen anything like this before, was moved; Edd and I were astonished. We were glad to have heard one of the last surviving masters of a long-dead tradition, one of the only people alive who still played the blues the way he used to in the first half of the twentieth century.

Yet something has always bothered me about my part in this transaction. Everything about Jack Owens, from the trucks in his yard to the lyrics of his blues, smacked of the genuine earthiness of the rural working-class African American life, the earthiness of a forgotten and vanishing world of which he seemed the last living relic. I have always enjoyed birdwatching, and the thrill I get from seeing an uncommon bird is not unlike the thrill I got from seeing Jack Owens in his native habitat. He was my ivory-billed wood-pecker—the last of an endangered species.

But when we view musicians as exotic animals, can conde-scension be far behind? I feel certain that my appreciation of Jack Owens was quite unlike my appreciation of, say, Wayne Shorter. For rather than appreciating Owens only for his artistry, I was appreciating him in large part for his authenticity.

And in that, I was much like the blues fans of the 1960s.

THANKFULLY, THINGS HAVE changed to some degree. Though the emphasis on the Rolling Stones's favorite musi-cians still endures, a largely white audience now embraces blues in all its variety. Yet John Hurt is still seen by some as a Delta blues musician with no conceivable connection to white music—or to the violence of his lyrics. The most complete Web site devoted to him is entitled "Mississippi John Hurt and the Delta Blues"—this man who was entirely unrepresen-tative of the Delta, of the blues, and of his race, is still held up as an authentic example of all three.

And so the myths persist. Even the most dedicated blues fans will tell you that John Hurt eschewed popular songs and stuck to traditional material that had been sung for years before his birth; that he developed his material within a wholly black milieu; and that his material was more or less "pastoral" in nature. In fact, as we have seen, Hurt played popular songs that postdated his birth, were probably gleaned from his exposure to them at popular entertainments such as medicine shows, and were in no sense "traditional" at that time; he often played together with whites; and if his material could be said to be preoccupied with one idea, it was death, and usually a violent one.

So what made Hurt so popular, the most beloved of the "rediscovered" blues musicians? It wasn't just his guitar playing. It was more likely that his fans saw in him an authentic representative of a forgotten black America at the same time as he gave them music that was familiar to their white ears simply because it wasn't so purely black. (As Calt puts it, "Because Hurt's wispy singing . . . was racially nondescript, it posed no barrier to his 'folk' popularity. His guitar playing . . . had all the prerequisite familiarity necessary to engage coffeehouse patrons.") Listening to Hurt may have confirmed in whites a feeling of racial optimism. His mild, genial music posed an image of blackness diametrically opposed to that of Malcolm X and all the other angry young black men of the time.

Unlike their forebears John Lomax and Cecil Sharp, these folkies saw themselves at the forefront of the Civil Rights movement and were trying to embrace cross-racial brotherhood and equality. And Hurt became a much more convenient symbol to them of the goodness of black folk than the other rediscoveries of the day. Lonnie Johnson was too citified, not down-home enough to be authentic; Skip James was too sullen and superior, and his dignified manner struck many as putting on airs; Son House was unable to handle his liquor. In contrast, Hurt's gentleness seemed almost messianic to some: Stefan Grossman, a Jew who studied guitar with Hurt, called him "very Christlike and perfect," bizarrely enough. It's not hard to discern a desire here that all blacks could share Hurt's characteristics.

None of this adoration, however, helped Mississippi John Hurt in the end. During a midwinter gig in Chicago, he contracted pneumonia and died, just three years after his rediscovery, at the age of seventy-three. His death may have been hastened by the strain of his extensive performing schedule.

IS IT INEVITABLE, then, that when whites experience and appreciate the art of black Americans, cultural condescension is part of that appreciation?

Only if whites valorize the black musicians they listen to as "authentic." Tom Hoskins and Mike Stewart, for example, appreciated John Hurt primarily as a brilliant guitarist, not as an authentic representative of a bygone folk culture. When most people listen to Duke Ellington or Wayne Shorter records, they're not appreciating them for their "blackness" or their otherness, but for their sophistication, skill, grace, and beauty. Even for self-acknowledged "blues tourists" like myself, condescension can be easily overcome. There is so much to be appreciated about blues musicians: the pathos and humor of their lyrics and delivery; the brilliance of their guitar, vocal, or piano work; the energy and drive of their performances; the way they engage and play with the expectations of their audience.

But all too often, whites find themselves in the position I found myself in when I visited Jack Owens: as tourists. They check out the flora and fauna, the exotic locales, taking pictures they can share with their friends, instead of appreciating the unique artistry of the musicians they're listening to.

And soon a few of these musicians start giving their audience what they so clearly want: a taste of what the audience considers an "authentic" black experience. At the point at which these musicians begin doing that, they become the contemporary equivalents of blackface minstrels, who fulfilled exactly the same function once upon a time.

These audiences forget that there is no "authentic" black culture in America, and there never has been. Black culture is a many-splendored, vibrant, changing thing, and is inseparable from the American culture with which it has always interacted; and its essential dignity lies, in large part, in the negotiation of that interaction, not in any notion of its "authenticity."

AND SO WE come to the conclusion of our tangled tale. As of this writing, black music and white music in America are perhaps farther apart than ever. Black musicians play R&B and hip-hop, white musicians play country and rock, and they share little if any common repertoire. American music, which was once a racial stew exemplified by songs such as "Nobody's Dirty Business," has become two entirely separate musics, one black and one white.

And, as we've seen, the reasons for this disjunction aren't only the usual commercial ones. The language of authenticity has played an enormous part as well. In defining America's most "authentic" musics as those that seem most racially pure, cultural authorities ranging from the most racist to the most well-meaning have repeatedly isolated certain strains of American music out of the racial stew, and subsequent musics have been built on those foundations. With the exception of disco, every time a new genre is invented—jazz, blues, country, rock'n'roll, hip-hop—it eventually becomes the "authentic" music of one or another of our two major races, no matter how much the other race contributed to its invention.

What can explain this hunger for segregation? We—particularly the Americans among us—seem to have been born with a desire to categorize all cultural products as either authentically black or authentically white. We remain confused by those that are authentically mixed, as if that were some kind of logical impossibility. Some of them we call "odd" or "mysterious"; some we call "groundbreaking" or "revolutionary." At times we deny that any mixture ever took place: many of the artists who crossed racial boundaries the most—like Jimmie Rodgers and Mississippi John Hurt—have come to represent nothing but the music of their own color. There are those we recognize as masters of racial mixing—Elvis Presley, Jimi Hendrix, and Eminem being the most obvious—but instead of accepting them as integrated Americans and therefore heroic figures, Hendrix gets accused of Uncle Tomming and Elvis and Eminem of "appropriation." Even scholars, who should know better, almost always consider "black music" a field of study entirely separate from the rest of American music.

Is there any way out of this trap of our own devising?

Perhaps there is. Musicians are by nature restless people, always searching for new sounds no matter where they come from. Typically, they don't care whether a sound is authentically black or white before adopting it as their own. John Hurt was undoubtedly one such musician. If we could all start listening to music with musicians' ears, if music education were the norm rather than the exception, and if we learned the real history of American music, perhaps the racial authenticity of the music we listen to would begin to be less important, and the racial mysteries of American music would cease to be "nobody's dirty business."

CHAPTER THREE

T.B. BLUES

The Story of Autobiographical Song

San Antonio, January 31, 1931

> When Jimmie Rodgers sang "T.B. Blues," his
> audiences knew that he meant it—and that was
> one of the things, amid all the hillbilly hokum
> of the day, that distinguished him from the
> likes of Vernon Dalhart and Carson Robison. It
> is what country music fans mean today when
> they bestow their highest accolade on an artist
> by calling him "sincere."
>
> NOLAN PORTERFIELD, *Jimmie Rodgers*

BY 1931, JIMMIE RODGERS was probably the most famous
musician in the country. He wasn't a very inventive guitar

player or singer; he couldn't compose new songs very well, almost always enlisting considerable help; he was short, almost completely bald, and in very poor health; his musical trademark was a rather gimmicky yodel—in short, he would seem, to our eyes, to have had little to recommend him. Yet he inspired the same kind of frenzy as Sinatra and Elvis would years later.

For Jimmie Rodgers personified a particular type of American hero. He had been a hardworking man—a brakeman on railroad lines—but he had also traveled and roamed, living the peripatetic life. There was a romance about him that was easy to make into myth—the myth of the rambling man, who goes from town to town and from girl to girl, always heeding the call to wander on, but nonetheless misses his Mississippi home and the sweet woman he left behind. Jimmie Rodgers vicariously gave his listeners the freedom they envied while affirming the comforts and values of their quotidian lives.

But it wasn't only that. Jimmie Rodgers sang the blues. He sang them honestly and without affectation, making them his own without imitating anyone else, and imbuing them with what we can only call "personal authenticity"—the feeling that they were made out of his own tears and laughter, his own memories and dreams, his own life and everything in it. Of course, things weren't that simple, but somehow he convinced everyone that they were.

By 1931, though, after three years of unprecedented fame, there was one major aspect of his life that Jimmie Rodgers had not yet sung about or even spoken about in public: his health. Other aspects of his life he'd dealt with in his customary breezy manner, never getting too specific or delving too deeply, either maintaining a studied nonchalance or indulging in sentimental simplification. But now he was going to give his public a dose of reality—he was going to sing about the disease that was killing him by degrees, a disease that many of his fans already knew he had.

Nolan Porterfield, whose biography of Jimmie Rodgers is nothing less than a masterpiece, has written,

> Mention a song called "T.B. Blues" today, and most people give you a brief look of disbelief, followed by sniggers and curious shakes of the head. Boy, what those oldtime hillbillies couldn't think of! The notion of a prominent entertainer singing about the disease that was killing him . . . strikes them as a rather literal (and pathetic) sick joke, on the macabre order of, say, Nat King Cole huskily warbling some merry ditty about lung cancer.

But tuberculosis was no stranger to Jimmie Rodgers's listeners. For decades it had been the leading cause of death in the United States, and it had killed 3.5 million Americans between 1900 and 1925. At the turn of the century up to ninety percent of American adults had had tuberculosis at one time. Nor was it that uncommon to sing about sickness—a different "T-B Blues" had been a hit for blues star Victoria Spivey in 1927 (and had been covered by Willie Jackson as well; Spivey recorded a follow-up, "Dirty T.B. Blues," two years later), Bessie Tucker had recorded a "T.B. Moan" in 1929, and others had also sung blues songs about illnesses. The lyrics to Rodgers's "T.B. Blues" were mostly adapted from previous blues lyrics—there was nothing essentially new here.

Except for one thing. Previously, when singers had sung

about having tuberculosis—or for that matter, about being lovesick, or having the blues, or missing their home—they may not have been singing about themselves. Victoria Spivey, for instance, did not have tuberculosis. Songs about illness were typically as full of generalities as a love song ("Oh now, the T.B.'s killin' me—I want my body buried in the deep blue sea," Spivey sang); few of them divulged intimate details. Blind Lemon Jefferson's "Pneumonia Blues" blames his condition on "slippin' 'round the corners, running up alleys too, watching my woman trying to see what she goin' do," which is clearly fiction. Lonnie Johnson saw fit to sing about a shipwreck he was on but not about the flu epidemic that killed almost his entire family; like most blues singers, he was not given to writing songs about his personal life. But in Jimmie Rodgers's case, his listeners either knew or quickly inferred that he was singing about his own illness. This lent the song an authenticity that Spivey's had not possessed.

At the same session, Rodgers sang another song he'd recently cowritten, "Jimmie the Kid." It's not one of his greatest songs. In it, he gives some not very interesting facts about his life, including naming a number of the train lines he'd traveled on, and he couches the whole in the third person. But it's unusual in one important respect: it is, in its way, an autobiography. It doesn't include just a detail or two—it's his entire life story.

These are autobiographical songs: songs that are truly about the singer (or writer) more than about anything else, that tell the truth, and that refrain from bleaching out facts through generalization. For example, Percy Sledge's "When a Man Loves a Woman" doesn't quite qualify as autobiographical—although Sledge wrote it about his own experience, he bleached out all specifics so that the song could apply to anyone. On the other hand, "The Ballad of John and Yoko" is a sterling example of autobiographical song.

Taken together, "T.B. Blues" and "Jimmie the Kid" represent a fascinating moment—a crystallization of sorts—in the development of personal authenticity in popular music. At the time, there was no good reason to think that the person singing on a particular record was really who he or she appeared to be: records were disembodied voices, not real people, and those voices could—and usually did—sing fiction. Public performances were likewise entertainments that had little if anything to do with the personal experiences of the entertainer. By singing about his own life in a way that audiences could call truthful, Rodgers was, intentionally or not, vouchsafing that he was as genuine as the record they were holding.

Today, after decades of music partially defined by ideas of sincerity, this may not seem very unusual. We have become accustomed over the last forty years to hearing autobiographical songs, ranging from Loretta Lynn's "Coal Miner's Daughter" to Nirvana's "Pennyroyal Tea" to Usher's "Confessions Part II." Performers often use autobiographical song now as a talisman of their personal authenticity, parading their insecurities and problems through song in order to boast of how "real" they are. But it was not common to give such detail in song until relatively recently, especially not in songs aimed at a mass market.

LET'S LOOK AT an example that parallels "T.B. Blues." In the entire history of American popular music, why have so few blind singers sung about being blind? Sleepy John Estes recorded "Stone Blind Blues" in 1947, and Sonny Terry recorded "I Woke Up One Morning and I Could Hardly See" in 1962. But besides these two songs, the only other instances seem to be a couple of gospel songs by Blind Gary Davis and Blind Roger Hays, and a wordless composition by jazz multi-instrumentalist Rahsaan Roland Kirk.

Of course, there have been plenty of brilliant blind song-writers, ranging from pioneer bluesmen Blind Lemon Jefferson and Blind Willie McTell to more recent artists such as Stevie Wonder. In fact, one scholar has counted no fewer than thirty-two blind prewar blues and gospel singers. Few of these artists have been reluctant to sing in the first person or to tell stories in their songs. But there is one subject they almost all avoid, the one that is absolutely central to their identities. Why?

You see, the reason blind singers rarely sang about being blind is simple: there was no audience for such a song. Who could relate to it? The number of blind listeners was undoubt-edly far fewer than the number of listeners who'd been jilted by a lover.

This desire to "relate" to a song is essential for understand-ing the meaning of the blues—and "T.B. Blues" *is* a blues.

BLUES IS SAID to be a very personal music. There's certainly some truth to this view—blues songs of the first half of the twentieth century were generally more personal than other songs, and early autobiographical songs were almost always blues or blues-related. Yet it would be a mistake to view the blues as primarily either a confessional mode or a kind of collective autobiography of black Americans, two views that seem prevalent today.

For early blues, like early cowboy songs, were mainly about a certain set of people, mostly black but sometimes white (like Jimmie Rodgers), both male and female, who lived largely itinerant lives, traveled from town to town, job to job, partner to partner; a people who thought far less of morality than of enjoyment; a people given to sex, violence, and hard liquor; a people inured to poverty and injustice, and expecting little else. Blues songs were generally not about hard-working and sober laborers, church-going women, homeowners, young men attending vocational school, soldiers, sailors, or civil servants. Instead they focused on social outcasts.

Naturally enough, many blues singers were themselves social outcasts—respectable folks wanted to have nothing to do with them. And social outcasts have nothing to lose. Far less invested in their reputations than their peers are, they can afford to be forthcoming about their sins, hard times, and sensual joys. Blues thus lends itself very well to gritty first-person narrative, narrative that purports to be autobiographical. And the large majority of blues songs fit this mold.

But those narratives usually either were fiction (Blind Willie McTell's "Writing Paper Blues" is one of the best storytelling blues songs ever, but McTell couldn't write), were too vague to be strictly personal, or concerned an event in which the singer was only a peripheral figure (Charley Patton's "High Water Everywhere" concerns a flood, Lonnie Johnson's "Life Saver Blues" a shipwreck). Autobiography certainly wasn't out of the question, but it was relatively rare: I would estimate that only about one to three percent of prewar blues songs could be called autobiographical. And few blues songs really tell compelling stories—most of them are so unrevealing as to be opaque.

Interestingly, most prewar autobiographical blues songs deal with prison experiences or run-ins with the law, perhaps because this subject matter naturally lends itself to specificity. But blues songs tended to be about situations to which listeners could relate, rather than situations peculiar to the singer.

The songs blues singers wrote specifically about themselves tend to stand out because of their uncommonness. In 1930 Charlie Jackson sang a compelling account of performing at a dance and being arrested and jailed; apparently it was so unusual to write autobiography that the song was entitled "Self Experience." And in 1940 Booker White, prompted by a recording director who was dissatisfied with the repertoire of standards he had brought to the studio, composed on the spot a handful of autobiographical songs such as "Parchman Farm Blues," "When Can I Change My Clothes," and "District Attorney Blues," suggesting that White didn't commonly perform material of this nature.

Another autobiographical blues song provides perhaps the closest contemporary parallel to "T.B. Blues." The Memphis Jug Band's 1930 "Meningitis Blues," written and sung by Memphis Minnie, is not only a moving and very personal account of a near-fatal illness, it tells a truly autobiographical story—which she seemed to acknowledge when she rerecorded it a few days later as "Memphis Minnie-Jitis Blues." It begins with an extraordinarily personal verse: "I come in home one Saturday night, pull off my clothes and I lie down; and that mornin' just about the break of day that meningitis began to creep around." It is as if she were pulling the listener right into her life—and her suffering. Spelling out all the details, she describes her pain, how her companion took her to the doctor and then to the hospital, and how the doctors gave up on her.

Memphis Minnie's accomplishments are plentiful: she was an extraordinarily skilled songwriter (she wrote Led Zeppelin's "When the Levee Breaks" and Chuck Berry's "I Wanna Be Your Driver"), an ingenious guitarist, a fine singer, and an astute businesswoman. Although she was just as rough and rowdy as her male counterparts, her recordings emphasize sexual satisfaction, domestic banter, and mellow good times, rather than the gratuitous violence expressed by many of her predecessors. And perhaps this explains why she was a huge star in the 1930s, during which she continued to record the occasional autobiographical song.

She was soon joined by fellow Memphian Sleepy John Estes, who began to sing songs about his lawyer, his blindness, and other personal matters. Robert Johnson's "Crossroads Blues" gives every indication of being about his own experience, although Johnson hid more than he revealed; the mystery he created with his seemingly autobiographical but actually remarkably opaque songs left thousands of fans and researchers *Searching for Robert Johnson*, as one book title has it.

As for Lightnin' Hopkins, who began recording in 1946, one gets the feeling that the reason he turned to autobiography was that he couldn't actually remember other people's songs very well (with the exception of those of his mentor, Blind Lemon Jefferson). His songs usually weren't well thought out like Johnson's, Memphis Minnie's, or Rodgers's—they were extemporized on the spot, just strings of made-up and free-associated verses, rarely hanging together or completing a picture. As Francis Davis puts it, "Practically anything you'd ever want to know about [Hopkins], no matter how trivial, is in a song somewhere. . . . In general, [he] was the least bardic of the great blues singers: less interested in telling a story than setting a mood and speaking whatever happened to be on his mind the second the tapes started to roll."

Since blues songs purport to be autobiographical, it would only make sense if occasionally singers sang directly about their lives. Yet as most of these examples attest in their own ways, autobiography was more the exception than the rule.

WHAT ELSE DID people sing about in this era if so few of them sang about themselves? Most of them sang songs they learned from others: from Tin Pan Alley, from fellow musicians, from family. If you wanted to write your own song, you might have taken Woody Guthrie's advice from his 1943 memoir, *Bound for Glory*: "If you think of something new to say, if a cyclone comes, or a flood wrecks the country, or a bus load of school children freeze to death along the road, if a big ship goes down, and an airplane falls in your neighborhood, an outlaw shoots it out with the deputies, or the working people go out to win a war, yes, you'll find a train load of things you can set down and make up a song about." Or you might have written a love song, or a sentimental parlor ballad. But it probably would never have occurred to you to write a song strictly about your own experiences.

It's certainly possible that a few of the hundreds of nineteenth- and very early twentieth-century cowboy, frontier, and sailor ballads may have been autobiographical when they were first written: "The Old Chisholm Trail," "The State of Arkansaw," "The Buffalo Skinners," "The Ballad of the Erie

Canal," and so on. Unfortunately, we know nothing about who wrote them. The same goes for even older first-person ballads.

By the twentieth century, hillbilly or old-time music generally was far less autobiographical than blues. It stuck much closer to established traditions, and the subject matter of the songs reflected this. But occasionally a singer might inject autobiographical detail into a song. Uncle Dave Macon, the first star of the Grand Ole Opry, made a frequent practice of spoken interludes interjected between, before, or in the middle of his tunes. His 1928 "From Earth to Heaven" is a fascinating example: he begins by giving the name and address of his wagoning firm, then sings about his daily routine. But then he claims to have sworn off drinking and dedicated his life to God, neither of which he actually did. (He also disparages the motorcar since it ruined his wagoning career; but at the same session he sang a paean to "The New Ford Car.") The means may be autobiographical, but the aim of "From Earth to Heaven" is spiritual, and the song, which begins with the truth, ends with fiction.

Besides Macon and Rodgers, perhaps the only other hillbilly singer who sang anything approaching autobiography was Goebel Reeves. Reeves was one of dozens of yodeling singer-songwriters following Jimmie Rodgers's path, among them Jimmie Davis, Cliff Carlisle, and Gene Autry. Calling himself "The Texas Drifter," he recorded "The Texas Drifter's Warning" in January 1930. A well-educated Texan from a wealthy family, Reeves had chosen the life of a hobo not out of necessity but because of its romantic appeal. In his "Warning," he sings of how he ran into a cop in West Texas who took all his money and then got a job picking cotton for next to nothing. Reeves was an excellent yodeler and had once played with Rodgers. But his songs and singing were far more studied, with little of Rodgers's charm. "The Texas Drifter's Warning" may well be autobiographical, though Reeves was prone to embellishing facts. If anything, it's surprising that there weren't more such songs in this period. After all, ever since he began having hit records in 1927, Jimmie Rodgers had made the central pretense of the blues—first-person narrative centering on the performer's own experience—into an important pretense of hillbilly music too. Before him, it simply hadn't been that way.

FROM VERY EARLY in his life, Jimmie Rodgers had wanted to be a musical entertainer. Every chance he got, he'd take out his guitar and sing for anyone who'd listen. As a business, though, that kind of playing was worse than nothing at all. No aficionado of traditional mountain or "old-time" music, Jimmie specialized in Tin Pan Alley hits, minstrel numbers, or other songs popular among city folk. But in order to earn a living, he spent most of his time working on the railroad, traveling throughout the South, where he was exposed to all sorts of music, often playing with and for African Americans.

He auditioned for Ralph Peer of the Victor Talking Machine Company in 1927 in Bristol, Tennessee, and recorded a couple of unremarkable songs. A few months later, he traveled to New York, gave Peer a phone call, and pretended that he just happened to be in town and had a little time to record a few more sides. The session, held in Camden, New Jersey, was not at first a success: Peer was looking for either original or traditional but forgotten material that he could copyright, and all Rodgers could perform were other people's songs.

Finally, he relaxed enough to perform a ditty whose opening lines were, "T for Texas, T for Tennessee; T for Texas, T for Tennessee; T for Thelma—the gal that made a wreck out of me." Peer was unimpressed, but released the song anyway under the title "Blue Yodel," since Rodgers yodeled after each verse. Perhaps because it was a blues with a gimmick, the song was an enormous hit that catapulted Rodgers to unprecedented fame. Hit followed hit, and Jimmie Rodgers quickly became a household name, his appearances, particularly in the South, creating a sensation.

Besides his "blue yodels" (he recorded thirteen), Rodgers hardly wrote any of his material by himself. Between 1928 and 1930, his most frequent collaborator was his sister-in-law, Elsie McWilliams, but he obtained songs from a variety of other sources, too. If he had been left to his own devices, he may not have written a single song. He was happier, it seems, performing other people's material.

But he hadn't reckoned on being tied to a businessman as astute and farsighted as Ralph Peer.

IS IT A coincidence that the first black vocal blues hit record, the first hillbilly hit record, and the first records by the artists who would define modern country music (Jimmie Rodgers and the Carter Family) were all recorded by the same man? Was Ralph Peer truly an American visionary, or did he stumble onto all this more or less by accident? Or was he simply a brilliant businessman?

Here are the facts. Peer was born in Kansas City, Missouri, in 1892, the son of a music dealer. As a teenager, he began working with Columbia Records, but by 1920 he had become the assistant to Fred Hager, the recording director of the OKeh label. In February of that year, a twenty-six-year-old black pianist, songwriter, and music publisher named Perry Bradford convinced OKeh's president to allow Mamie Smith, a black female singer, to record a song he'd written—even though Hager advised against it, fearing a boycott against any label that broke the color bar. "Crazy Blues," backed by a black band Perry had organized called the Jazz Hounds, was the first blues record sung and played by blacks. And, in part because of Peer's promotional efforts, it was a huge success.

Three years later, an Atlanta record dealer named Polk Brockman saw a newsreel at the Palace Theater in Times Square of a Virginia fiddler's convention; Brockman called OKeh Records and asked them to come down to Atlanta to attempt a few recordings. So in June 1923, Peer conducted the first commercial location recording with portable equipment (recording both black and white performers). One record made at that session, Fiddlin' John Carson's "The Little Old Log Cabin in the Lane" coupled with "The Old Hen Cackled and the Rooster's Going to Crow," was the first country music hit (although the genre wouldn't be called *country* for a number of years). It sold so rapidly in Atlanta that Peer started making frequent trips to the South (as did the representatives of other record companies).

But late in 1925, Peer and OKeh had a falling out, and Peer left to pursue other business, without success. In 1927, down on his luck, Peer contacted the Victor Talking Machine Company with a brilliant idea. As he later wrote, "The arrangement was that I would select the artists and material and supervise the hillbilly recordings for Victor. My publishing firm would own the copyrights, and thus I would be compensated by the royalties resulting from the compositions which I would select for recording purposes." In return, he would work for Victor for nothing—a nominal salary of $1 per year.

From then on, Peer was on a quest for *new songs*. They could be old, traditional songs—as old as the hills—so long as they had never before been recorded or published as sheet music. Or they could be new, or purloined. No matter—what was important was that Peer could have them copyrighted in the artist's name. The agreement he made with the artists he recorded made him the publisher and therefore assignee of the copyright of each new song, without any initial outlay on his part. In return, he arranged for the artists to record these new songs, and advanced them money on the royalties.

Peer was completely uninterested in songs whose provenance was known and established, for he himself could make no money on these. If his artists recorded previously copyrighted or public domain songs, they would only stand to make $50 per side (at best)—Victor's standard fee (which was far higher than that of other record companies)—and he would make nothing. He later recalled that "Jimmie would bring in some famous old minstrel song and just do it word-for-word, and of course I'd stop that immediately. I'd say, 'You didn't compose that.'"

With the songwriting royalties that Peer guaranteed his artists for original songs, they could make a half cent per record—not bad if you released twenty or thirty sides a year and each disc sold thousands of copies. Peer, as publisher, made three times that amount—about a million dollars a year—and generously loaned some of his cash to his favored artists.

So that's why Peer pushed Jimmie Rodgers into recording original numbers almost exclusively, most of them cocomposed by Rodgers himself, thus spurring Rodgers to constantly come up with new topics for songs. Eventually one of those topics would turn out to be his own life.

JIMMIE RODGERS arrived in San Antonio fresh off a brief but intense benefit tour for victims of drought and the Depression, a tour headlined by Will Rogers, an entertainer Jimmie Rodgers idolized. Jimmie Rodgers's change in direction on January 31, 1931—his recording of material that was more autobiographical than anything he'd attempted before—may have resulted from his close contact with America's most popular entertainer.

When I say "most popular," I don't just mean that Will Rogers was the most popular entertainer of his day—there's no doubt of that. I mean the most popular American entertainer ever. His best biographer, Ben Yagoda, claims as a "fact" that Rogers "was loved more than any American has been loved before or since," and the claim appears entirely plausible. When he died in a plane crash in 1935, Yagoda writes,

> the magnitude of the reaction, in point of fact, was such as you would expect the passing of a beloved President to engender. Will Rogers, fifty-five years old, had a radio show, wrote a daily newspaper column, acted in the

movies. Years earlier he had been a rope-twirling monologist in the *Ziegfeld Follies*, before that a vaudeville gypsy. Yet people had come to depend on his presence— his absence was making them realize—more than that of any politician.

One of the keys to Will Rogers's popularity was undoubt- edly the sense his audiences got that he was being "authentic," being *himself*. When he first appeared in vaudeville in 1911, he "was like nothing else on the vaudeville stage." Where other monologists told humorous stories in "carefully constructed personas," Will Rogers, "self-effacing and understated, was always himself, or something very close to it. . . . His remarks appeared insistently extemporaneous, almost improvisa- tional." (In this, he was following an old American tradition, joining Davey Crockett, Abraham Lincoln, Mark Twain, Walt Whitman, Buffalo Bill Cody, and many others.)

And being himself included being autobiographical. In fact, back in 1921, Will Rogers had made what is most likely the very first film that portrayed the life of its maker, *One Day in 365* (whose working title was *No Story at All*), which is a bit like an episode of *The Osbournes*. As Yagoda describes it,

Not only did Will star in it and write the script but the cast was his own family and the only set was his own house. The script (no complete print survives) [describes] a day in the life of the Rogers family. Will desperately tries to find a suitable scenario for a picture due to start shooting that day, but he is constantly inter- rupted. . . . By 1:30 in the morning, there's still no script;

in a final close-up, Will speaks into the camera. "Some of these days I'm going to put on a story from real life—but then no one would believe it."

By the time Jimmie Rodgers appeared onstage with Will Rogers, the latter was also the most widely read columnist in the country, with his daily columns appearing in more than four hundred newspapers. Once again, he wrote whatever came off the top of his head, never bothering to construct a persona any different from who he was. The same held for the talking films he made in the early 1930s, which were more popular than those of any other actor. He didn't *act* in these films—he improvised and behaved naturally. That he was aware of the difference between himself and others in this respect seems borne out by the name of the imaginary political party he invented when *Life* magazine had him pretend to run for president in 1928: Anti-Bunk.

Nobody in the 1920s or 1930s, then, embodied personal authenticity better than Will Rogers. And that was bound to rub off on the man whose career was beginning to depend on precisely that same quality.

BILL MALONE has written of Jimmie Rodgers, "If he sang 'I've Ranged, I've Roamed, and I've Traveled,' his listeners were sure he had done just that. When he sang 'Lullaby Yodel,' many people were convinced that he was singing to an estranged wife who had taken their child with her (even though his wife's sister wrote the song!). 'High Powered Mamma,' of course, just had to be about that same wife who 'just wouldn't leave other daddies alone.'"

Indeed, there was some basis for this belief. Many of his sentimental songs, largely written by McWilliams, were based on elements of his personal history, though in a decidedly vague way: "My Little Old Home Down in New Orleans," "Daddy and Home," "My Rough and Rowdy Ways." And he sang them with a heartfelt delivery that made them seem to describe not only his own life, but that of his listeners too. As Porterfield explains, "To many, Jimmie Rodgers made 'sincerity,' 'honesty,' and 'heart' the compelling forces of country music."

Jimmie Rodgers was the first celebrity singer whose songs, one and all, were widely taken to be about his own life. And that became the modus operandi of several generations of country singers—Woody Guthrie, Hank Williams, Loretta Lynn, Dolly Parton, Merle Haggard, and many others. But Rodgers didn't start out being autobiographical: it was only after he became a celebrity that he started singing about his battle with tuberculosis, for it was only then that his audience knew enough about him to care about his personal problems.

Let's put it another way. Jimmie Rodgers started out just like any blues musician: singing songs about wild women and rambling men, fast trains and lonely nights. But at a certain point he might have reflected upon the facts of his celebrity. His listeners all thought he was singing about his own life, even when he sang other people's songs, even when he sang about imaginary situations and unfamiliar places and women he'd never met. Why not, then, actually do what they already thought he was doing? Why not actually sing about dying? Couldn't he then take his listeners to a new level? They were buying his records, after all, not just because they liked his music, but because they wanted to learn more about *him*. So why not sing about the most important fact of his life?

One reason so few blind singers ever sang about being blind is precisely this: no blind singer ever had a following like Jimmie Rodgers's. No blind singer was ever confronted with millions of fans telling him that the reason they bought his records was that they believed he was singing about his own life and they could relate to him. But Jimmie Rodgers was. And that may be why he decided to record two songs about his own life on that January day in 1931.

JIMMIE RODGERS left the tour he was on (with Will Rogers) in Dallas, having learned that Peer was on his way to San Antonio with portable recording equipment. Probably Peer had planned his trip primarily to record Rodgers, but hoped to find some other local talent as well. Rodgers had a day or two to rest and prepare for the session, while Peer lined up some local musicians to accompany him.

The sessions were held at the Texas Hotel, and for the first number, "T.B. Blues," Jimmie was accompanied by an excellent local steel guitarist, Charles Kama. He opened the song with a line that could have come from any number of songs: "My good gal's trying to make a fool out of me." But what followed exemplified Rodgers's ingenious mix of humor and tragedy: "Trying to make me believe I ain't got that ol' T.B." From there, the song became increasingly morbid, ending with the couplet

> Gee, but the graveyard is a lonesome place.
> They put you on your back, throw that mud down in
> your face.

Perhaps to signify that this wasn't one of his usual novelty numbers, Rodgers uncharacteristically refrained from yodeling on this song, instead singing the chorus, "I've got the T.B. blues," in a yodeling manner.

A year or two earlier, Jimmie Rodgers had written to one of his correspondents and collaborators, a Texas prisoner named Ray Hall, asking for his version of "T.B. Blues," together with any old random verses Hall could remember. Hall sent Rodgers what he had, and, as he later recalled, "Jimmie changed words here and there and some of the phrases—that's the way he worked." The concluding graveyard phrase, for instance, came from another Rodgers song, "Blue Yodel No. 9." The result was an altogether new composition, though largely made up of common blues phrases. Porterfield persuasively comments,

> "T.B. Blues" is at once intensely authentic and yet calmly impersonal, as if the ominous disease and certain death are someone else's afflictions. How otherwise could he sing, so eloquently, so stoically, "I've been fighting like a lion, looks like I'm going to lose—'cause there ain't nobody ever whipped the T.B. blues"? . . . From beginning to end, . . . "T.B. Blues" is both an artistic achievement and the most eloquent evidence of Jimmie Rodgers's tragic vision. It was a vision borne of his own courage and will, of his great zest for life and his own coming to terms with the transience of it, a vision substantial enough to elevate him to the ranks of those poets and painters and artisans whose work illuminates and eases all our human lives.

There is a fine line between self-mythologizing and self-revelation. Somehow, it is easier to believe in a confession if it's about trouble. And nothing could be more troubling than one's own imminent death. By singing about it so eloquently, Jimmie Rodgers provided a convincing testament of his dedication to reveal himself to his audience.

RODGERS NEXT RECORDED a number called "Travellin' Blues," written by a friend, Shelly Lee Alley, who played fiddle on the record together with his brother Alvin. Finally Rodgers turned to a song whose basic idea had been suggested to him by another one of his San Antonio buddies, Jack Neville: "Jimmie the Kid." For both numbers he was accompanied not only by Kama, but by local musicians M. T. Salazar on guitar and Mike Cordova on bass.

"Jimmie the Kid" is pure gleeful hokum. It begins, "I'll tell you the story of Jimmie the Kid—he's a brakeman you all know," and then details all the railroad lines he yodeled on. After a while, he tells us that he has a "yodelin' mama so sweet" and "a beautiful home all of his own—it's the yodeler's paradise." He concludes by both yodeling and singing about it.

"Jimmie the Kid" is the logical outcome of the process that Peer and Rodgers had initiated back in 1927. From the idea of performing only original songs, it's just a short step to the idea that the songs should wear that originality on their sleeves—and what better way to do that than to sing a song so conspicuously autobiographical that nobody else could possibly sing it?

■ ■ ■ ■

RODGERS WAS NOT the first to record a song with his name in the title—a number of vaudeville performers did the same. One excellent if obscure example is "Jasper Taylor Blues," recorded in 1928 by the Original Washboard Band with Jasper Taylor, an African American percussionist from Texas who was based in Chicago. Composed by Taylor along with established songwriters Clarence Williams and Eddie Heywood, the lyrics, sung by Vaudeville singer Julia Davis, celebrate Taylor's sexual prowess: the chorus runs, "Jasper Taylor, Jasper Taylor—oh, how that boy can love." Of course, the lyrics are pure braggadocio, yet the song shows that early performers were by no means hesitant to promote themselves in song. Whether any of these songs were truly autobiographical, though, is a question I've been unable to answer.

In about 1933, Bonnie Parker wrote a very frank and autobiographical defense of her and her husband's conduct entitled "The Ballad of Bonnie and Clyde." We don't know if she wrote any music to go with the lyrics, but it's likely she wrote it as a song rather than a poem. The pair were well-known music lovers. Although the song was widely published, nobody recorded it for decades. Of course, it could have been influenced by "Jimmie the Kid," but more likely both songs drew on a long tradition of outlaw ballads: "Billy the Kid," "John Hardy," "Steamboat Bill," "Sam Bass," and "Jesse James." Another question, of course, is whether any of these numbers ended up influencing John Lennon and his "Ballad of John and Yoko."

AFTER THIS SESSION, Jimmie Rodgers lived another two years and recorded dozens more songs. But none of them were quite as autobiographical as "T.B. Blues" and "Jimmie the Kid." These were, perhaps even for Rodgers himself, little more than novelty numbers. Something unusual had happened in those two songs, but it was simply too unusual to be repeated very often.

IN 1937, six years after "T.B. Blues," a then-unknown folksinger named Woody Guthrie wrote a parody of it called "Dust Pneumonia Blues" to the melody of Jimmie Rodgers's signature "Blue Yodel (T for Texas)." In it, Guthrie sings, "Now there ought to be some yodelin' in this song, but I can't yodel for the rattlin' in my lungs" (perhaps echoing the fact that Jimmie Rodgers had deliberately left his usual yodel out of "T.B. Blues"). Three years later, Guthrie recorded three hours of conversation and songs (including "Dust Pneumonia Blues" and Rodgers's "Blue Yodel No. 4") with Alan Lomax for the Library of Congress, discussing only two entertainers at length: Jimmie Rodgers and Guthrie's fellow Oklahoman Will Rogers. In these conversations, it seems that Jimmie Rodgers was something of a musical father figure for Guthrie. But Guthrie, who may have learned from Rodgers how to project honesty in song, resented the way Rodgers's fictions could mislead. He talked about how Rodgers's "California Blues" ("Blue Yodel No. 4") had painted a false picture of paradise for millions of Southerners who, when they arrived in California, found themselves exploited. Guthrie was taking a very different approach to autobiographical song.

"Dust Pneumonia Blues" became one of Guthrie's *Dust Bowl Ballads*, a group of fourteen sides he recorded in 1940 as an album. Many of these songs sound autobiographical: most of them are in the first person and contain intimate details of the narrator's life—which is more than one could say about most songs of the era. But Woody Guthrie was not, at this time, a celebrity of any kind—the album sold only about two thousand copies—so the listener had no way of telling which of the experiences he sang about he'd lived himself, and which were experiences of people he'd met. And that was his point: these songs were meant to encompass the experiences of a people. Even a truly autobiographical narrative like Guthrie's later "Talking Sailor," which humorously relates how he shipped out with the Merchant Marines during World War II, was, in a way, less about Guthrie's own experiences than about an average American going out to fight the Fascists.

I don't want to imply that Guthrie refrained from celebrating himself. He was as much of a showman as Rodgers (or, later, Bob Dylan, for that matter) and he was equally concerned about his image. But he made sure that each of his songs had a larger point to make. He wasn't simply celebrating himself or singing only about his troubles and joys for the pleasure of his fans. Rodgers reveled in celebrity; Guthrie, to some degree, eschewed it. This, of course, in no way makes him less of an autobiographical artist than Rodgers, or less personally authentic. In fact, Guthrie projected his own personality as a bedrock of authenticity that made his artistic and social vision credible and solid. It does help explain, though, why he was far less influenced by commercial considerations.

Guthrie was probably just as central a figure in autobiographical song as Rodgers. He better exemplifies personal authenticity, and he had more of an impact upon the 1960s scene (though that impact would not be strongly felt until after he had become terminally ill and was no longer as creative a force). But Guthrie was quite clearly in Jimmie Rodgers's debt—one can hear Rodgers's influence all over Guthrie's recordings.

MEANWHILE, IN EARLY country music authenticity was still an issue, but it was not until Hank Williams's appearance in the late 1940s that personal authenticity—the basing of a performer's appeal on the artist's integrity and honesty—became its touchstone. Until 1949, country music wasn't yet called "country"; it had outlasted its previous labels, "old-time" and "hillbilly," and was now known as "folk." As Williams, for whom Rodgers was a primary inspiration, defined it in 1952, "Folk music is sincere. There ain't nothin' phony about it. When a folksinger sings a sad song, he's sad. He means it. The tunes are simple and easy to remember, and they're sincere with them." Thus Williams eliminated in large measure the "novelty" tone of much of Rodgers's work; not only did Williams sing his songs as though he meant them, he sang as though his life depended on it.

While Williams's songs are indeed sincere, they're not strictly autobiographical, though audiences could catch hints of his real life in many of them. In this sense they were very much like the Jimmie Rodgers songs that Elsie McWilliams had helped him write—Williams's signature "Ramblin' Man" was an updated (and far more lonesome) version of Rodgers's "Rough and Rowdy Ways." Williams, like Rodgers, had a way of taking his own experiences and making them universal; the autobiographer, however, makes them particular.

So outside of Woody Guthrie and the blues, there just wasn't much autobiographical song, even by the early 1960s. Was the recording of "Jimmie the Kid" and "T.B. Blues" a fluke, then?

IN SEPTEMBER of 1960, a nineteen-year-old Bob Dylan recorded a handful of songs in his house in Minneapolis. Woody Guthrie's influence is clear: among them are four of Guthrie's songs, including the frankly autobiographical "Talking Sailor." But Dylan also recorded an improvised number about his roommate, "Talkin' Hugh Brown"; Jimmie Rodgers's "Muleskinner Blues"; and the Memphis Jug Band's "K. C. Moan." And on his very first album, recorded just fourteen months later, Dylan, in an homage to Guthrie, performed a frankly autobiographical song called "Talking New York." As we've seen, Rodgers, Guthrie, and the Memphis Jug Band all had important roles to play in the history of autobiographical song, and Dylan's tip of the hat to them signifies that something was in the air. It was as if he were tracing the provenance of the mantle that was being passed to him.

Of course, Dylan's aim in "Talking New York" was not self-revelation but a satirical look at New York City. And Dylan has not recorded many truly autobiographical songs. His liner notes to his second album and "Ballad in Plain D" from his fourth are frankly autobiographical, but after that, he lowered the veil on his personal life. The cult of personality built up around him was based mainly on guesswork and interpretation, for Dylan saw celebrity as a trap. The songs he based on his own experiences were almost always replete with metaphors, disguises, and fictions, and even the publication of his first volume of memoirs in 2004 left most questions intentionally unanswered. But plenty of other folksingers took a more straightforward approach.

By the early 1970s, with the maturity of the "singer-songwriter" genre, everyone was singing autobiography. "The Ballad of John and Yoko" came out in 1969, and Lennon followed it with such autobiographical numbers as "Cold Turkey" and "Mother"; but he had already tentatively ventured into autobiography with "Norwegian Wood" and "Julia." Folk-rockers were recording autobiographical song back in 1967, the year of Arlo Guthrie's "Alice's Restaurant," Bobbie Gentry's "Chickasaw County Child," Paul Revere and the Raiders' "The Legend of Paul Revere," and the Mamas and the Papas' "Creeque Alley." In 1968, Van Morrison released *Astral Weeks*, a revelatory record full of autobiography, and one that may remain unmatched in terms of the album as memoir. By the end of 1971, Dolly Parton had cut "Coat of Many Colors," Loretta Lynn had come out with "Coal Miner's Daughter," and James Taylor had had a minor hit with "Fire and Rain," a song whose press release advertised its autobiographical nature. And these are just a few examples out of hundreds. The floodgates had now opened, and autobiography would remain as conventional a subject for song as love.

WHY DID IT take almost forty years for the autobiographical song to flourish? Why didn't Hank Williams write a single song that gave us the detail we get from "Meningitis Blues" or "Jimmie the Kid"? Why was Woody Guthrie so alone in telling his own story? Why were blues just about the only autobiographical songs one could find in the 1950s?

In part, it's because, even at this late period in recording history, both Williams and Guthrie had seen themselves as writing *folk* songs, songs that anyone could sing, and this was true for Dylan as well. The songs had to strike the right balance between being personal and being universal. The change only began in the 1960s because of the explosion of singer-songwriters, with Dylan and the Beatles leading the pack. It was only then that it became not only acceptable but required for singers to write their own songs.

This imperative was much like Ralph Peer's four decades earlier, and produced similar results. Personal authenticity now became vitally important. Artists were using autobiography in much the same way as Rodgers had—as a style that emphasized their humanity, realness, and honesty. And the increasingly global nature of celebrity and the music business made it less of a problem if a singer-songwriter's songs would be hard for another artist to cover.

Just as it became inevitable that blues singers, who sang first-person narratives that purported to be autobiographical, would really begin to sing about themselves on occasion, it soon became inevitable that singer-songwriters would turn their attention not only to generalized love songs, which had long been the domain of songwriters who were not singers, or political messages, which had long been the domain of protest singers such as Pete Seeger, but to their own lives, especially with the strong, positive value put on self-examination in the 1960s.

By now, it's almost de rigeur to sing about one's own life, even if one has nothing to say. In 2004 alone, superstars Ashlee Simpson, Usher, and Alicia Keys all had number-one hit albums entitled, respectively, *Autobiography, Confessions,* and

The Diary of Alicia Keys. Artists ranging from Kurt Cobain to Jennifer Lopez to Fifty Cent have used songs as the equivalent of press releases, telling their fans exactly how they want their real lives to be perceived (even when they didn't write all the songs themselves). Of course, this is exactly what Rodgers and Lennon did too. But while it was once rare, now it's the name of the game. Is it possible that things have changed so fast? Is it possible that the autobiographical song is really such a recent innovation?

Indeed, it's more than possible: it's quite likely. If, in 1925, you were to take a cross-section of Americans, sit them down in a room, and ask them to write a song that tells a story, probably fewer than five percent of them would have written a song about themselves. Instead, they would have written songs about the *Titanic*, a great flood, a famous outlaw, a local election, or perhaps some woodland animals acting out an old fable. If, in 2007, you were to do the same thing, my guess is that seventy-five percent of them would sing a story about themselves.

Why? Perhaps it can all be traced back to that day in 1931. For the songs Jimmie Rodgers sang then established him as personally authentic, more so than any of the songs he had sung before. Rodgers's records clearly influenced Woody Guthrie, who in turn influenced Bob Dylan, who in turn influenced Bobbie Gentry, Van Morrison, John Lennon, Tim Hardin, James Taylor, and a host of others. Following a different track, Rodgers's records clearly influenced Hank Williams, Tom T. Hall, Loretta Lynn, Dolly Parton, Merle Haggard, and a host of others. The line may not be unbroken or even all that clear. But it never is, is it?

Although the story of autobiographical song may seem

disjointed, peculiar, and unnatural, one point is inescapable. Autobiographical song is relatively new and postdates almost every other element of popular song lyrics as we know them.

What does this tell us about the quest for personal authenticity, then? Simply that revealing oneself in song, a goal that we now all take for granted, is a rather recent and comparatively artificial development in the history of popular music. We now think of autobiographical song as a natural form of expression, but as anyone who has ever tried can attest, writing a song based on one's own life, with a verse and chorus structure, that will appeal to a mass-market audience is no simple matter. It is far easier to sing about almost anything else.

IN RETROSPECT, we can isolate seven functions of or impulses behind autobiographical song, and by doing so we can make it easier to understand the differences between "Meningitis Blues," "T.B. Blues," "Jimmie the Kid," "Talking Sailor," "Pennyroyal Tea," and "Jennie from the Block." Some autobiographical songs may partake of only one of these, others of all seven.

First, there's the primal need for *confession*, an essentially private impulse that is basic to all of us.

Second, there's what we can call the *blues impulse*. The blues is, as we've seen, a first-person song about quotidian yet troubling experiences with which the audience can sympathize. It was also the basis for Jimmie Rodgers's appeal. The reason some people sing the blues is in many cases exactly the same reason they'll introduce autobiographical elements into their song.

Third, there are market forces that pressure singers to be

original, and being autobiographical is a logical outcome of that pressure. This is exemplified both by Ralph Peer's pressure and the situation created by the popularity of Dylan and the Beatles in the 1960s.

Fourth, there's the Will Rogers phenomenon, *realness*—the desire to be genuine, to present not a persona but who you really are to your public. Related to this is the desire to make an intimate kind of music.

Fifth, there's what I call the *press release* function. "T.B. Blues" was Jimmie Rodgers's way of telling his fans that he was dying. Before he recorded this song, they would have had to rely only on rumor. This function, like the last, is intrinsically tied to and dependent on notions of celebrity.

Sixth, there's plain old *boastfulness.* This applies to songs like "Jimmie the Kid," the vaudeville numbers that preceded it, and a large number of hip-hop songs.

Seventh, there's *social comment.* This was not a function of Jimmie Rodgers's autobiographical songs, but was a major feature of those by his primary successor, Woody Guthrie.

IT IS NOT HARD to assume that the more autobiographical singers are, the more honest or authentic they are. Certainly Memphis Minnie's "Meningitis Blues" was more confessional than Victoria Spivey's "T–B Blues," and Jimmie Rodgers's "T.B. Blues" was more personal and heartfelt than most of his blue yodels. Yet there's also something highly artificial about certain autobiographical songs, ranging from "Jimmie the Kid" to "The Ballad of John and Yoko" to "Jenny from the Block." Are artists who go to great lengths to construct a song around those aspects of their lives that are already public knowledge being more honest than those who sing about fictional or universal subjects? Or are they self-consciously attempting to control their public personas through song?

There is no one-to-one correspondence between being true to yourself and singing about yourself. Using elements of autobiography in song to show how real one is, as most of the artists discussed in this chapter did and so many more do these days, can sometimes be less honest than simply singing about whatever comes most naturally.

And, as the example of Lightnin' Hopkins shows us, even that can get a bit boring after a while. We need some theatricality in the music we listen to. Autobiographical song, as in the case of "T.B. Blues," can sometimes provide us with that. And perhaps that—pure, simple *entertainment*—is its eighth and most important function.

CHAPTER FOUR

HEARTBREAK HOTEL

The Art and Artifice of Elvis Presley

Nashville, January 10, 1956

Rock and roll may BE meticulously choreo-
graphed insincerity, like that's what it *is* (for all
else it might sometimes be) . . .

       RICHARD MELTZER, *A Whore Just Like the Rest*

In April [1956] came a song that overwhelmed
everybody. . . . It was no use at all for jiving. It
spoke only of loneliness and despair. Its melody
was all stealth, its gloom comically overstated.
He loved it all, the forlorn, sidewalk tread of the
bass, the harsh guitar, the sparse tinkle of a barroom piano, and most of all the tough, manly
advice with which it concluded: "Now if your

baby leaves you, and you've got a tale to tell,
just take a walk down Lonely Street . . ." For a
time AFN [Armed Forces Network] was playing
"Heartbreak Hotel" every hour. The song's self-
pity should have been hilarious. Instead, it made
Leonard feel worldly, tragic, bigger somehow.

IAN McEWAN, *The Innocent*

ELVIS PRESLEY wasn't feeling very heartbroken when he
recorded "Heartbreak Hotel." He'd never worked in the RCA
studio before, but he wasn't scared. He had turned twenty-
one just two days earlier, he had a single, "I Forgot to
Remember to Forget," climbing to the top of the country
charts, and the guys he'd been playing with for months were
in the studio with him. A month ago he had told an audience,
"This is going to be my first hit," before breaking into the
song, which he'd first heard a month before that. Now he was
brimming with enthusiasm and confidence, having just
careened through a wild version of Ray Charles's "I Got a
Woman." It was almost the exact opposite from the situation
in which a nameless Miami man had found himself a year earlier—a man whom Elvis was about to pretend to be.

Sometime in 1955, an aspiring songwriter named Tommy
Durden had met with Mae Axton, a Florida schoolteacher
who worked as a music promoter in her spare time, in order
to enlist her help with a song. He showed her a recent story in
a Miami newspaper about, as Axton wrote later, "a man who
had rid himself of his identity, written a one-line sentence, 'I
walk a lonely street,' and then killed himself." Somehow

Heartbreak Hotel appeared at the end of that street, and the song that would define Elvis's career came into being.

But there was one thing Elvis did have in common that day with the suicide who had so haunted Durden—they had both erased their identities. The suicide had done so, I assume, by getting rid of any documents that might have identified him; Elvis did so by pretending not just that his baby had left him and he was so lonely he could die, but that he was a half-crazed, hopped-up, libidinous equivalent of the movie stars—James Dean, Marlon Brando, Richard Widmark—who were capturing his and his generation's imagination. In truth, he was a soft-spoken, well-mannered Southern kid (of the poor white rather than genteel variety) with no particular anguish tormenting him. But he, unlike the honchos at RCA—who unanimously disapproved of Elvis's choice of song for his first major-label single—knew what his audience needed. He had seen the movies *The Wild One, Rebel Without a Cause, The Blackboard Jungle*, and others over and over again, and he knew that only souls in torment could light up the screen with the kind of menace that would have girls wetting their panties. "I've made a study of Marlon Brando," he confided to Lloyd Shearer a few months later. "I've made a study of poor Jimmy Dean. I've made a study of myself, and I know why girls, at least the young 'uns, go for us. We're sullen, we're brooding, we're something of a menace. I don't understand it exactly, but that's what the girls like in men. . . . You can't be sexy if you smile. You can't be a rebel if you grin."

IN THE FIVE SINGLES Elvis had cut prior to this session, all for Sun Records in Memphis, he had gradually transformed himself from a naïve crooner to one of the most original—and bizarre—vocalists of his era. There had been an extraordinary evolution in Elvis's voice through these singles: "That's All Right," "Good Rockin' Tonight," "Milkcow Blues Boogie," "Baby Let's Play House," and "I Forgot to Remember to Forget." On the first of these numbers, a bluesy R&B song from the 1940s, Elvis sang in a straightforward if ingenuous manner, sprightly and energetic, melodious and not terribly idiosyncratic. In "Good Rockin' Tonight," he first attempted the hoarse shout common to black bluesmen. In his October 1954 appearance on the radio show *Louisiana Hayride*, he added a few extra wild touches to his Sun songs. But by April 1955, the date of "Baby Let's Play House" (his first national hit record, though only a minor success), Elvis had lost all his ingenuousness and sounded certifiably Martian, singing a baritone baby-talk with a hypnotic stutter and a vibrato that would have made Sarah Vaughan blush.

As for "Heartbreak Hotel," it sounded like it was recorded underwater, with Elvis's repeated gurgle of "be so lonely, baby"—a vocalism that can only have been influenced by Vincent Price—undulating over the sparsest instrumentation for a number-one hit since the musician's strike of 1943.

What Elvis came up with in his vocal style in 1955 and 1956 was as revolutionary as what Louis Armstrong had come up with in the twenties, what Hank Williams had come up with in the forties, or what Ray Charles had come up with at roughly the same time as Elvis: a unique vocal vocabulary. Most of its major features may be heard in slightly less exaggerated form in the stylings of Clyde McPhatter of the Drifters, especially on their 1953 hit "Money Honey," which Elvis also covered at his first RCA session; but there was something new here, a kind of parody, even self-parody, an overstatement that justified Elvis's famous remark, "I don't sound like nobody." The main ingredients of this vocabulary were two completely distinct approaches to the upper and lower registers: a baritone quaver that sounded like someone was pounding him in the chest, and a tenor so pure it was ghostly. This mixture was peppered with a hiccup even more abrupt than Hank Williams's patented my-voice-is-crackin'-'cause-I'm-cryin' (indulged most famously in "Lovesick Blues"), an ease with blue notes that few other white singers had ever displayed, and an amplification of every sentiment into "shameless melodrama," as Greil Marcus puts it.

At one point in his book, *Last Train to Memphis: The Rise of Elvis Presley*, Peter Guralnick describes Elvis's voice well: "'Baby Let's Play House' virtually exploded with energy and high spirits and the sheer bubbling irrepressibility that Sam Phillips had first sensed in Elvis' voice. 'Whoa, baby, baby, baby, baby, baby,' Elvis opened in an ascending, hiccoughing stutter that knocked everybody out with its utterly unpredictable, uninhibited, and gloriously playful ridiculousness."

Marcus calls "Baby Let's Play House" "a correspondence course in rock'n'roll, and it was by far the most imitated of his first records." Virtually every white rock'n'roll—or rockabilly, which amounted to the same thing—singer of the 1950s adopted at least some of Elvis's peculiar mannerisms. As Stephen Tucker puts it, "They sang most often with a strong southern accent complemented by a gaggle of vocal gymnastics—hiccuping, gliding into a lower register, swooping up to a falsetto, growling, howling, and stuttering." At Sun Records, there were Roy Orbison, Charlie Rich, Carl Perkins, Billy Lee Riley, and Warren Smith; elsewhere, there were

Eddie Cochran, Gene Vincent, Wanda Jackson, George Jones, and dozens of other little Elvises mushrooming across America. And the key thing about them all was their "utterly unpredictable, uninhibited, and gloriously playful ridiculousness." Buddy Holly hiccupped nursery rhymes, Jerry Lee Lewis played Satan, and from "Ubangi Stomp" to "Flying Saucers Rock 'n' Roll," they all reveled in other worlds. As Sun's publicist Bill Williams put it, "All of 'em were totally nuts. I think every one of them must have come in on the midnight train from nowhere. I mean, it was like they came from outer space." Beamed here by an Elvis ray, one supposes, for Elvis's otherworldly voice spawned rockabilly in the same way that Charlie Parker's saxophone spawned bebop or Jimi Hendrix's guitar spawned hard rock.

LAST TRAIN TO MEMPHIS is likely to remain the most authoritative book on Elvis Presley's early life for a long time. It's a remarkable work not only for its startlingly vivid evocation of a bygone age and landscape but because it finally cleared up many of the paradoxes surrounding Elvis's rise.

But those paradoxes still seem puzzling, even if we now know all the facts in detail. A nineteen-year-old whose professed ambition was to be another Dean Martin suddenly reinvents rock'n'roll. Sam Phillips, head of Sun Records, who reportedly said that if he could find a white man who could sing like a black man he could make "a billion dollars," sits on Elvis's first acetate for a year without calling him and, after a handful of singles, sells his contract for $35,000. A talent marketed to a country-and-western audience sings primarily rhythm-and-blues numbers; an innocent, clean-cut young man is derided as a satanic pervert; a conventional balladeer at heart invents a completely new style of singing that puts sixteen-year-old girls into a sexual frenzy. Where did that voice, that style, come from? Who taught him to dress that way, sing that way, shake that way? Was he Sam Phillips's brainchild or a sui generis genius?

The answer to most of these questions is Elvis's conception of himself as an actor, someone who's just playing a part. There's no contradiction between Dean Martin and rock'n'roll if they're both just roles. It's clear that Sam Phillips wanted to mold Elvis to "sing like a black man," and that Elvis didn't want to be limited to that. He wanted to sing not just country and rhythm-and-blues, but pop music—he wanted to try on different personas, ranging from down-home country boy to respectable young man to moody rebel to sex-crazed juvenile delinquent. As Barbara Pittman, one of Elvis's early girl-friends, told Ken Burke, "Elvis could imitate anybody. He could do Hank Snow, Dean Martin, Mario Lanza, Eddy Arnold, the Ink Spots, anybody."

Pittman is clearly talking about Elvis's voice, not the way he moved or acted. And that voice is the key to understanding who Elvis was, where he was going, and how he gloriously galvanized American music. Apart from the above quote about "Baby Let's Play House," however, Guralnick barely discusses the subject.

The world of *Last Train to Memphis* is, like the world in most of Guralnick's books, one of Americans to whom music comes more or less as naturally as breathing—good Americans often defeated by the pressures of the music industry but just as often thriving despite them. In his books one rarely finds musicians who spend hours trying to perfect their technique, or struggle with self-destruction and violence, or put on different masks for different audiences; his is a largely pastoral vision of American music, at once awe-inspiring and everyday.

In his author's note, Guralnick writes that Elvis "sang all the songs he really cared about . . . without barrier or affectation," which makes Elvis sound like an idealized country or blues singer. In an early and enormously influential 1976 essay, "Elvis Presley and the American Dream," Guralnick says that Elvis "never recaptured the spirit or the verve of those first Sun sessions, [which] were seriously, passionately, and joyously in earnest, . . . pure and timeless." By contrast, the RCA sides were characterized by "musical excesses and [a] pronounced air of self-parody, [and] were also fundamentally silly records." And in another essay, "Faded Love," Guralnick writes that the Sun years were characterized by "a kind of unself-conscious innocence. . . . On the Sun sides he [threw] in everything that had made up his life to date." Guralnick is essentially ignoring "Baby Let's Play House," Elvis's most influential Sun side, and saying that the real Elvis was the one of "That's All Right, Mama"—an authentic Elvis who sang from his soul and imbued his songs with his own essence.

And plenty of other writers seem to have agreed. Bobbie Ann Mason, in her short biography of Elvis, writes that "everything he did seemed so natural and real. . . . The sounds that came hurtling out of Elvis's unfettered soul were so real and refreshing." Pamela Clarke Keogh, who rightly points out that "Elvis was almost pure style" in her illustrated biography, goes on to say that his style "was, essentially, himself." It is often taken for granted that any singer who can convey Elvis's energy and passion must be singing from the bottom of the heart.

But if one listens closely, Elvis's voice just doesn't fit these descriptions. The most successful Sun and early RCA singles are overwhelmed by vocal tics, mannerisms, postures—and a radical new style. Perhaps Elvis's peculiarities no longer sound like affectations because we've become so familiar with them, both in his own records and in those of his musical descendants; but compared to the singing of Hank Snow, Carl Smith, Eddy Arnold, Dean Martin, or Frank Sinatra, Elvis sounded completely crazy. He sounded evil.

He was neither. He knew perfectly well what he was doing. He knew how to inject a snarl into his voice, just as he knew how to put a sneer into his smile. An arrogance came across in his singing, an arrogance that was—especially when compared to the obsequiousness he displayed in interviews—an act.

THE RCA STUDIO in Nashville was in a dilapidated building, home of the United Methodist Television, Radio and Film Commission; it had, in Howard DeWitt's words, "a dark, eerie quality to it," most fitting for the debut of "Heartbreak Hotel." But January 10 wasn't the first time Elvis had been in it. He'd arrived in Nashville five days earlier to prepare for the session and to check things out. Steve Sholes, RCA's main A&R man and Elvis's main RCA contact, later recalled that "Elvis walked into the studio and smiled. Then he started tapping his foot as he looked around the room."

When he came back to the studio on the afternoon of January 10, his band, the Blue Moon Boys—Scotty Moore on guitar, Bill Black on bass, and D. J. Fontana on drums—were all there. In addition, Sholes and Elvis had decided to add two other musicians for this session: famed session guitarist Chet Atkins and equally famed pianist Floyd Cramer, both well-established country musicians. Elvis still felt somewhat nervous, understandably enough. It was his first time recording outside the familiar Sun Studios, and he spent the first ten minutes pacing around the room. Finally, in order to calm down a little, he sat down next to Cramer and started playing the piano and singing spirituals—"I'm Bound for the Kingdom," "I'll Tell It Wherever I Go." After that, Sholes told Elvis to choose his first song. All the nervousness was now gone, and Elvis was ready.

The set of sessions lasted nine hours—from two to five that afternoon ("I Got a Woman," "Heartbreak Hotel"), from seven to ten that evening ("Money Honey"), and from four to seven the following afternoon (two ballads Sholes and Elvis had chosen from Sholes's list of potential songs for the date, "I Was the One" and "I'm Counting on You"). The studio was full of observers, including Elvis's manager, Colonel Tom Parker; Parker's assistant, Tom Diskin; Mae Axton; and various RCA executives, trying to assess their latest acquisition.

At first, Elvis danced around the room, full of energy and good spirits. Sholes halted the taping and explained that here, unlike at Sun, Elvis needed to stand in one spot, a large "X" taped on the floor. But of course, that didn't work at all. Sholes had the studio remiked, and now Elvis could dance around as much as he wanted. He took his shoes off, cut his finger on a guitar string, refused to take a break when Sholes suggested it, and cut take after take. He took charge, actually directing the session. Sholes was no longer calling the shots—if he ever had been. "I Got a Woman," a song Elvis had been performing since its original release a year earlier, was recorded within an hour.

The result was nothing short of spectacular. When you listen to "I Got a Woman," it's almost impossible to imagine Elvis standing still. The way he was dancing around the room is audible in his voice, It's a restless record, hopped-up and irrepressible, one of the most energetic numbers he ever recorded. The words mean nothing, less than nothing to Elvis. The whole song is about the beat, and about Elvis's voice: its quiver, its almost Sinatra-like phrasing, stretching the phrases beyond the bar line—then chopping up the beat, feather-light one moment and dropping down to an unintelligible stutter the next. It's a record all about playfulness and freedom, the limitless possibilities of the human voice when animated by the right groove.

"Heartbreak Hotel" was a strange contrast. Here the energy was tightly controlled; and instead of triumph, the subject of the song was utter defeat. DeWitt describes the session well: "Colonel Tom Parker was unusually quiet during the taping. Steve Sholes rubbed his neck nervously. The musicians looked bored."

In Nashville, the usual procedure was to record four sides per three-hour session. Yet only two sides had been recorded in the afternoon session, and the entire evening session was devoted to recording "Money Honey," a huge R&B hit in 1953, without getting a satisfactory take (the released version is spliced from two different takes). Clyde McPhatter's version could have served as a kind of template for Elvis's vocal style, and Elvis had been performing it live for over a year; but somehow he couldn't capture the joy and freedom of the original.

The next day, Elvis inserted all sorts of exaggerated quivers, swoops, stutters, and even some slightly off-key notes into two pallid ballads, rendering them practically unfit for release.

SHOLES WAS NOW over a barrel. He needed to release a single to prove to his superiors at RCA that Elvis was worth the money he'd spent on him. He had been careful to steer Elvis in the right direction: a few weeks earlier, he'd sent Elvis a note proposing ten titles for the session, accompanied by lead sheets and acetate demos. These included, besides the two ballads, songs like "I Need a Good Girl Bad," "Shiver and Shake," "Old Devil Blues," "Automatic Baby," and "Wam Bam Hot Ziggety Zam." But what Elvis had now recorded was nothing Sholes felt at all confident about: two covers of well-known R&B songs; the two ballads, which Elvis had badly mangled; and "Heartbreak Hotel." No less an authority than Sam Phillips, Elvis's producer at Sun, pronounced that song a "morbid mess . . . only a damned fool would release it." Nobody seemed to like it—not Sholes, not Atkins (the nominal producer of the session), not Gordon Stoker, who had provided background vocals on the ballads. And Sholes's superiors were so put off by the session that they wanted him to go back to Nashville. "They all told me ['Heartbreak Hotel'] didn't sound like anything, it didn't sound like his other record[s], and I'd better not release it, better go back and record it again." (The song had previously been turned down by the Wilburn Brothers too, who called it "weird"; and even Colonel Parker had been unconvinced when he'd first heard it.) In short, "Heartbreak Hotel" sounded nothing like what Elvis was supposed to sound like, and what he'd sounded like until now: vibrant, upbeat, exuberant.

On the other hand, the record perfectly captured the teenage angst that was sweeping the country. James Dean had died on September 30, 1955, and *Rebel Without a Cause* had opened less than a month later. Fan clubs sprang up around the world, including twenty-six in Indiana, Dean's home state, alone. Thousands of kids tried to look, dress, and act like Dean. At least six memorial pop records were released, including "Jimmy Dean's First Christmas in Heaven." There was, in short, mass hysteria. And everybody was wondering who'd be the next James Dean.

With "Heartbreak Hotel," Elvis, who knew *Rebel Without a Cause* by heart, proved he fit the bill perfectly. By April, the song had reached number one on *Billboard*'s pop and country-western charts, and number three on its R&B charts. And its almost unequaled success in crossing these genres (only two songs in American history have performed better on all three charts: Elvis's third RCA single, "Hound Dog," and Jerry Lee Lewis's "Whole Lotta Shakin' Goin' On") was no accident. When Elvis came to RCA, he was given far more artistic freedom than he'd had at Sun, and he used that freedom with a deliberation and assurance that can only be considered astonishing coming from such a novice entertainer.

"HEARTBREAK HOTEL," like "Baby Let's Play House," "Hound Dog," and "All Shook Up," has a meaning beyond its existence as a consumer product. These early songs helped define a new generation with a message of liberated desire; and Elvis Presley used all of his powers of exaggeration, exuberance, and bravery to create a hitherto unheard music that would, yes, change the world.

Like most innovators, Elvis Presley had a vision, a vision that continuously evolved, yet always remained true to its founding principle. At its heart was his voice, with its inimitable combination of playfulness, arrogance, and desire. Perhaps it was this mixture that set his music apart from that of his predecessors—there certainly wasn't much arrogance in the popular music of the early 1950s, and the songs of playfulness and desire seemed to inhabit two different worlds.

This mixture not only precluded any sort of personal authenticity, it seemed to be a reaction against it. In order to make arrogance and desire palatable to American listeners, they could not be genuine; moreover, it's difficult to be simultaneously earnest and playful (perhaps only certain hip-hop artists have pulled this off successfully). By embellishing country music's plainspoken style with all sorts of mannerisms, Elvis deliberately moved his music away from the this-is-God's-truth mode of country delivery and the cult of authenticity that went with it. His casual delivery and the way he slurred his words are reminiscent of Dean Martin's later records. But while much of Martin's charm lay in the fact that he sounded just as drunk as he appeared to be, Elvis sounded like a cartoon version of a drunk.

It only made sense, then, that the songs he and his managers chose rarely, if ever, bore any relationship to the events of his personal life—a sharp contrast to the modus operandi of Hank Williams or Jimmie Rodgers. In fact, rock'n'roll songwriting—with the exception of the songs of Leiber and Stoller, who also wrote many of the greatest rhythm and blues hits—moved away from the storytelling mode so predominant in country and rhythm and blues, adopting instead the bland ingenuousness of mass-market pop. And as for Leiber and Stoller's records, they took the real-life situations earlier blues songs had elaborated on and injected them with a rebellious humor that made them seem cartoonish and absurd.

In other words, rock'n'roll was at its core self-consciously inauthentic music. It spoke of self-invention: if Elvis could reinvent himself, so could others; if he could assume a mask, so could anyone. Its inauthenticity gave it staying power.

Much the same could be said of a later musical phenomenon—disco. Both genres delighted in absurdity; both engendered record-smashing and unreasonable tirades from the keepers of the status quo; both reflected the tastes of marginalized social groups (hillbillies and adolescent delinquents in one case, gays and blacks in the other); both were wild, uninhibited, and explicitly rejected all previous musical genres; both made radical breaks with past styles in clothing and décor; and both ignored the idea widely accepted as central to country, blues, folk, and much of later rock music: that one's music should reflect one's own *real* life and personality and world. Instead, rockabilly and disco created their own peculiar, unique worlds, populated by cartoonish characters, lots of sex, partying, and generally uninhibited behavior.

And the cult that developed around the King, unlike the later cults of Kurt Cobain and Tupac Shakur, was fully cognizant of Elvis's love for inauthenticity, for artifice. Would Elvis have spawned so many impersonators if he had sung just what came naturally to him, without affectations? In fact, like his voice, every other aspect of his life—the gaudiness of Graceland (which would soon become his own personal Heartbreak Hotel), his need to be surrounded by hangers-on, his drug-taking and spiritual quests, the way he twitched while he was singing, and his obsessions with police and kung-fu—

seemed to be symptoms of one thing: the fear of being alone. "I'll be so lonely, I could *die*." The road of personal authenticity is a lonely one; Elvis avoided it like the plague.

And rock'n'roll largely followed in his footsteps. For the first ten years of its history, the question of authenticity was raised only by the music's detractors.

THE MASSIVE SUCCESS of "Heartbreak Hotel" overshadowed all previous rock'n'roll—the song gave the genre a new definition, setting it apart from everything that had gone before. (Even John Lennon credited "Heartbreak Hotel" with igniting his love for the music.) But it wasn't the playfulness of the song that accomplished this: earlier rock'n'roll hits such as "Maybelline," "Rock Around the Clock," and "Bo Diddley" had been playful enough. It was the song's exaggerated melancholy, the melancholy that had so scared the brass at RCA. In his repeated "be so lonely," Elvis was creating an unreal, artificial world, marking rock'n'roll as a genre free from introspection or confession.

As a result, rock'n'roll was shunned by those who sought authenticity: it was anathema to folk, jazz, and blues purists, not to mention the defenders of the pop-music status quo. Blues and folk scholar Jeff Todd Titon writes, "In the late 1950s when I was a teenager, . . . folk music was in vogue; it offered a meaningful musical alternative to rock and roll's vapid insistency"; and his reaction was far from uncommon.

More contemporaneous examples are numerous. Frank Sinatra, a staunch defender of traditional jazz, wrote in 1957 that rock'n'roll "smells phony and false." *Time* magazine, also in 1957, called it an "epileptic kind of minstrelsy." The same year, Mitch Miller, the head of A&R at Columbia Records, who had made Sinatra sing ridiculous numbers like "Mama Will Bark" and "Tennessee Newsboy," called Presley a "three-ring circus" and rock records the "comic books" of music. As late as 1964, Peter Yarrow of Peter, Paul and Mary called the typical rock'n'roller "an unscrupulous modifier of folk songs whose business it is to make this type of song palatable for the teenage delinquent mother-my-dog instinct." (Of course, Yarrow himself was none too scrupulous a modifier of folk songs.)

The funny thing about these comments by Elvis's hypocritical detractors is that they were all on the money. For rock'n'roll as performed by Elvis and his followers had introduced, via its perennial use of artifice, a host of brand new concepts to the American musical stage, concepts that, rather than debasing the music, helped it become fabulously entertaining: preening puerility, nonsense as heroism, a mirror-gazing joyousness, sex for preteens. None of these applied to much pop or folk music—or culture—before Elvis; but after Elvis, these concepts ruled America—and the world.

IF "HEARTBREAK HOTEL" marked rock'n'roll as a genre that delighted in inauthenticity, Ray Charles's original version of "I Got a Woman," along with its flip side, "Come Back Baby," had marked the birth of soul as a music that came to define authenticity for a host of later performers. With these and subsequent singles, Ray Charles popularized a raw, bluesy style that emphasized the voice's natural imperfections when overcome by emotion, introducing a level of personal authenticity into black music that was entirely foreign to performers such as Clyde McPhatter. Prior to that session, Charles, whose voice was far from resonant, had been performing in a smooth style indebted to Nat "King" Cole and Charles Brown. "I Got a Woman" seemed to come out of the blue. As Charles later told David Ritz,

> [Around this time,] I became myself. I opened up the floodgates, let myself do things I hadn't done before, created sounds which, people told me afterwards, had never been created before. If I was inventing something new, I wasn't aware of it. In my mind, I was just bringing out more of me. . . . Imitating Nat Cole had required a certain calculation on my part. I had to gird myself, I had to fix my voice into position. I loved doing it, but it certainly wasn't effortless. This new combination of blues and gospel was. It required nothing of me but being true to my very first identity.

In fact, in 1947, when he was only seventeen, Charles had recorded four songs, his very first—original piano-and-vocal blues ("St. Pete's Blues," "Walkin' and Talkin'," "Wonderin' and Wonderin'," and "Why Did You Go?") that display every characteristic of his mature recordings. In other words, with "I Got a Woman," Ray Charles had gone back to singing the blues.

So while both Ray Charles and Elvis appeared to be reinventing pop music vocal styles at the same time, founding new genres with ease and assurance, and while both of them were messing with the blues, singing songs of desire and loneliness, Ray Charles's style was actually far older.

By saying that Ray Charles was striving for authenticity and Elvis wasn't, I don't mean to suggest that Ray was actually drowning in his own tears when he sang "Drown in My Own Tears," a song whose melancholy is every bit as exaggerated as that of "Heartbreak Hotel." Yet he actually did cry when performing this and other songs. Perhaps he was simply a better actor than Elvis.

More likely, though, his vocal style was more conducive to raw emotion—it was a style of grunts and sobs, the sounds of sex and weeping, of succumbing to deep feeling. The late classical music scholar Henry Pleasants describes how this works:

His records disclose an extraordinary assortment of slurs, glides, turns, shrieks, wails, breaks, shouts, screams and hollers, all wonderfully controlled, disciplined by inspired musicianship, and harnessed to ingenious subtleties of harmony, dynamics and rhythm. . . . It is the singing either of a man whose vocabulary is inadequate to express what is in his heart and mind or of one whose feelings are too intense for satisfactory verbal or conventionally melodic articulation. He can't *tell* it to you. He can't even sing it to you. He has to cry out to you, or shout to you, in tones eloquent of despair—or exaltation. The voice alone, with little assistance from the text or the notated music, conveys the message.

Elvis's style, on the other hand, emphasized playfulness—witness how he delivered his high and low notes in entirely different manners—and the feelings expressed were exaggerated to the point of ridiculousness. Richard Middleton, perhaps the most astute analyst of Elvis's vocal style, gets at the difference between Elvis and previous singers succinctly: in "Baby Let's Play House," what he calls Elvis's "boogification" "is deliberately exaggerated so that it now expresses not instinctive enjoyment but self-aware technique: Elvis's confidence in his own powers is so unquestioned as to reach the level of ironic self-presentation."

IT CAN'T BE only a coincidence that Elvis chose to cover Ray Charles and Clyde McPhatter at his first RCA recording session—after all, he was trying to define himself as a brand new kind of singer, one for whom conventional vocal inhibitions did not exist. Clyde McPhatter represented one vocal extreme: a florid, mannered style characterized by exaggeration and heavy on vocal effects. (Charlie Gillett, writing about the Drifters' hit "Such a Night," describes McPhatter's voice best: "The singer slightly overdid the ecstasy, feigning innocence of the humour in the situation yet somehow also communicating the sense that he was aware of his own ridiculousness.") Charles represented another—a hoarse voice soaked in blues and gospel, a voice of black experience. Both sounded dynamic, wild, unconstrained, and both indulged in remarkable vocal techniques. Elvis wanted to encompass all this and more in his voice: melodrama, earthiness, blackness, power, joy.

But none of this had anything to do with who he really was at heart. Elvis didn't see himself as another Clyde McPhatter or Ray Charles, both black singers singing for a black audience. Prior to "That's All Right," he'd recorded six songs of his own choosing, all of them conventional pop or country ballads written by whites, and his repertoire consisted mostly of songs made famous by white singers like Bing Crosby, Dean Martin, Eddie Fisher, Perry Como, Hank Williams, Eddie Arnold, and Hank Snow. Contrary to myth, Elvis probably did not frequent blues clubs on Memphis's Beale Street while in high school; he was a white boy through and through.

While Elvis was only one of dozens of white artists who recorded R&B songs in the mid-1950s, by the time of "Heartbreak Hotel" he was beginning to see himself as a unique figure in popular music history. This white country boy wasn't making black songs blander, like Pat Boone or Bill Haley. Instead, he was bringing the joy and excitement he heard in black song to white America undiluted. And the only way he could do so was to pretend to be black.

That pretense, though, had to be obvious in order to succeed. In this Elvis resembled nobody more than the performer who would personify white rock'n'roll ten years later, Mick Jagger. For both of them continued and updated an age-old tradition in American music: blackface minstrelsy.

The white minstrels who played blacks on stage seldom really tried to imitate or represent blacks. Everything they did was exaggerated as much as possible, whether it was their makeup or the lyrics of their songs and sketches. Elvis and Jagger were no different: their aim was to liberate whites from what they saw as their staid, all-too-polite manners and engage them in a kind of entertainment that personified the "primitive" qualities they saw in blacks: from the casual swagger to the unadorned leer, from the whoops of joy to the jive talk, from the "riddim" in their bones to the good times in their bottles.

The minstrel tradition is far from an unbroken one in

America: its life has been characterized by any number of sudden stops and starts, transformations and collapses. What white rock'n'roll did with it was to shift it a little bit away from its most obvious referents (poor, uneducated blacks) and make it more general (Americans as a whole). Elvis, like many others both before and after him, repositioned the minstrel as an all-around entertainer, not just a parodist of a certain group of people. Elvis wanted to be all things to all people. So he shucked off many of the most obvious signifiers of stereotyped blackness that previous minstrels had employed: he didn't blacken his face, he didn't dress in rags, and his jokes were those of a nice southern boy, not a stuttering lazy idiot. Elvis thus freed minstrelsy from much of its racist essence— his early RCA singles were high on the R&B charts, were played on R&B radio stations, and were bought by black Americans in large numbers. He made neither black nor white music but American music that could appeal to everyone on earth with a new message of youth, liberation, desire, and joy.

And for the next ten years or so, that's precisely what rock'n'roll did. Whether black (Little Richard, Lloyd Price, Fats Domino, Chuck Berry, Ray Charles, Sam Cooke, Jackie Wilson, James Brown) or white (Jerry Lee Lewis, the Everly Brothers, Buddy Holly, Roy Orbison, the Beach Boys), the rock'n'roll performers that immediately followed Elvis's success all sang songs that specifically revolved around one persona: the teenager in love. There were few attempts to explore that persona in depth, though; this theme was simply an excuse to be as exuberant and ridiculous, as sexed up and charged up, as you could get. This wasn't innocence, the way so many nostalgic commentators think of those early days.

This was a music full of knowing winks, vaudeville tricks, novelty gimmicks, and sex, sex, sex.

All that would change in the mid-1960s, when the spectre of authenticity grabbed hold of the reins of this runaway genre, and rock music became what it remains today: a mode of performance characterized by a strong desire to stop acting and get real. Of course, there have been exceptions: the Rolling Stones and the Who in the 1960s, glam, art rock, and heavy metal in the 1970s, much of new wave in the 1980s. By now, though, Elvis's aesthetic seems to have all but vanished. If a band doesn't at least pretend to "get real" from time to time, they lose their credibility—and their fans.

As for Elvis himself, he never did get real—he remained an actor to the end. And as an actor, he was a great singer. Because he cared deeply about his performances, he put his heart and soul into the task of bringing life to songs as absurdly varied as "Bossa Nova Baby," "It's Now or Never," "Old Shep," and "Peace in the Valley." Occasionally, we'd even seem to glimpse Elvis's reality in his songs: "Suspicious Minds" and "Hurt" hinted, however accidentally, at Elvis's troubles. But from "Baby Let's Play House" and "Heartbreak Hotel" to "Burning Love" and "American Trilogy," Elvis's art was artifice, and it served him well.

CHAPTER FIVE

SUGAR SUGAR

Faking It in the Age of Singer-Songwriters

Los Angeles, January 1967

Call us synthetic because, dammit, we are!

MICHAEL NESMITH

IMAGINE A CALIFORNIA RADIO STATION in the summer of 1969. The song playing is "Sugar Sugar" by the Archies, a non-existent band created to give a children's TV cartoon a pop soundtrack. All summer long the song has been playing on high rotation—an infuriatingly catchy moment of perfect pop music—anodyne, exotic, unforgettable, and about as "inauthentic" as one can get.

"Sugar Sugar" was popular with the target audience—the younger brothers and sisters of teenagers, paying for the record with their pocket money. But it was also bought by people from all walks of life, even hippies who deluded themselves into believing that they could hear a veiled drug reference in the line "pour a little sugar on me." This inane yet brilliant song would go on to sell close to ten million copies worldwide.

Many felt repelled by the song's childish jauntiness and naked commercialism and couldn't allow themselves to embrace it as a simple thing of beauty. In the late 1960s a lot of people were taking themselves seriously: the personal was political, and everyday likes and dislikes could be spun into pseudo-social theories overnight. "Bubblegum" became widely used as a term of abuse, as in bubblegum cinema, bubblegum politics, bubblegum fashion. It meant fake, without depth, or manufactured for public consumption.

The Archies were, of course, the epitome of a manufactured pop group. A studio band—a varying gang of session singers, musicians, and writers—they were assembled by musical svengali Don Kirshner following his notorious split from the Monkees. The Archies were a simpler vehicle for Kirshner, who enlisted songwriter Jeff Barry and singer Ron Dante as their core.

The TV cartoon was based on Archie, a comic character who dated back to the 1940s. Now, together with Betty, Veronica, Jughead, and Reggie, he formed a high-school band. Each episode featured at least one of the band's songs, animated in the semi-psychedelic style of the time. There was no pretense that this was a real band—the singles were promoted by cartoon clips. As imaginary characters in a children's show, the Archies had no independent existence and could be trusted not to undermine their pop perfection in their real lives.

■　■　■　■

THE MONKEES, however, were a different story. Kirshner's problems with the band had started for this exact reason— they weren't cartoons, and they weren't happy being seen as fakes. Kirshner had helped to create the Monkees' huge pop success, providing the songwriters, producers, and musicians for their biggest early hits. But the Monkees had opinions and personalities of their own.

Television producers Bob Rafelson and Bert Schneider had originally recruited the four members by undertaking an exhaustive search for the stars of their projected television series about a youthful pop group. Two actors (David Jones and Micky Dolenz) and two musicians (Michael Nesmith and Peter Tork) had been selected and quickly thrown into the filming of the show. It was a highly entertaining program, full of unexpected camera tricks and cuts, usually featuring two songs in each episode, with largely improvised visual accompaniments that prefigured many later developments in music video.

From an early stage, the fact that the four Monkees weren't allowed much of a role in making their records had been a bone of contention for the group. This might not have been the case if they had simply been depicted as actors engaged in a role, but the producers played deliberately with the ambiguity of the situation. The band's first single, "Last Train to Clarksville," was released before the first show aired, and was a huge hit. When the show was criticized as representing a fake Beatles, the Monkees were asked to undergo a rehearsal crash-course in order to become "a real band," performing gigs in their own right. While they had only sung on the records, which were otherwise played by session musicians, they were now expected to replicate the songs in real-life situations. This gave Nesmith and Tork some degree of satisfaction as they were able to demonstrate their musicianship—although the gigs were chaotic affairs, mostly inaudible because of the hysterical audience reaction.

Even within the show this ambiguity was emphasized. The four played comedic characters but kept their real names. The pilot episode featured segments from Nesmith's and Jones's screen tests for the show, and many subsequent episodes featured brief inserts in which the four Monkees answered questions as their real selves. Rafelson and Schneider had decided that audiences, seeing the Monkees in real life, would be encouraged to view the members of the group as individuals and thus would bestow their affection more readily. Yet at the same time, the producers tried to keep the four from speaking to the press, and the physical improvisation featured in the musical segments of the show, like the scripts themselves, played heavily on the idea that the four actors were real musicians acting as themselves, just as the Beatles had acted as themselves in *A Hard Day's Night* and *Help*.

As a result of this confusion, Nesmith and Tork in particular felt that their status as "real musicians" was being undermined, and that they should at least be allowed to play instruments on their own records. Nesmith turned this into a public argument at a press conference in early 1967 when he announced that the Monkees were "being passed off as something we aren't. We all play instruments, but we didn't on any of our records. Furthermore, our company doesn't want us to, and won't let us." A meeting was called at the Beverly Hills Hotel to clear the air. Kirshner was generally reluctant to leave New York and fly to Los Angeles. This contributed to his distant relationship with the members of the group. But on this occasion he made the journey. Afterward he recalled that "I had given them royalty checks for over a million dollars at a time—kids who previously had nothing." These were the proceeds from the band's early records. He felt that they should be pretty happy with this and couldn't understand why they were so worked up about playing their own instruments. His feeling, perhaps unreasonable, was that if they didn't want to keep doing things his way, they shouldn't take the money.

At this point, Kirshner's assistant Herb Moelis waved a contract in Nesmith's face and reminded him that it meant that he could be legally suspended for his actions. Nesmith punched his hand through a door to show how deadly serious he was about the issue. "That could have been your face," he blustered to the record company man.

It's hard to imagine anyone being very impressed by his little tough-guy act, but it has gone down in history as the defining moment of the controversy. In fact, the story was slightly more protracted, as the Monkees appealed to Abe Schneider, the president of Columbia Pictures, via Bert Schneider, who happened to be his son. The Monkees were allowed to go into the studio without Kirshner to try and prove themselves. Playing their own instruments, they recorded two songs ("I'm Just One of Your Toys" and "The Girl I Knew Somewhere") that they wanted to be their next release. Schneider warned Kirshner not to put out the Neil Diamond song "A Little Bit Me, A Little Bit You" as the next Monkees single. But Kirshner had promised Diamond that if "I'm a Believer" went to number one, Diamond would get the follow-up, so Kirshner ignored Schneider's directive. This was the last straw, and shortly afterward Kirshner stopped working with the band.

Schneider and Rafelson both said later that Kirshner was too egotistical in wanting to take full credit for the Monkees' music. This attitude clashed with the illusion they were still trying to maintain. Rafelson said, "My feeling was, fine, just don't take the credit for it because you'll eliminate half your audience—authenticity, integrity and a certain kind of pop truth being the slogans of the day." Kirshner always had a gift for self-promotion. Ironically, his departure was hastened precisely because his desire for recognition risked revealing the fakery.

Peter Tork has said, "What Donnie didn't know was that he could have gone right on being the same guy he was, doing the same things he did. . . . All we wanted to do was be the musicians in the chairs. But for some reason . . . he saw that as a challenge." But this comment was perhaps disingenuous. Don Kirshner was exactly the kind of guy who didn't want to work that way. It was always going to be his way or no way.

Prior to the Beverly Hills Hotel meeting it seems that Kirshner may have intended to record "Sugar Sugar" with the Monkees, although this could just be a mischievous story he put out later. The least one can say is that if they had continued to work with Kirshner, the Monkees might have ended up recording the song instead of the Archies. But the Monkees got their way and started to play on their records and even to write some of their own songs.

One can understand how Michael Nesmith felt. It must have been strange to receive acclaim for records on which he had had so little involvement—he must have felt like an impostor. But by wanting to get involved beyond this level, the Monkees made the mistake of believing part of the hype—that they were already stars and therefore capable of doing the whole show themselves.

Perhaps Nesmith was just too close to the process to enjoy the early Monkees records. He was a competent and successful songwriter in his own right, although the pure pop of the Monkees didn't come naturally to him. The band had had a succession of glorious pop songs, from the absurd proclamations of the "Monkees Theme" through the upbeat wistfulness of "Last Train to Clarksville" to the catchy brilliance of "I'm a Believer." They had been served well by excellent songwriters such as Neil Diamond, Goffin and King, and Boyce and Hart, and they probably imagined that their own attempts would be equally good. Or else they failed to see the quality of the songs, believing that they were successful as a band only because of the exposure the songs received on the weekly show.

It is true that the Monkees records weren't hits only because of the good songwriting. The four band members' sole contribution was the vocals, but perhaps because this was all that they were asked to do, they performed the songs with a joyous and infectious enthusiasm. "I'm a Believer" was a simple, effective pop song, built around a basic three-chord shuffle and a classic, cheesy organ riff. But Micky Dolenz's lead vocal gave the song a real tenderness that was slyly underwritten by the comical "do-do-do's" of the bridge, and the song finished triumphantly with Dolenz freaking out with gusto on the improvised outro. Without these vocals even this fine song might have fared less well. The Monkees' justifiable pride in their performances perhaps gave them confidence that, in spite of an inauspicious start, they could somehow get themselves taken seriously as a band once they took over the reins.

But after Kirshner's departure, the Monkees' career started to slide down the greasy pole, and the TV show was canceled the next year. In late 1968 their overblown and absurd film *Head* was released to terrible reviews. Its story, insofar as it had one, centered around an imaginary suicide of one or all of the Monkees. As a film, the old insult "the longest suicide note in history" is a pretty fair description. Schneider later said that "we were quite satisfied to see the movie be the last thing the Monkees ever did . . . this was the cap and then we're finished and if we can destroy the group in the process of making the movie, all the better." Perhaps Schneider was rationalizing the movie's failure. But Bob Rafelson, who also worked on *Head*, seemed equally delighted to lay his uncool Monkees period in the grave with this acid-influenced series of random skits. By 1969 he had moved on, along with *Head* screenwriter Jack Nicholson, to the start of a new credible film career by helping to make the super-hip *Easy Rider*, a film that was thus partly funded by the proceeds of the Monkees' TV series.

The original teen Monkees fans were just confused by *Head*, but the groovy, politically aware audiences the Monkees wanted to impress were not prepared to accept the ex-fakes as the genuine article. The film was a commercial failure. There was one more TV show—the special *33⅓ Revolutions Per Monkee*. Director Jack Good, legendary in the UK as the founder of rock'n'roll television with shows such as *6.5 Special* and *Oh Boy!*, took the opportunity to unleash a messianic critique of the decline of pop music since rock'n'roll. The special was, like its creator, both bizarre and fascinating, but it failed to turn the tide. By the late summer of 1969 the Monkees' only television presence was in Kellogg's cereal advertisements. The original show would soon be rerun, and continues to be to this day, but in late 1969 Nesmith left the band and the original incarnation of the Monkees was finished.

Who are the heroes and villains in this story? One imagines that, as Don Kirshner watched the cash pile up from "Sugar Sugar" and saw the Monkees falling apart, he felt vindicated by the turn of events. He has generally been depicted as the villain, the evil genius who kept the Monkees in captivity until Nesmith punched his way free. And he fits the villain role perfectly. But it is hard to see what the Monkees really achieved by liberating themselves from Kirshner's control. As a pop phenomenon, a band created for a mere television show, they made some really good pop records. As an authentic band, they were rarely more than humdrum.

Nesmith, who had started life "dirt poor" but was now guaranteed wealth from his Liquid Paper inheritance—his mother had invented the mistake-erasing potion—was rather more than a spoiled rich kid, but in this episode, he showed that being wealthy and famous was not enough for him—he wanted respect too. He was thus a good representative of a generation coming of age in an era whose affluence allowed them the unprecedented liberty to express and indulge themselves and to be taken seriously, too. Having inadvertently helped to get *Easy Rider* made, Nesmith should at least have been able to belatedly sympathize with Peter Fonda's inarticulate statement of hip disillusionment—"We blew it . . ."

Regardless of whose side you take in this story, the really interesting question is why it was so important to the Monkees to prove that they could be a real band.

PRIOR TO THE 1960S record companies created hits primarily by taking a songwriter's song, finding the right singer, and hiring session musicians to play the music. Pop singers weren't expected to choose or write the song or do anything much except turn up on the right day to sing it. They were primarily pretty faces used to sell the song. But by the late 1960s, it had become uncool or "phony" to behave in this way.

The main catalysts in this change were Bob Dylan and the Beatles. Dylan's emergence from the folk movement into the mainstream had brought his personal and poetic visions to a wider audience. While earlier folk and country had revered icons of integrity and self-expression going back through Hank Williams and Woody Guthrie all the way to Jimmie Rodgers, rock'n'roll had been fundamentally a joyously inauthentic music, as embodied by Elvis Presley and his followers. Dylan's move to rock'n'roll was a significant step toward bridging this gap. But even more than Dylan, it was the Beatles who, by writing and performing their own songs, transformed the music industry from one in which the congruence between singer and songwriter was irrelevant to one in which it could not be ignored.

Contemporary bands such as the Byrds, the Kinks, and the Beach Boys didn't always play their own instruments on their records, but at least enjoyed the credibility of being songwriters. In 1967, the Kinks ("Session Man") and the Byrds ("So You Want to Be a Rock and Roll Star") both recorded ambiguous songs that made a mockery of music business fakery, revealing a degree of discomfort with their own situations.

But when the Monkees felt that their status as "phonies" was an embarrassment, they were ultimately comparing themselves to the Beatles, the band in whose image they had been created.

LOOKING BACK OVER the careers of John Lennon and Paul McCartney, it is easy to focus on the unique period of creativity from *Rubber Soul* to *The White Album*. But while the songs of this period have the most influence on musicians today, the early songs such as "From Me to You" and "I Wanna Hold Your Hand" gave them global fame and helped to establish the group of singer-songwriters as the dominant archetype in rock music.

Of course, aspects of their style ranging from early rock'n'roll and skiffle to fifties pop originated earlier. But they managed to combine all these elements in a way that seemed completely new and unexpected. And the sheer scale of their success caused the music business to undergo a paradigm shift. Now every A&R department and label chief was on the hunt for groups whose members wrote and performed their own songs, rather than singers performing songs written by professional songwriters.

Listening now to the early records, one is constantly amazed by the ingenuity and skill with which Lennon and McCartney skipped beyond the obvious, using existing styles and making them sound fresh, and creating striking songs with great economy and verve. From the start of their career in the late fifties up to 1965, they wrote songs in standard styles, mostly love songs, but they manipulated the form to its limits, trying every hook, harmony, repetition, and twist they could imagine.

Paul McCartney was the more polished and emotionally distanced of the pair. A skilled songwriter, he could imitate and adapt any style he cared to. He varied from the straight rock'n'roll of "I Saw Her Standing There" to a great ballad like "Yesterday." Songs like "The Night Before" and "Things We Said Today" had a cinematic feel, reminiscent of the kitchen-sink dramas of the period. His songs were accomplished from the start, but the extra layer of gloss meant that they revealed less about the writer's personality than Lennon's did. And later in their careers it was Lennon's pursuit of honesty in his songs that established his enduring mystique.

WHEN WE KNOW singers are performing their own songs, we are invited to feel that they may be speaking directly to us, and telling us about their own lives. John Lennon's early songs are mostly straightforward love songs. But through the edges, you can catch frequent glimpses of a real twenty-year-old—often emotionally insecure but covering up with aggression and sarcasm.

Lennon had a problematic childhood and was known for his caustic insults and jokes. His mother died in a car crash in 1958, soon after he had reconciled with her. After that Lennon was especially unstable, regularly getting into drunken fights. His erratic behavior continued at least into the early years of the Beatles' career. This complex individual is visible in Lennon's early songs: he says to a girl who has spurned him, "If I could see you now, I'd try to make you sad somehow," then threatens to take out his grief on every other girl he meets ("I'll Cry Instead"). "You Can't Do That" crudely expresses a young man's bullying jealousy, while "She Loves You" captures the world of teenage crushes and rejection, with its echoes of local "he said / she said" gossip. As Dave Marsh comments in his book *The Heart of Rock and Soul,* Lennon's caustic sentiment also has undertones of something more bitter than advising a friend to apologize to a girl. "What Lennon sings boils down to a warning to his friend: You'd better appreciate this woman's friendship, because if you don't, I will."

Separated from the music, the words of these songs are sometimes quite bleak, painting an uncomfortable but very familiar picture of relationships between inarticulate, repressed youths. This is why they hit a chord with adolescents who recognized the feverish, slightly hysterical tone of reporting on latest boyfriends and girlfriends or the Friday and Saturday night scenes that provided drama in their lives.

Before the scale of their fame became apparent, Lennon and McCartney had anticipated that they might end up as jobbing songwriters. For a while their efforts were almost as focused on producing songs for other artists as on writing for themselves. McCartney was quoted as saying that they aspired to write songs as good as those of Gerry Goffin and Carole King (whose classic "Brill Building" songs—produced by a legion of lyricists, songwriters, producers, and others in the business who all worked in one New York building—had made as much money for Kirshner as for themselves).

Goffin and King wrote an array of hits in varying styles. The nearest they came to the Beatles' early subject matter was perhaps in songs like "Oh No Not My Baby" and "Will You Love Me Tomorrow," where the stories are told from the point of view of uncertain young girls. In the second of these, a girl ponders whether or not to spend the night with a man, knowing he might be taking advantage of her, but wanting to believe that he will still respect her in the morning. In the first, a girl tells how her friends and family are warning her off a man because he is unfaithful to her, but she refuses to believe them. In both songs the narrator is young and confused, and the fascination comes from the way we can empathize with their naïve hope, but still see that they are fooling themselves. These are very knowing songs, in which the songwriters have deliberately allowed us to see this emotional confusion. By contrast, the Beatles' early songs are less sleight-of-hand, showing their emotions in a more direct way.

The two Beatles also idolized Leiber and Stoller, who had written songs that Elvis performed, including "Jailhouse Rock" and the original version of "Hound Dog." They also wrote rock standards such as "Yakety Yak" and "Along Came Jones," among a series of hits for the Coasters, a band they created to perform their songs. Leiber and Stoller's songs were rarely earnest: they often took a playful idea and created a hook out of it. The early Beatles songs had a similar playfulness in the twists and turns of the music and in the absurd "yeah yeah yeah" screams and "ooh's" that made their vocals distinctive. This kind of songwriting harked back to Elvis's early records and to another of Lennon's heroes, Little Richard. But lyrically, the playfulness was less evident in the early Lennon and McCartney songs, as the subject matter stayed rooted in love and relationships.

Given the way that Lennon and McCartney had revered these great songwriting teams, it is ironic that their own extraordinary achievements as songwriting performers helped to shift the focus of creativity away from the songwriter and toward the artist. With the success of the Beatles, it was no longer sufficient for artists to merely interpret a song; now it had to be their own song, their own self-expression, giving the audience a different expectation of the music's level of intensity and significance.

The Beatles were also influenced by Buddy Holly and Roy Orbison, both of whom sang their own songs, as had many previous country and blues artists. As we might expect, their personalities—Buddy Holly's sunny confidence and the more insecure persona of Roy Orbison, whose love songs often expressed his fear of rejection or failure—were clearly visible through their songs.

In later years, Orbison could never comprehend how David Lynch could have appropriated his "In Dreams" to such disturbing effect in the film *Blue Velvet*. "They're beating people up to this pretty song," he said. "I didn't quite understand it." He thought he had sung a sweet song of romantic longing, but it also had notes of something slightly weird and obsessive. And this is the kind of dislocation that becomes more intense when singers perform their own songs, inviting us to peer between the lines, listen to the emotion in their voices, and work out for ourselves who they really are. Often they reveal more than they realize about themselves.

This heightened identification of the singer with the song

also changes the kind of songs that can succeed. Songs that are very personal and private work better for a singer-songwriter than songs that tell a universal story from a more objective viewpoint. We start to hear songs as pages from the singer's diary rather than seeing the singer as an actor playing a role or as a simple entertainer. As a result, we start to prize honesty and become more fascinated by the real personalities of emotionally powerful artists.

It would be a mistake to be misled by great writers like Goffin and King, Leiber and Stoller, and Burt Bacharach and Hal David (who wrote classics such as "Walk On By" and "Say a Little Prayer") into thinking that this was a golden age that passed simply because of the rise of singer-songwriters. The great songwriters of the fifties and early sixties should perhaps be seen as the last flowering of the classic American songwriting tradition of the pre- and post-war period. Gershwin, Kern, and Rodgers and Hart had operated at a time when the musical theater was still a strong force, and had written both for the popular market and for shows. However by the late fifties the only real outlet for songwriters was recorded popular music, and a great deal of what was produced in this period was cynical or inane. The fifties were notable for novelty hits and preposterous dance crazes. The initial excitement of rock'n'roll was soon blunted as many of its key performers were put out of action—Elvis in the army, Chuck Berry in jail, Buddy Holly dead, Jerry Lee Lewis disgraced—and replaced by bland music business stooges like Fabian. The poor quality of much of the music and the payola scandals of the period contributed to an increasing feeling in listeners that what they were being sold was not "the real thing."

It was this feeling that helped fuel both the folk and blues revivals—and the hysteria that surrounded the Beatles.

Some songwriters thought that this lean period, produced by the demand for groups performing their own work, was a mere fad that would soon pass. But Gerry Goffin has recalled seeing Dylan perform in New York and immediately realizing that the ground had shifted for good. In his opinion it was the Beatles, the Stones, and Dylan who basically brought the Brill Building era to an end, and while Goffin, King, and Kirshner were all able to move on to different phases of successful careers, the business would never be quite the same again. Carole King ended up becoming a performer of her own songs, as did Randy Newman and James Taylor, two more fine songwriters who might perhaps have stayed in the background in an earlier era. Professional songwriting was by no means dead, but for the time being, everything had changed.

AS THE BEDLAM of the Beatles' fame spread around the world, the songs they wrote started to change. Competing bands such as the Rolling Stones and the Beach Boys were starting to stretch the limits of what could be done with a pop song, and the Beatles were forced to try some extraordinary things to keep their preeminent position. They had by now stretched the love song to its breaking point, and by 1965 they were looking for ways to take their songwriting into different territories.

Lennon was by this stage deeply frustrated with the band's lovable public image, feeling that people didn't see the real person behind his persona. He believed that he was not taken seriously and that his true self was being submerged into the collective identity of the Beatles. The suits and polite bows that Brian Epstein had imposed on the band seemed fussy and conformist to him. They grated against his rebelliousness and contrariness, as did Epstein's natural deference to authority and tradition. Lennon had been struggling to find ways to express himself outside the straitjacket of Beatles songs—his two books of nonsense poetry and drawings (*In His Own Write* and *A Spaniard in the Works*), published in 1964 and 1965, demonstrated his more anarchic side. The sense of absurdity that Lennon shared with the other band members had initially been visible only in interviews, press conferences, and moments from their wacky Dick Lester–directed films. But now he started to find ways of expressing this part of himself in song.

Lennon and McCartney songs such as "Help" and "We Can Work It Out" had already marked a steady progression. Released in June 1966, "Paperback Writer," a McCartney song with Lennon's "Rain" on the reverse side, was the first Beatles single that didn't contain a love song. Influenced by Bob Dylan and by their expanded use of drugs, the two songwriters moved on in the mid-sixties from these early doggerel experiments to more impressive songs. Through the period of *Revolver* and *Sergeant Pepper*, the Beatles' subject matter returned less frequently to the love song; instead they used a bewildering variety of styles and subjects, from the prosaic Liverpool poetry of "Penny Lane" to the existential gloom of "Nowhere Man" to the narrative elegy of "Eleanor Rigby."

"Norwegian Wood" was a key transitional song for Lennon because for the first time he found a way to write a song directly about himself. The actual lyric is somewhat guarded, partly because he was speaking about a one-night stand and, as a married man, was reluctant to be too confessional. But the song is rooted in a recognizable version of Lennon's real life and has a confessional tone, in spite of its surreal turn. In "Norwegian Wood," we can see the seeds of a more direct approach that led to the styles and attitudes Lennon adopted a few years later.

However, Lennon's great songs of this period tend to reveal little about his real life. While the odd song like "Help" and "Nowhere Man" did have clear personal relevance, songs like "I Am The Walrus," "Strawberry Fields Forever," "She Said She Said," "Tomorrow Never Knows," and "A Day In The Life" relied on tangential imagery that dropped clues and red herrings, but gave little away. In searching for a style of his own, Lennon found himself close to the English absurdist tradition of Edward Lear and Lewis Carroll. He took his sarcasm and verbal invention, coupled to a fascination with fragmented details of culture and history, and channeled them into tuneful, memorable pop songs. Their playful aspect is emphasized by "Glass Onion," in which Lennon mocks the earnest interpreters who had searched for hidden meanings in Beatles songs. Even "All You Need Is Love," acclaimed as an anthem for the Summer of Love (1967), was more of a verbal game than a political statement, with its clever wordplay and riddle-like verses.

At the same time as Lennon was finding a way to express himself, he moved to a more indirect form of songwriting. But occasionally he wrote some far more revealing, direct songs. The haunting ballad "Julia" was a rare moment of self-revelation, merging his feelings for his lost mother Julia and new partner Yoko into a touching expression of love, even though here, as in "Everyone's Got Something to Hide Except Me and My Monkey," Yoko is referred to only indirectly. "Norwegian Wood" had been a breakthrough song for Lennon, but when he did talk about his own life at this stage he still tended to emulate its coded autobiographical approach. Nonetheless, by the time he wrote "The Ballad of John and Yoko," it was clear that he was becoming increasingly interested in a more personal kind of songwriting.

IN JANUARY 1967, when the Monkees held their meeting at the Beverly Hills Hotel, the Beatles were at the peak of their creative powers. Their most recent albums, *Rubber Soul* and *Revolver*, were critically acclaimed and represented some of the most remarkable popular music that had ever been made. They were working on *Sergeant Pepper* and about to release the single that coupled "Strawberry Fields" with "Penny Lane."

The Monkees had been set up as a copycat Beatles and had been very successful at selling records. But they didn't have anything like the credibility or integrity of the Beatles, even if the furor that erupted around their fakeness was somewhat hypocritical, given the widespread use of session players by other contemporary bands. And now they were falling behind the Beatles in terms of innovation as well.

The irony of the comparison was painful because the Beatles actually liked the Monkees. They enjoyed the absurd humor of the television show, and Lennon once told Nesmith that he had never missed an episode. At this stage, the authenticity that Nesmith aspired to was simply to be in a band of real musicians, playing on their own records and writing their own songs if at all possible. Nesmith's desire was not for honesty and autobiography, or any kind of soul-baring.

Deeply personal songwriting was still relatively rare in the pop music of the mid-sixties. The odd exception that, if anything, proves the rule is "Moulty" by the Boston band the Barbarians, an archetypal garage band of the mid-sixties, whose name derived from their scruffy, antifashion, sandal-wearing style. It was the basic garage style of bands like the Barbarians that would later be co-opted into the bubblegum sound, but with the edges smoothed down and the lyrics replaced by bland, child-friendly ones. However the original garage music was rougher, with more of a punk energy to the performances.

Moulty, the drummer and singer, had lost his hand at the age of fourteen, apparently when a pipe-bomb he was manufacturing went off too soon. The band recorded some decent garage records, clumsy covers of songs such as "Mr. Tambourine Man" and "Suzie Q." They achieved a minor U.S. hit with "Are You a Boy or Are You a Girl," a song that made fun of both the fashionable British Invasion and the Barbarians' own long-haired look.

Doug Morris, the band's producer, asked Moulty to record a song Morris had worked on—about Moulty's disability. The rest of the band was in Boston while Moulty worked in New York with Morris on what was intended only as a rough version. The Hawks, who were later to become the Band, were drafted to play the backing track. Meanwhile, Moulty simply "did my thing, rearranged the words, did my talking, making it real." The result was a strange soliloquy in which he speaks about how bad things had been for him in the days after losing his hand and how he had nearly given up, but had found salvation in music and in starting his band. Then the song spoke directly to anyone who felt "different or strange," urging them not to give up or turn away.

Moulty believed he had an understanding with the record company that they wouldn't release the song without his consent. When they subsequently broke this agreement he was so infuriated that he flew straight back to the Laurie Records office in New York and allegedly chased the president around his office, breaking copies of the single over his head.

The single, however, touched a chord with a mass audience and became a hit. The Barbarians were forced to learn it by listening to the Hawks' version so they could respond to live requests. In retrospect Moulty realized that something in the song had spoken directly to teenagers going through a bad time, feeling different or strange and misunderstood. Fans came up to Moulty in tears after gigs to tell him how the song had helped them through difficult periods. In spite of the song's bogus credentials with the band—which had neither written nor performed it—it became the Barbarians' finest moment. If nothing else, "Moulty" showed how the rock audience could be affected by a song they perceived as being truly personal.

BY 1968, John Lennon was starting to chafe at the bounds of his group and to castigate himself for failing to achieve what he now really wanted: genuine self-expression. Over the next few years, as the Beatles started to disintegrate, he began to reappraise his situation. In 1967 he had started living with

Yoko Ono, and she helped influence him to take a closer look at the way he had been living his life. He felt free for the first time to escape from some of the traps he had been caught in: the endless touring, the smooth polish applied to his songs by George Martin's production, and Paul McCartney's sugar-coated pop songs. He had already changed a great deal from the difficult lad he had been a few years earlier, partly from the necessity of dealing with his public role. He had come to be seen as someone with artistic sensibilities who held controversial political and religious views in his own right, rather than being a mere pop puppet.

Now he wanted to live up to the possibilities created by this new improved public image. Encouraged by Yoko, he wanted to express himself artistically in a more honest and direct way, and to make significant statements through his art and music. The open autobiography of "The Ballad of John and Yoko," despite its flippant treatment of some difficult experiences, showed the more personal direction he was moving in. In late Beatles songs such as "I Want You," he started to restrict himself to what he saw as a more truthful, minimalist way of expressing himself. He worked on several avant-garde albums with Yoko—including the unlistenable lo-fi *Two Virgins*, on the cover of which they posed naked—and became more involved in the art scene.

In his solo music he increasingly searched for ways to return to the raw roots of rock'n'roll (perhaps forgetting how playful those roots had actually been) and to make personal and political statements. While the surrealism and humor of his mid-period Beatles songs, with their layered production values and instrumentation, had represented a high point of his career, he now looked for ways to cut through the masks and layers of sound to communicate in a simpler, purer way, in order to show his audience his "real self."

At the same time, Mike Nesmith was attaining the degree of self-expression he had been aiming for. He released some interesting and respectable songs, both with the Monkees and in his subsequent solo career, only to find that Lennon and the rest of the world had moved on again—to work that was far more introspective and intense.

Nesmith's solo material was mostly country-rock. For the past few years, various musicians and producers had tussled with the problem of how to bring the "authentic" feeling of country music into rock. The Nashville sound had been the country establishment's reaction to rock'n'roll and to country's subsequent marginalization. Leaving out some of the more grating elements of traditional country and replacing them with syrupy strings, artists such as Jim Reeves and Patsy Cline (although she disliked the smoothness of her Nashville sound recordings) had achieved a degree of pop success. However, they had in the process alienated the part of their audience that saw this as a betrayal of the authenticity evident in genuine country.

Now the merging of country and rock was attempted from the other direction: musicians such as Gram Parsons and Nesmith brought a country sensibility to rock music. One end of this particular trail was the hugely successful 1970s West Coast sound of the Eagles and their contemporaries. But the earlier attempts at country-rock have a greater charm, even as they attempted to exploit country's supposed authenticity to bring extra gravity to rock music.

On the sleeve notes to his later album *And the Hits Keep on*

Coming, Nesmith wrote, "I have tried to make music as honest and beautiful as I know how . . . but I am afraid to admit that I did it for me." This statement reveals both the hollow feeling left by an unquenchable thirst for authenticity and a dawning realization that, in spite of making some sporadically fine music, he hadn't been able to find the holy grail of authenticity for which he had been searching.

In country music, Nesmith was looking for something purer, something that came directly from the heart, or from the land and the people, rather than from the ego or mere skilled craftmanship. He remembered a childhood of poverty but had subsequently become wealthy. Perhaps he suffered from the misapprehension that he now lacked something essential that poor people had—that there is something innately authentic about the lives and music of the poor and downtrodden, and that this music somehow emerges fully formed from the soul, from deep wells to which the affluent no longer have access.

If this misapprehension is the basis of an individual quest for authenticity, it is doomed to end in disappointment. Not only is it based on a mirage, it also involves trying to become a different person by taking on the surface attributes of those who live entirely different lives.

Even if folk, blues, and country actually contained the essence of integrity and honesty that have been projected onto them, it would still not be possible to acquire this authenticity simply by adopting one of these styles. One can't help but be reminded of Pulp singer Jarvis Cocker's later taunt in "Common People" that they are laughing at you because of "the stupid things you do, because you think that poor is cool."

In some respects Nesmith had the last laugh. He at least learned from his disillusionment, managing at last with his subsequent career in video to get one step ahead of the game instead of lagging one step behind. He won the first video Grammy for his influential video album *Elephant Parts* and was instrumental in inventing the idea of video-based music television, creating the *Pop Clips* show for Nickelodeon, which Time Warner later used as the basis for developing MTV. Being intelligent and self-aware, the irony can't have escaped him that he had come full circle. After his time as a real musician, the original manufactured pop star had returned to establish the principal forum for the most manufactured era yet in popular music.

MEANWHILE, WITH his first few solo releases, in particular the single "Cold Turkey" and the *Plastic Ono Band* album, John Lennon confronted his listeners with a presentation of his self as naked and rubbed raw. The results were almost unbearably tender in some cases and hate-filled in others. Never before had a pop star displayed personal complex emotions with such intensity. *Plastic Ono Band* was mostly written at the same time as John and Yoko were undergoing the controversial primal scream therapy at Arthur Janov's California institute. The patients were asked to revisit painful episodes from their childhood and to give vent to the resultant emotion by screaming. This therapy had a powerful influence on Lennon's reevaluation of his life and art.

A song like "Mother" feels like an entry in a therapy diary so private that we shouldn't be allowed to hear it. It is hard not to flinch as Lennon's final repetition of "Mummy don't go, Daddy come home" descends into screams of distress. The closing track, "My Mummy's Dead," is shorter and more deadpan but no less upsetting. These recordings take the belief that music should be personally authentic to an unusual extreme.

The lyrics also demonstrate John's feeling that he was finally expressing himself in a truthful way. "Now I'm reborn . . . I was the walrus, but now I'm John," he sings in "God." In that song, the list of concepts and people in which he no longer believes progresses from magic, Jesus, mantra, Bob Dylan ("Zimmerman"), and yoga through "I don't believe in Beatles" until all he can say is "I just believe in me. Yoko and me." Perhaps this lyric simply reflects the narcissism that prolonged therapy tends to induce, but it's also a powerful statement of the idea that art must come from deep inside your own self or soul.

The idea that stripped-down instrumentation expresses the self more powerfully and directly is evident on *Plastic Ono Band*. The album influenced later artists not just in its screams and emotional torment (which we can trace forward to Kurt Cobain's later, more commercial recordings) but also in its emphasis on musical simplicity as a kind of honesty or purity. In this respect it is a direct precursor of *MTV Unplugged* and the increasing reverence for acoustic and stripped-down musical styles; it also points toward the way punk's simplicity would be seen as a signifier of integrity. "Well Well Well" mimics the simplest blues styles, in particular the John Lee Hooker trick of having the voice follow a guitar line over a repetitive thud, while "Working Class Hero" adopts a folk-influenced two-chord drone. Throughout the album the instrumentation is sparse and the music is basic, conspicuously avoiding complex chord patterns or melodies.

Lennon wanted to be personally authentic, but in these songs he adopted the accoutrements of cultural authenticity to reinforce the message. And by using music that derived from folk and blues in this way, he reinforced the idea that these past musical styles could function as badges of integrity.

A COMMON PROBLEM with self-expression and autobiography in songs is that however honest we may be, we tend to project a mixture of the person we are and the person we want to be, or want to be seen to be.

Compare this to the way we react to people in general. In daily life we are used to judging people's character by watching how they act and what they say and do (or don't say and do). We use these clues to build up a picture of the real person, even when hidden behind masks and conventions.

But when performers come right out and say, "This is the kind of person I am, and what do you think of that," we react differently: we wonder why they want to make this statement about themselves and what they might be hiding. The very fact that they consciously assert something about themselves makes us treat their statements as deliberate attempts to project a certain persona, and we are led to question whether this is the truth, a self-deception, or a construction intended for public consumption.

In *Plastic Ono Band*, Lennon focused on his childhood and on his relationship with Yoko. If, for instance, his break-up with his first wife, Cynthia, and separation from his first son,

Julian, was on his mind, we hear nothing of it in these songs. It's not fair to castigate him for this omission—clearly he wrote about what was preoccupying him at the time—but it exemplifies an aspect of his life that he didn't address in song.

Lennon's increased self-awareness and focus had led him to a more earnest and serious idea of what a song ought to do. *Plastic Ono Band* notably lacks the sense of humor that had defined even his late Beatles songs. Lennon's subsequent solo career was very uneven. There were some great songs, but there were also some far weaker moments that resulted from an excess of earnestness or self-absorption.

Lennon's early solo material had a touch of born-again fervor about it. An indirect man had learned how to be direct. And a natural-born individualist was trying to learn how to be (or refuse to be) one of the voices of a generation—no easy task, and one that he approached with wildly varying degrees of success. On the release of the next album, *Imagine, Rolling Stone*'s Ben Gerson saw a problem in Lennon's modified approach to music, saying, "I fear that John sees himself in the role of the truth-teller, and as such can justify any kind of self-indulgent brutality in the name of truth." Gerson was referring to the tracks "Gimme Some Truth," in which Lennon rails against hypocrites, politicians, and prima donnas in general, and "How Do You Sleep?" in which Lennon issues a series of insults calculated to hurt his erstwhile friend Paul McCartney. Lennon's faith in his own honesty encouraged him to revert to his earlier aggression but now with a self-righteous tinge that was uncomfortable to observe.

By contrast, many of Lennon's best solo songs were those in which he put the earnestness and sanctimony to one side and recovered some of the playfulness he had exhibited in the Beatles songs, tying this to either his politics ("Give Peace a Chance," "Happy Xmas, War Is Over," "Imagine") or his emotions ("Oh Yoko," "Number 9 Dream," "Instant Karma"). "Imagine" faintly echoed "All You Need Is Love" in using riddles and mental games to lead in to a message so simple that it can be taken in different ways by different people. "Give Peace a Chance" and "Happy Xmas, War Is Over" were basic nursery-rhyme-style songs that were playful at the same time as they made serious and important points. Even the apparent simplicity of "Happy Xmas, War Is Over" is based on a koan-like puzzle—"War is over," but only "if you want it"—that invites us to ponder the reasons why war isn't over, rather than simply demanding peace in a more direct way. In these songs, rather than preaching or berating the listener, Lennon managed to leaven his message with a gentler approach.

BY THE LATE SIXTIES, following the success of the Beatles, the non-singing songwriters were in retreat. The tradition of the house songwriter persisted in soul music issued by Tamla Motown Records and elsewhere, but it came under some pressure even there in the late sixties and early seventies from artists such as Marvin Gaye, who was extraordinary enough to take creative control of his own music and make *What's Going On*. Most everywhere else the singer-songwriter was in charge.

This became one of the points around which subsequent pop and rock music became differentiated. The Beatles had a foot in both camps for most of their career, something that would become more difficult for later artists to achieve. Much of their early period (especially hits such as "She Loves You" and "I Wanna Hold Your Hand") can be seen as a stage in the history of pop music aimed at the youth audience—a history that moved from the fifties teen idols and boy- and girl-bands to Beatlemania and on to the bubblegum period. In this kind of pop, authenticity is only invoked where it helps to build commercial appeal. The period during which pop music was dominated by singer-songwriters was relatively brief. The huge success of "Sugar Sugar" had a lasting impact. By the early seventies, the Osmonds, together with the Jackson Five and the Bay City Rollers, had confirmed the Archies' blueprint for pop success, and the bubblegum model has proven successful for boy- and girl-bands ever since.

The songs of the late Beatles were part of a different story: they encouraged imitators to put adolescent poetry to music, and to experiment with song structures and styles. The floodgates of autobiography and self-reference that were opened by Lennon, Dylan, and their contemporaries remained open. This was the path that led to rock music—as opposed to commercial pop—and in this sphere authenticity became ever more powerful. Artists not only had to perform their own songs, but these songs had to be meaningful and significant (even "heavy") to the older, twenty-something audiences that listened to the music.

Increasingly the fundamental purpose of rock music came to be self-expression. As a result, many bands and artists have created fascinating records based on their personal, poetic take on the world. Less talented musicians have used this goal to justify self-indulgence and obscurantism, producing songs that are meaningless to anyone but themselves. But it has generally gone unquestioned within rock music that performers must be artistically creative in their own right and that the power of their music must be intimately connected to the power of their personality.

The two diverging paths that led to pop and rock—the paths of "Sugar Sugar" and of "Mother"—created an increasing dislocation in popular music. In the 1990s, Nirvana felt the need to apologize for and deride their popular appeal. In the same decade in the UK, Supergrass became one of the most popular bands of the Britpop period with "Alright," a wonderfully cheerful pop song that directly recalls the best moments of the Monkees. On the basis of the preposterous video for the song, Steven Spielberg offered Supergrass the chance to star in a Monkees-style American TV show produced by his company. However, they declined the offer and then spent the rest of their career trying to play down the song and its cheesy appeal. They often refused to perform it and stressed with their subsequent music and interviews that they were a serious rock band for whom "Alright" had been a one-off aberration. Only occasionally have they allowed themselves flashes of the glorious pop that was so evident on their first few singles. Clearly the kind of stigma that the Monkees had felt was still as strong in the minds of musicians thirty years later.

Performers who took themselves seriously had increasingly abandoned pop in order to express themselves through rock, and it became even harder to achieve anything interesting within the bounds of pop music. In Lennon's distaste for McCartney's pop entertainments, in Supergrass's and Nirvana's embarrassment at their mainstream success, and in a thousand other rock voices, we can hear in retrospect the idea that it is inauthentic or inadequate to merely entertain, and that simple amusement or listening pleasure is not enough. The very distinction between rock and pop in the UK was based on a refusal among rock musicians and critics to be classified as "popular" as in "appealing to a mass audience," a strange state of affairs indeed.

There is a deeper question hiding here: How should we judge any artistic venture? Is the most important thing the artist's self-expression or the audience's appreciation of the final product? Art has to be evaluated by some criteria—some artists have always aimed to please their audience, while others have aimed to satisfy their own need to project their inner selves outward. The latter urge is no less valid than the former, but it cannot be called successful unless it connects with an audience, no matter how small—in other words, it must be tempered by some kind of audience consideration. Our ideas of how rock music should be judged came to be based increasingly on how successfully the artists expressed themselves; this was certainly responsible for some great records, but also for some truly self-obsessed music.

Lennon's shift to a more extreme kind of personal authenticity also influenced a further development in rock. It became increasingly important that artists bare their souls, and if they appeared to be tormented souls, all the better. Songs that delved into the tortured recesses of the artist's mental processes and problems became an indicator of the ultimate kind of authenticity. When artists performed such songs, the audience could believe that they were holding absolutely nothing back, that they were crucifying themselves in public for the sake of their art. Of course, like any tendency in music, this concept spawned many fakes and imitators. It became increasingly common for artists to invent or exaggerate the turmoil of their lives in order to make themselves sound more interesting. A quiet middle-class upbringing without incident was never going to compete with an adolescence of drug-addled misery.

For many, the road to becoming a fascinating rock star has gone beyond this pose. Many have actually emulated the lifestyle, submerged themselves in problems, and got involved in drugs and violent situations for authenticity's sake. Sid Vicious (of the Sex Pistols) and G. G. Allin (of the Jabbers and the Scumfucs, among others) are just two extreme examples—both intentionally lived lives of danger and excess as part of the process of making themselves into rock stars. Pete Doherty (of the Libertines and Babyshambles) now seems determined to play a similar game.

And across a wide variety of genres, the idea of the tormented artist has had one of its most irritating outlets in therapy music. From Tori Amos to Roger Waters to Sting, from the worst grunge to rappers' self-examinations, it has become more and more common for musicians to use their music as the equivalent of the confession box or psychiatrist's couch. Where 1970s and 1980s heavy metal was a crass, entertaining, and hugely "inauthentic" style, the top-selling metal bands of 2003—Staind, Nickelback, Evanescence, and the like—all concentrated on heavy adolescent introspection. As the leader of the parody-metal band Satanicide put it, "It's gotten to the point where all we hear about is everyone's problems. Rock'n'roll has become this personal therapy that we all have to take witness of."

In this context, we may contrast Kurt Cobain's emotional torment with the cheerful anarchy of the Pixies, a band that was in many respects more remarkable and groundbreaking than Nirvana. The Pixies pretty much invented grunge's dynamics, and Cobain confessed that his "(Smells Like) Teen Spirit" was an attempt to mimic them, their "Gigantic" being the most obvious reference point. But their songs were often humorous, involving the singer Black Francis in a series of masks and discussing absurd subject matters such as superheros and alien landings rather than making personal revelations. Musically, the band was more obviously accomplished than Nirvana, which perhaps also distanced it from the more punky approach of the grunge bands that followed them. As a result, audiences that saw themselves and their angst reflected in "(Smells Like) Teen Spirit" didn't warm to the Pixies as much as they did to other groups, and their success was considerably more limited.

ARTISTS SEARCHING for authenticity tend to look back to a mythical golden age of innocence, when music was less self-conscious and was created in a simpler, purer way. This attitude often masks their feelings of inadequacy or frustration: they are deeply conscious of the gap between who they feel they are and how they are perceived by others.

Michael Nesmith and John Lennon both tied themselves in knots to demonstrate that they were anything but fake, and in consequence they invited us to judge them on how real they managed to be. Seeing firsthand the smoke and mirrors that held the music business together and understanding how music fans were increasingly aware of this fakery, both reacted by parading their own authenticity. They did this partly by relying on the perceived authenticity of past musical styles and partly in the way they projected themselves and their music to the public. And both, while promising to give us the whole truth and nothing but the truth, were able to tell us only part of the truth, as they came up against the obstacle of conveying matters of artistic seriousness through the simple forms of rock music while still entertaining their audience.

Meanwhile, the Archies responded to the fakery of the music business by making no attempt to be anything other than fake. As cartoons they could hardly have done otherwise. But beyond this, the Archies' records simply arrived without baggage, entertained for three minutes, and then departed. They did exactly what they were asked to do and nothing more or less. While Lennon and Nesmith at times lapsed into pretentiousness and simulation in their efforts to "keep it real," the Archies never inflicted their performers' egos and anxieties on us. In a perverse way one might even say that they were the most honest of the lot. As cartoons, they lacked self-consciousness, giving them a unique innocence that couldn't be re-created by real people.

But musicians tend to be real people who are projected to the public as though they were cartoons or caricatures. Through the 1960s and '70s the heightened scrutiny and awareness of performers' personalities meant that the more sensitive performers became even more acutely aware of the gap between their public personas and private selves. This may partly explain why the quest for personal authenticity in music escalated so dramatically in this period.

This was also the period in which the young turned away from the postwar social consensus toward a more self-centered culture and counterculture. One can endlessly debate the reasons for and enduring influence of the "me generation," but it seems clear that the changes in popular music also partly reflected deeper changes in society. However it had come about, pop and rock music in the early seventies looked very different from that of a decade earlier. Songwriting had become a much more autobiographical, soul-baring process, faking it was widely seen as a mortal sin, and country, folk, and blues were more than ever pigeonholed as the wellsprings of genuine music.

John Lennon's personal quest for authenticity shows some of the difficulties that lie in the way of putting your self into your music. In his songs we see a great many facets of a complex personality. Even in the songs where he tried to strip his self bare, we hear unintended echoes and ironies. By inviting us to consider his personality as a central aspect of his art, he also invites us to reach our own conclusions about his faults and qualities. He probably didn't need to record "Mother" for us to know that he had painful early experiences of loss and rejection. We could already hear that in "Julia," and in his aggressive reaction to the prospect of desertion in the early Beatles songs. His attempt at sincerity in "Woman Is the Nigger of the World" showed us only how hard he had struggled to overcome his earlier misogyny and how he channeled this through his love for Yoko. The complexity of his personality continues to fascinate, but simultaneously keeps his real self out of reach.

Is Lennon showing us his true self on *Plastic Ono Band*? Or is he showing us an accurate picture of one stage of his development, one aspect of an ever-changing personality that couldn't be pinned down easily, even by himself? This album is a convincing portrait of someone emerging from harrowing therapy. The self projected here is almost autistic in its self-obsession and emotional incontinence. But Lennon didn't live his whole life in this frame of mind. We can gain our own insights into different phases of his life, even when he wasn't consciously baring his soul. And we may prefer not to believe that the most tortured representation he gave us was necessarily the most "authentic."

A song represents a tiny fragment of thought, but it is the friction between that tiny moment and the larger picture that creates sparks of fascination. A song can't tell us the whole truth about a person, nor can it be truly profound. The amount of information contained in a song is simply too small to convey a grand system of thought. But when we hear a song against a background knowledge of its creator's life, we sometimes hear greater levels of profundity than the song itself can carry. After Lennon's death, the repeated playing of "Imagine" on the radio carried a cathartic wave of emotion. But the same song can, on a bad day, seem like no more than a meaningless, empty nursery rhyme. A song can only stand as a signpost toward a real person, and as a record or reminder of something more profound. "Imagine" was never going to change the world, any more than Lennon was about to give away his possessions. However it can still be heard by different people as a daily inspiration or comfort.

Gram Parsons, who had a greater claim than Michael Nesmith to being the real pioneer of country-rock, once described his musical inheritors, the Eagles, as "bubblegum," saying that their music had "too much sugar in it. Life is tougher than they make it out to be." While the Eagles may have deserved his derision, his words could be taken to imply that great music should be difficult and harsh rather than sweet or consoling. Early country and folk music had in fact always mixed up tragedy with comedy, murder ballads with dancing songs and absurd entertainments. Music in hard times often plays the role of allowing mental escape and momentary joy as well as reflecting the people's suffering. Gram Parsons clearly knew this—even the heartrending, brilliant *Grievous Angel* album is a bravura mixture of tragedy and wry comedy. What he was really objecting to in the Eagles, apart from their imitation of his own sound, was that they were too smooth and flawless to be genuine country. But in looking for the words to attack their music, he took the easy path of attacking them for not being serious enough, echoing the Lennonesque idea that being purely popular or entertaining was in some way dirty or wrong. Perhaps it is the luxury of a more affluent age to see suffering and misery as glamorous or authentic attributes. Whatever the reasons, from the 1960s onward the retrospective quest for authenticity tended to disregard the light and frothy aspects of earlier music, focusing only on the serious, tragic, or intense.

But pop songs don't exist only to change people's lives or to change the world. They can also convey simple, banal emotion, and a stupid song like "Sugar Sugar" can sometimes light up the day like a moment of condensed happiness and light, without our needing to think any further about where this song comes from or why it makes us happy. There is no good reason to despise the song for making no attempt to do anything other than this.

Lennon said of his song "Imagine": "Anti-religious, anti-nationalistic, anti-conventional, anti-capitalistic, but because it is sugar-coated it is accepted. . . . Now I understand what you have to do. Put your political message across with a little honey." He was justifying the commercial approach of the song's music and lyrics, claiming that it was just as fundamentalist as the *Plastic Ono Band* material beneath its sugar-coating and that rather than "selling out," he was using the song's commercial nature to smuggle through his political message.

Lennon may have been misunderstanding the universal power of his own song. "Imagine" is able to rise above the particular political moment and be applied in different ways because it is abstract and speaks in riddles and questions rather than in bald statements. Can we imagine no possessions? Even when we know that the man who wrote the song had a room full of fur coats? Well, maybe we can for a moment, and see where that line of thought takes us. It may not be exactly where Lennon intended us to go, but is that such a bad thing? In this song, Lennon had taken a step away from the extremes of self-expression and hard-line politics and created a fable that could be applied to any listener. It is political only in the same way that a Zen parable or children's story might be political, by raising questions rather than by giving answers. In fact, Lennon wasn't disguising a moment of authenticity and self-expression beneath commercialism—he was taking a healthy step away from authenticity and self-absorption in order to communicate a message while still entertaining us. It is partly for this reason that "Imagine" is still a powerful song and one that will last a long time.

Is it a better song than "Sugar Sugar"? It seems almost ridiculous to compare the two, as the intentions behind them are so different. "Imagine" was a song that had some real content beneath its shiny surface—it was thought-provoking even if, in the process of becoming a classic, it didn't achieve all that Lennon intended it to. On the other hand, both songs have a simplicity that makes it hard to imagine a time when they didn't exist, and both succeeded partly because of an excess of sweetness. Perhaps the gap between the two songs is not as wide as one would automatically assume. Lennon didn't share many qualities with Don Kirshner, but at least when he wrote and recorded "Imagine," he showed his understanding of something that Kirshner had always known: that sometimes you need a spoonful of sugar to get through your day.

CHAPTER SIX

TONIGHT'S THE NIGHT

Neil Young and Being "More Real"

Los Angeles, August 26, 1973

Oppress'd with myself that I have dared to
  open my mouth,
Aware now that amid all that blab whose
  echoes recoil upon me I have not once had
  the least idea who or what I am,
But that before all my arrogant poems the real
  Me stands yet untouch'd, untold, altogether
  unreach'd,
Withdrawn far, mocking me with mock-
  congratulatory signs and bows,
With peals of distant ironical laughter at every
  word I have written,

> Pointing in silence to these songs, and then to
> the sand beneath.
>
> WALT WHITMAN,
> "As I Ebb'd with the Ocean of Life"

THE 1970S was the decade in which all of rock music's potential—for both greatness and awfulness—came to fruition. In the 1960s, rock had evolved from a rude melding of a wide variety of popular styles into an art form that considered itself on the same aesthetic level as poetry and classical music. But in the 1970s this art form would go to its greatest extremes.

The 1970s saw the birth and rapid rise of funk, glam, disco, electro, ambient, new age, heavy metal, prog rock, punk, new wave, and hip-hop. Arguably, no radically new pop genre has emerged since then—all can be said to be subgenres of one of these. This was, of course, also the decade that featured much of the most banal and cliché-ridden rock ever, along with some of its most deafeningly experimental moments. Name any possible quality of rock music, from schlocky to heavy, from hard to soft, from clever to dumb, from ecstatic to depressing, and you'll find unparalleled examples in the 1970s.

Perhaps it was simply that natural point in the evolution of a genre: if rock was born in the early 1950s, it was now in its late teens and early twenties, the period when experimentation and creativity are often at their peak. But there were also important political and social factors. The hopeful dream of the 1960s collapsed in the years 1968 to 1974, with the assassinations of Martin Luther King Jr. and Robert Kennedy, the election (and reelection) of Richard Nixon, the escalation of the war in Indochina, the suppression of the student revolts at Berkeley, the killing of students at Kent State, and the recession following OPEC price rises. The music of the 1960s came to an end with the disastrous concert at Altamont—where riots resulted in four deaths—and a period of disenchantment seemed to have taken hold. But instead of putting an end to experimentation and creative energy, this disenchantment somehow forced musicians into a new and darker direction: there was a desperation in the early 1970s that had been missing from the 1960s, and it fueled the music, took it to new heights and depths.

There were, of course, changes in the way music was listened to and played—the age of the three-minute single was effectively over, supplanted by album-oriented rock, and this gave groups the freedom not only to stretch out, but to conceive of their music as high art. In addition, the groups that had dominated the 1960s, the Beatles and the Rolling Stones, no longer ruled the scene, and dozens of equally ambitious bands—Led Zeppelin, Pink Floyd, CSNY, Creedence Clearwater Revival, Black Sabbath, the Who, Jethro Tull, the Doors—vied to take their place. Rock was now free to break up into subgenres: hard rock and soft rock, California rock and New York rock, Black rock and Southern rock, heavy metal and glam. The major labels were entering a period of prolonged confusion resulting from the unprecedented success of single-less albums by groups like Led Zeppelin; some of them, including Warner Brothers and Atlantic, simply let many of their artists make any kind of music they wanted to, subjecting them to no strictures whatsoever. And a huge number of these artists were making money hand over fist.

Then there were the drugs. The marijuana that had fueled the 1960s was now so common that if you didn't smoke it, you were ostracized. Heroin and cocaine made huge advances in the 1970s; speed and quaaludes, alcohol and acid were all wildly popular and readily available. To be a musician and not be in an altered state was so uncommon as to be almost unheard of. The desperation of the time fueled excess, the excess fueled desperation, and both fueled an unprecedented degree of nonconformist creativity.

One extreme among many that surfaced in the early 1970s was an extreme looseness. This aesthetic, which was almost the exact opposite of that which had driven the Beatles' singles, emphasized spontaneity and collective improvisation; it was exemplified by the West Coast jams of Jimi Hendrix, the Grateful Dead, Sly and the Family Stone, Captain Beefheart, and Neil Young. This aesthetic later devolved into a kind of aimlessness, but for a few years it was driven by drugs and desperation, and was held together by ambition—just the right balance to produce masterpieces. And one of those masterpieces was the strange and wonderful hymn to death and failure called *Tonight's the Night*.

Tonight's the Night was the apotheosis of the 1970s: drugged-out, driven, and death-soaked. Moreover, it somehow seemed closer to "reality" than anything else created at the time. Recorded mostly in one six-hour drunken session, it was perhaps the rawest, most fucked-up, and most "honest" rock record of its time. In comparison to this, a lot of other popular acts—from Led Zeppelin to the Grateful Dead, from Elton John to the Carpenters, from Wings to Lou Reed to David Bowie—seemed to be in their own fantasy worlds. Neil Young may not have been the only one "keeping it real," but sometimes it seemed that way.

WHO WAS NEIL YOUNG?

Born and raised in Canada, Young began playing in high school with garage rockers, then turned to the Toronto folk scene without success. He soon moved to California, where he joined fellow Canadians Stephen Stills and Bruce Palmer to form the Buffalo Springfield. After the band's breakup in 1969, he released an eponymous solo record that was painstakingly composed over hours in the studio and was unlike anything else he would ever attempt.

Only with his second album, *Everybody Knows This Is Nowhere*, recorded with a backup band he formed called Crazy Horse, did Young find his true calling: simple, evocative songs; extremely basic rhythms; extended and suspended chords, but only a handful of them—unlike, say, in the complex songs of Paul Simon or Joni Mitchell; nonvirtuosic yet intense guitar solos; lyrics that were open to be read in many different ways; a countryish twang to the music; an unhurried intensity; and an emphasis on the darker side of life.

He proceeded to join Crosby, Stills, and Nash, cutting *Déjà Vu,* one of the best-selling albums of the decade, with them. His next two solo albums were among his most successful: *After the Gold Rush* and *Harvest* cast him as the dark horse—

and the most compelling member—of CSNY. But he then proceeded to fuck everything up. He recorded the tour that followed *Harvest* as *Time Fades Away*, and the album, consisting only of new songs, documents some of the most depressing music ever made. It sold badly, and his next solo tour consisted almost exclusively of as-yet-unreleased songs from the *Tonight's the Night* sessions. Young's following album, *On the Beach*, was equally stoned: the second side consisted of three long, slow, depressing stream-of-consciousness blues songs; and near the end of it came lyrics that seemed to sum it all up: "You're all just pissin' in the wind; you don't know it but you are; and there ain't nothin' like a friend who can tell you you're just pissin' in the wind."

The next album Young planned to release would have been his most commercial since *Harvest*. *Homegrown* included the potential hit "Love Is a Rose"; but instead he released *Tonight's the Night*, which combined nine numbers from the drunken sessions eighteen months earlier with two numbers from the *Time Fades Away* period and a live song co-written by the late Danny Whitten of Crazy Horse and featuring him on guitar and lead vocals. *Homegrown* was never released, though a half-dozen numbers from it later appeared on other records, and Linda Ronstadt had a hit with "Love Is a Rose." *Tonight's the Night* was followed by *Zuma*, a comparatively direct—and fierce—hard rock album with Crazy Horse. But Young then quit in the middle of a sold-out tour with Stephen Stills, canceling a score of dates simply because he didn't like the music he was playing. It was hard to see how anyone could possibly sabotage his own career more successfully than Neil Young was doing (though, as we'll see, in the 1980s he took that tendency to new heights). Then, after an unsatisfying record called *American Stars 'n' Bars* that was half previously recorded numbers and half new and raunchy but relatively dull rock songs, he released a greatest hits three-record set called *Decade* and a laid-back and rather boring country record called *Comes a Time*. His last two records of the decade were his reaction to punk: a loud, brutal, and intensely creative effort called *Rust Never Sleeps* and a two-record live summation of his career called *Live Rust*. The 1970s were over, and Young had helped define the decade. But who was he, as a man and as a musician?

Jimmy McDonough's *Shakey,* one of the best biographies ever written of a rock star, amply answers that question in its eight hundred pages. And McDonough's answer appears to be, at first, very simple: Neil Young is *real.* "Being real: This is what Young constantly strives for," McDonough writes. "Few other musicians of his stature have gone to such lengths to keep things real. . . . Young has abandoned entire albums, dumped bands and tours in a heartbeat, walked away from massive success to release drunk, out-of-tune albums guaranteed to sell three copies, all to follow his muse."

This is not just McDonough's point of view. Elliot Roberts, Young's manager, puts it this way: "Neil's run by his art. If Neil perceives he's being jive, he can't do it." Surf-guitar pioneer Link Wray echoes this sentiment: "If he wanted to be a phony, he could. Not this guy. He chooses not to. Neil's always been real." And Neil Young himself remarked about his second record, *Everybody Knows This Is Nowhere*, "I started just tryin' to be real instead of fabricate something. . . . Since then I've just been striving to get realer and realer on record. As in More Real."

But what does "More Real" mean? Doesn't Neil Young have to play a part just like every other performer? It's easy to see how Neil Young is realer than, say, David Bowie, with his make-up and theatrical personas. But how is he realer than any of the American superstars that were his contemporaries— Gregg Allman, Bob Dylan, Jerry Garcia, Joni Mitchell, Bob Seger, and Bruce Springsteen? None of them were especially "phony."

And then there was one other American superstar of the 1970s who was also emphasizing honesty at all costs and saw himself as the avatar of a new, white soulfulness. Also a self-professed loner and intensely private person with a massive ego, he too was subject to frightening spells of anger and pique. Like Young, he was born in the 1940s and his dad left the family when he was a kid; like Young, he avoided heroin but indulged heavily in alcohol. He too was reluctant to sing at first, thinking of himself primarily as a songwriter and band member; after his first few records, he too preferred to record live with a minimum of overdubs. Both became stars who dedicated themselves to constantly reinventing their music and image; both reacted to the advent of punk rock in the late '70s by releasing records that were far angrier and louder than what had preceded them.

Neil Young was voted artist of the decade by the *Village Voice* in 1979. But Billy Joel had outsold every other performer in history.

■   ■   ■   ■

THIS COMPARISON must seem like outright heresy. Whatever Neil Young and Billy Joel may have in common, it's not their fans. Yet their careers, as outlined above, have parallels too striking to ignore, even when you look at their songs. Young's "Don't Be Denied" and Joel's "Piano Man" are both baldly autobiographical statements about the tragedy and heroism of being musicians; both became their signature numbers for a period. Joel's "Honesty" and Young's "Heart of Gold" are two of the most indelible songs ever written about searching for truth and goodness in an untruthful world; Young's "The Loner" and Joel's "The Stranger" muse on the impossibility of ever really knowing oneself; Young's "Tired Eyes" and Joel's "Captain Jack" are both epic songs about drug use and dealing. Like Young's, Joel's hatred of phoniness and insistence on honesty are all over his songs, from "Just the Way You Are" to "The Entertainer" and "Big Shot."

The critics, however, have canonized Young while dismissing Joel. Young produced a decade's worth of the most critically acclaimed records in rock history, while Joel produced a comparable string of critically reviled albums—in Jimmy Guterman and Owen O'Donnell's *The Worst Rock-and-Roll Records of All Time,* he wins the prize as The Worst Rock-and-Roller of All Time. If the aesthetic of authenticity has any meaning, why is there such a gulf between the critical reception of two such "honest" and patently autobiographical singer/songwriters?

Part of the reason, of course, has nothing to do with "honesty" at all. In his music, Billy Joel often comes across as the kind of guy one tends to avoid at social events, obnoxious and bullying. Most of what he sings is either cliché or bombastic, mawkish or lecherous. And there is something terribly taste-less about the Irish touches in "The Entertainer," the Italian accent in "Big Shot," the synthesized Caribbean steel drums in "All You Wanna Do Is Dance," the classical touches in "Angry Young Man," the Latin accent in "Rosalinda's Eyes." When Billy Joel quotes from the Ronettes' "Be My Baby" in "Say Goodbye to Hollywood," it's a look-at-how-clever-I-am quote, while when Neil Young steals a melody, he modestly acknowledges it: "I'm singing this borrowed tune I took from the Rolling Stones," he sings in "Borrowed Tune," which takes its melody from "Lady Jane"—"alone in this empty room, too wasted to write my own." Young's vocals are the essence of vulnerability, while Joel's are full of bravado (this comes across in their lyrics too). Compare, for example, Young's "Borrowed Tune" and Joel's "Souvenirs," both slow, touching songs for piano and voice alone. Young's is a folk-rock voice: high and slightly hoarse, artless and pleading, sad and direct, wavering in pitch and intensity. Joel's is a Broadway voice: strong and clear, deliberate in its effects, with well-controlled vibrato.

But a good part of the reason for the critical distance between the two has to do with a different degree of authen-ticity from that implied by the word "honesty." Billy Joel is doubtless being "honest" in most of his songs, but there are two very different kinds of honesty: earnestness and self-revelation. It's the difference between an answer and a ques-tion: earnestness is saying, "This is who I am, and I really want you to believe me," while self-revelation is saying, "I wonder who I am—could you help me find out?" For obvious rea-sons, the latter is a far more inviting position.

Consider, for example, the difference between the following phrases. In "Honesty," Joel sings, "I don't want some pretty face to tell me pretty lies: all I want is someone to believe." In "World on a String," Young sings, "It's just a game you see me play, only real in the way that I feel from day to day." For Joel (just as for John Lennon), there's a very clear dividing line between truth and fiction, and Joel is firmly on the side of truth. For Young (just as for Bob Dylan), being real means being true to whatever he feels at the moment, and that can and will change.

Tonight's the Night, which includes both "Borrowed Tune" and "World on a String," exemplifies Young's idea of truth. The record, most of which was recorded on one day— August 26, 1973—was largely inspired by the heroin-related deaths of Danny Whitten, the guitarist for Crazy Horse, and Bruce Berry, a CSNY roadie; and by the deaths of three men shot in a cocaine deal in Topanga Canyon, Young's hippie neighborhood. The musicians on the record were all intoxicated from a combination of tequila, cocaine, and marijuana, and they played as if they were only inches away from complete collapse. The songs were often recorded in one take, and most of them featured glaring mistakes. Listeners have learned to associate authenticity with a kind of clawing at the essence, an attempt to expose the rawest of nerves. Billy Joel wore his heart on his sleeve, but he was a consummate professional, writing sophisticated melodies designed to appeal to the largest possible audience. Neil Young was anything but. Especially on *Tonight's the Night*, Young's music embodied a fuck-everything attitude that may have been more extreme than anything previously recorded.

■　■　■　■

ONE OF YOUNG'S secrets is his apparent ability to tap directly into his subconscious. Listen to his description of his song-writing technique:

> Songwriting, for me, is like a *release.* It's not a craft. Crafts usually involve a little bit of training and expertise and you draw on your experiences—but if you're thinking about that while you're writing, don't! If I can do it without thinking about it, I'm doing it great. . . . *I'm* waiting to see what I'm gonna do next. That should give you some indication of how much planning goes into it. . . . *It doesn't have to make sense,* just give you a feeling. You get a feeling from something that doesn't make any sense. . . . To start second-guessing yourself as it's coming out of you, you're gonna jam it up and it's not gonna come out. Thinking in songs—that's where it gets lost. Either playing it or writing it.

Of course, this is an old Romantic notion: Coleridge played upon it in his preface to "Kubla Khan," Shelley wrote of the skylark's "profuse strains of unpremeditated art," Keats cried, "O for a Life of Sensations rather than of Thoughts!" Keats, especially, was taken with the inherent authenticity of the imagination, with what he called "negative capability," or the ability of the poet to let the poem write itself "without any irritable reaching after fact & reason." "If Poetry comes not as naturally as the Leaves to a tree," he wrote, "it had better not come at all."

This notion has reappeared in lyric poetry again and again. Baudelaire adopted it; so did the surrealists; so did the existentialists; so did Walt Whitman and, much later, the beats. Even prior to the Romantics, inspiration was considered to come from the gods or the muses; now it came from a part of oneself—called at one point the imagination and later the unconscious—that was difficult to know.

Yet Keats's poetry certainly doesn't read as if it came "as naturally as the Leaves to a tree." It's damn clever stuff, involving regular meter and rhyme, which is why it's so effective. Thoughts, reason, facts—these are as essential to good poetry and good songwriting as inspiration.

When Young says, echoing Keats, "Thinking in songs— that's where it gets lost," is he lying? How could anyone compose such an indelible corpus of songs without thinking about it? Young is acting as if he were Lightnin' Hopkins, just making up lyrics as they come to him. But he's not. His songs are clearly well thought-out.

Yet perhaps Neil Young, like Keats, was really telling the truth, if only metaphorically. For writers, composers, and artists must always function on two levels: as creators on the one hand and as self-critics, editors, or mediators on the other. When one attempts to separate those two interlinked levels of thought—to allow only the first to function fully and to suppress the second—that's when one can feel as though one is writing "as naturally as the Leaves to a tree," that's when one can channel the imagination most fully, and that's when writing can become a "release" rather than a "craft." Young, like Keats, is trying to capture the innocent imagination of the child (and his songs about childhood—"I Am a Child," "Sugar Mountain"—bear this out). This is essentially a quixotic goal—one can never achieve the state of pure naturalness that romantics aspire to—yet the attempt to reach that goal can have profound consequences for one's art.

Young's susceptibility to these romantic notions also helps explain why he is so taken with constant change, why so few of his albums sound the same. Shelley wrote an ode to mutability; Keats called the poet a chameleon. The songwriter or poet who is "being real" tries to be simply a channel for "truth" or "the real" to course through, and that "truth" is constantly changing.

Another of Young's secrets to "being real" is to eschew recording technology, to record "live," largely avoiding overdubs, post-recording effects, and splicing. Everything Young said about songwriting he could equally have said about performing and recording: "If I can do it without thinking about it, I'm doing it great." Whether writing songs, recording them, or performing them live, Neil Young was trying to shut down, in the most effective way he could, the side of himself that functioned as an editor or critic and let the creative juices flow as naturally as possible. (Whether he succeeded or not is another question.) As he once said, "Cinema verité? I got into audio verité. The concept of capturing the moment on the camera? I just translated that right into the recording studio."

IT TAKES A LOT of dedicated work to make music, whether it be loose and spontaneous or heavily orchestrated. And musicians must be cajoled into doing things the right way, whether that means hours of practicing or being given the right impetus to improvise in just the right way. *Tonight's the Night* was no exception to the rule.

The band first tried recording in a conventional Los

Angeles studio, but the sound was "too stiff," according to the producer David Briggs. So they went down the road to Studio Instrumental Rentals on Santa Monica Boulevard, knocked a hole in the wall with a sledgehammer, backed a mobile recording truck into the alley, and ran the cables into the rehearsal studio. The band was recorded live from a small stage.

Jimmy McDonough tells the rest of the tale:

> Briggs and Young refused to let the musicians listen to playback of any of the recordings until it was all over. If Briggs liked a particular take, he'd mix it out in the truck.
>
> A picture began to develop, and with it came more new songs. "We didn't go down with the idea, 'Let's make a spooky record,'" said Briggs. "The album just kind of evolved." . . .
>
> Mind-altering chemicals were an essential component of this particular trip, with alcohol at the top of the list. Ben Keith set the tone when he popped the top off a bottle of tequila and threw it to the wind. "We won't be needing that anymore," he quipped. "A drunken Irish wake," is how [bassist] Billy Talbot described the sessions.
>
> Getting loose enough took time. On the two-track masters, Young initially sounds uptight and impatient with the band. . . . But as the days passed and the tequila flowed, so did the music.
>
> "We weren't stumbling or anything," recalls [drummer] Ralph Molina. "We'd just get to a point where you get a glow, just a glow. The head was fucking great, man. When you do blow and drink, that's when you get that glow. . . . No one said, 'Let's go play,' we all just knew it was time.

We never talked about what anybody was playin', who's playin' what part or any of that kinda shit. It was so fuckin' emotional—it wasn't like we were doin' sessions."

The music created at S.I.R. began to conjure up spirits. "The mood was hangin' in the air. You could cut it with a knife," said [guitarist Nils] Lofgren. "There was no need for Neil to lead us to the mood. We were all affected in our own ways by Danny Whitten and Bruce Berry dying. That's what the whole record was about— we didn't sit around and talk about 'Oh God, what a shame.' This was a chance for all of us to come together and get out of that stuff."

[Neil Young commented,] "What we were doing was playing those guys on the way . . . I mean, I'm not a junkie, and I won't even try to check out what it's like. But we'd get really high—drink a lot of tequila, get right out on the edge, where we knew we were so screwed up that we could easily just fall on our faces. . . . We were wide open . . . just wide open . . . I was able to step outside myself to do this record, to become a performer of the songs rather than the writer." . . .

Spontaneous, ragged, and headed for a cliff, this music was much further out than anything Young had attempted before. "With *After the Gold Rush*, even though the recording was done as live as possible, at least we rehearsed things and got pretty on top of 'em before we recorded," said Lofgren. "On *Tonight's the Night*, Neil took it a step further. He was kinda rebelling against everything. I remember talkin' to him and he said, 'Hey, I've made records where you analyze everything and you do it three thousand times and it's perfect. I'm sick of it. I want to make a record that's totally stark naked. Raw. I don't wanna fix any of it.' ". . .

The band holed up in the rehearsal hall, getting tanked, wearing sunglasses all night and playing drunken sets of new songs for a nonexistent audience. . . . "It was frustrating," said Lofgren. "It took me a while to latch on to the concept. As we learned the songs, we'd be recording. I'm sittin' there thinkin', 'Well, another five run-throughs and I'll have my part down,' and Neil would be like 'OK, next song.' I'd go, 'Wait a minute, wait a minute!' " Young would show the band the chords, the words, and work out harmonies—all simultaneously. "Just as we were learnin' a new song and trying to sing at the same time, he'd be rollin' tape, lookin' for a final take. It freaked us all out." . . .

Young was in the thick of it. Surrounded by friends, his subconscious unhinged, he had tuned in to the cosmos. Halfway through "Mellow My Mind," Young's ravaged voice cracks with emotion. "I still get chills when it gets to that fuckin' note," said Molina. "It's so real."

THE BAND THEN took the show on the road. As Young sums it up, "I was drunk outta my mind on that tour. Hey—you don't play bad when you're drunk, you just play real slow. You don't give a shit. Really don't give a shit. I was fucking with the audience. From what I understand, the way rock and roll unfolded with Johnny Rotten and the punk movement—that kind of audience abuse—kinda started with that tour."

Upon the album's belated release, Dave Marsh wrote in *Rolling Stone*, "The music has a feeling of offhand, first-take crudity matched recently only by *Blood on the Tracks*, almost as though Young wanted us to miss its ultimate majesty in order to emphasize its ragged edge of desolation. . . . There is no sense of retreat, no apology, no excuses offered and no quarter given."

And then there was the packaging. The sleeve "was printed on blotter paper," according to artist Gary Burden. "It's meant to age quickly and fall apart, because I guess Neil was around a lotta things that were just falling apart." There's a very strange insert in the record, a piece of paper folded in four, featuring a rambling letter to "Waterface" that starts out, "Welcome to Miami Beach. Everything is cheaper than it looks" and ends "I'm sorry. You don't know these people. This means nothing to you. . . . P.S. Please take my advice." The rest of the insert consists of an out-of-focus picture of a speeding Buick; what looks like a still from *Tom Sawyer* or *Huck Finn*; a photograph of Roy Orbison cut out of a bootleg cassette; the complete credits to Young's *On the Beach*, which had been released a few months earlier; a typewritten account of a bad dream; and an untranslated reprint of a Dutch review of a show from the tour. The actual musician credits for *Tonight's the Night* are on the record labels.

How does Neil Young explain this strange packaging? The answer should be obvious by now: "See, *Tonight's the Night* was the closest to art that I've come." This wasn't pop music—carefully crafted confections. It wasn't even rock'n'roll—that driving and often ridiculous music made by Elvis, the Beatles, and Led Zeppelin—anymore. This was deliberately off-putting, half-crazy weirdness, the kind of statement only an *artist* could make.

WHEN ARTISTS ATTEMPT to present their "real selves" to their audience, they must necessarily make some compromises. For a song is almost always a crafted rather than a spontaneous utterance. There are artists who, it is said, can walk on a stage and perform, without any preconceptions, exactly what they are feeling and thinking at that very moment, utterly spontaneously—Keith Jarrett or Lightnin' Hopkins, for instance. But even if this is true, they are not professional songwriters like Neil Young (or Billy Joel).

What separates the artist's real self from the self that is presented to the world we can call "mediation," and the artist who strives to be authentic will try to minimize the level of mediation to the greatest possible degree. With *Tonight's the Night*, that's exactly what Neil Young did.

Look at the songwriting. A fully crafted, or mediated, song that tells a story will do so artfully, progressing from a beginning to a logical middle to an end. If James Taylor, Joni Mitchell, or John Prine had written a song about the life and death of Bruce Berry, it would have followed a certain logic. "Tonight's the Night," however, follows only an internal, unknown, and probably drunken logic in its sequence of verses, and the chorus has no logical relation to the story told. Some of the verses rhyme and others don't, some of the lines scan and others run on or end too soon. "Early in the morning at the break of day he used to sleep until the afternoon," one line runs, evading not only syntax but logic. It sounds like a strange mistake—singing the wrong line at the wrong time—that Young just decided to leave in there.

And then there's the drunken performance of the song, with Young's voice wandering off-mike and off-key, the missed notes in his piano playing, the feeling that his fellow musicians, though all skilled, still don't know exactly where the song will go. For centuries, alcohol has been a reliable way for performers to shed their inhibitions, and Neil Young was relying on an age-old tradition. The result is a song that sounds as spontaneous, as unmediated, as a song can possibly sound. When you find out, halfway through the song, that Bruce Berry just died, you feel as though you're now present at his wake. The chorus, "Tonight's the night," seems now to refer to the drunken celebration of his death that we are hearing. This creates an unprecedented immediacy: not only is the performance and the songwriting seemingly unmediated, but the song itself is *about* the here and now, the absolute present. "Tonight's the night," in this context, means "Here we are."

All this may reflect Young's subconscious, but it results from his conscious choice to create music in this particular way. As Marsh put it in his review, "The jitteriness of the music, its sloppy, unarranged (but decidedly structured) feeling, is clearly calculated." The music is effective in part because Young's subject matter—the deaths of his friends—is not only emotionally compelling, it fits the approach so well. It might not have worked this way if Young had been singing about his childhood, for example, or his politics. We should think of his approach to the album *Tonight's the Night* as only one of his songwriting/performance techniques, as Young undoubtedly did himself. After all, when he sang about childhood, as in "Sugar Mountain" and "I Am a Child," he employed an altogether different technique, emphasizing simple melodies, lots of rhymes, and strummed acoustic guitar; and when he sang about politics, as in "Ohio" and "Rockin' in the Free World," he employed yet another technique, emphasizing a strong and distorted electric guitar line and very simple bass and drums.

Does this mean that those songs are less real, less authentic, than "Tonight's the Night"? Perhaps. But they're not necessarily any less emotionally compelling, so does realness make a difference? The real difference is that "Tonight's the Night" is the result of a conscious quest for authenticity, whereas "Sugar Mountain" and "Ohio" are simply great songs performed with authentic feeling.

BUT IS IT its authenticity that makes *Tonight's the Night* such a great album? If Billy Joel had passed around five bottles of tequila and a large number of marijuana brownies before a session, told some of the musicians to switch instruments, picked up a guitar instead of playing piano, and sung off-key songs offhand about the deaths of his friends, the result might have sounded just as authentic as *Tonight's the Night*. But would it have been as good?

Definitely not. *Tonight's the Night* is full of brilliant songs, brilliantly performed. The way Bruce Berry's death comes as a surprise in the middle of the title cut is just the beginning. "World on a String," despite—or because of?—the muffed harmonies on the chorus, is one of the most eloquent songs ever written about the mutability of existence; "Mellow My Mind" is a supremely touching plea for someone to stop the singer's inner agitation; "Tired Eyes," with its graphic yet self-questioning lyrics, is undoubtedly the best song ever written about a drug-related killing; sometimes "Borrowed Tune" seems like the loneliest song ever sung. The chord changes throughout are odd and compelling, the melodies perfect for the lyrics and unforgettable without them. And then there's Nils Lofgren's brilliant guitar playing, Ben Keith's haunting pedal steel, Young's oh-so-vulnerable and desperate vocals.

Are any of these things the direct result of Young's quest for authenticity, or is something else altogether going on: "craft," perhaps, or "thinking in songs"? The answer is a little bit of both. By this time in their careers, not only Neil Young but all the musicians he was working with were seasoned by hundreds of hours of working and playing, both together and with other groups, experienced in writing excellent songs and playing excellent music. And they drew on all this experience as they worked within the parameters of "realness" that Young had set for them—and for himself. In other words, they put all their craft, all their talent, at the service of the realness they were after.

This may sound like an outright contradiction, since Young defined realness in opposition to craft. But while performed with great skill, none of the songs on *Tonight's the Night* are as meticulously crafted as a Billy Joel song, and the performances, no matter how brilliant, all sound utterly spontaneous, rather than worked out in advance. No matter how beautiful are the harmonies on "New Mama," or how perfect is Lofgren's guitar solo on "Speakin' Out," or how great that extra two beats in the chorus of "Tired Eyes" sounds, none of these are the result of the kind of polished craft that characterizes Fleetwood Mac's *Rumours* or the Beatles' *Abbey Road*.

Let's look at a parallel example: that of Keith Jarrett, a jazz pianist whose solo improvised concerts are legendarily unpredictable—and rich in great music. Jarrett explains one key to keeping the music fresh: "Your brain will develop habit patterns and decide what's good and bad in the sounds that you're making. And if your brain is making those decisions you will not find the letter 'o' in the alphabet; you may end up sticking around 'b' and never get past it because you did not want something peculiar to happen." Yet eliminating habit patterns does not come easily—it takes years of experience. "If I can say I'm experienced at something, I guess [I'm experienced at] acting as a conduit. I know how to get to that place where that line is about as open as can be." Eliminating habit patterns and getting to "that place" where the "line is open" amount to the same thing, more or less. It's a Zen-like state that can be induced by meditation, alcohol, drugs, or self-discipline, but in each case it takes practice to get there. And *Tonight's the Night* is evidence of that practice.

TONIGHT'S THE NIGHT'S fuck-everything attitude was shared by a number of other breakthrough albums of the 1970s: Sly and the Family Stone's *There's a Riot Goin' On,* the Rolling Stones' *Exile on Main Street,* Big Star's *Sister Lovers,* Pere Ubu's *Dub Housing.* And that attitude found its apotheosis in punk. All of a sudden, at the close of the decade, Neil Young found that he had met his match in the "More Real" category.

His response was the second side of 1979's *Rust Never Sleeps,* with its punk cry of "It's better to burn out than to fade away." This was nothing like *Tonight's the Night*—nothing here sounded stoned or wasted, despondent or lonely. If *Tonight's the Night* was fuck-everything music, the word *fuck* meant *never mind, mess up; Rust Never Sleeps* was fuck-everything music with *fuck* meaning *fuck over, damage, hurt*. The music on *Tonight's the Night* had been complex both despite of and because of the abandon with which it had been created—not only were the songs complicated, but the collective improvisation throughout the album added a new layer of intricacy. By contrast, *Rust Never Sleeps* was almost moronic at times in its extreme simplicity, with Crazy Horse—including two of the players on the *Tonight's the Night* sessions, Billy Talbot and Ralph Molina—doing nothing but hitting the beats as loudly as possible. The result was an absolute foregrounding of Young's lyrics (which ranged from the rich and evocative "Sedan Delivery" and "Powderfinger" to the submoronic "Welfare Mothers") and filthy, distortion-heavy guitar playing. As McDonough puts it, "The punk zeitgeist had gotten a couple of hooks into Young's brain and out poured hopped-up, abrasive sludge. This was insane music. . . . Young's guitar attack changed completely with *Rust*. Gone were most of the lyrical epiphanies of the 1975–1977 period. In their place were massive sheets of noise—gunky distorto headache music."

Rust Never Sleeps is an amazingly rich record, simply because the songwriting is so brilliant. It was voted album of the year, and Young artist of the year, by both readers and critics in *Rolling Stone*. But it sounds static, monolithic, in comparison to the mercurial *Tonight's the Night*. In responding to the "realness" of punk, Young had adopted its aggression and simplicity, abandoning the freedom and interplay of *Tonight's the Night* and *On the Beach*. The result was "real" enough. But *Tonight's the Night* had been a virtual wake, putting the listener right at the center of death and the love that pours out afterward; nothing that either Neil Young or punk produced ever quite matched it in sheer immediacy. Nor, perhaps, has anything else since.

AFTER *RUST NEVER SLEEPS*, Neil Young put out a series of terrible records. Not only did these feature inept songwriting and lousy performances, uninspired music and idiotic lyrics, unemotional singing and transparent meanings, but they sounded terrible—overproduced, obvious, heavy-handed. Sometimes it seemed as though never before had an artist of Neil Young's stature gone so far astray.

Was Young still being "real" during this period, which lasted most of the 1980s? He claims he was, though in a peculiar way:

> I told Elliot [Mazer, Young's manager], "Let's tear the whole fuckin' thing down, let's tear it down. A couple of months' work and it'll be gone": my *career*.... "Let's just start over again—level it." It's a comforting thought to me. A clean slate....
>
> It's hard to tell what's real and what isn't. Actually, it's all real.
>
> Ellen Talbot [bassist Billy Talbot's sister-in-law] said to me once, "When you change from one style to another, people don't know who to believe. They don't

know whether you're being you or somebody else, and if you do that too much, nobody'll believe you." Which I thought was pretty astute. . . .

Part of me is kinda like an actor—if I don't have something happening directly about my life, I can take from experiences around me, and then, by way of becoming another person, another persona, I can express a buncha fuckin' feelings. And that's what I like to do. So does that mean I'm not being true to myself and that people should not know who to believe?

But how could Neil Young be "real" when he was putting all his music through a computer, or wearing pink and playing rockabilly, or supporting Ronald Reagan and playing hardcore country, or trying to be a soul singer with a horn section?

On the face of it, the answer seems obvious: of course he wasn't. Just as David Bowie wasn't being as real as Neil Young back in 1974, Neil Young wasn't being as real as David Bowie in 1984. Being real means not only getting emotionally involved in one's persona. It also means exploring oneself, revealing oneself, trying to get one's inner angels and demons into one's art.

It's almost as if Young's constant quest for authenticity had induced a kind of fever in him. After spending half of the 1970s releasing uncommercial records, and afraid of looking back at the past, he now figured that being real must entail releasing even *more* uncommercial records.

Finally, in the late 1980s and early '90s, Young made some good records again. On one of them, he sings a song whose chorus runs, "Why do I keep fucking up?" It's a legitimate question that brings up all sorts of possibilities. But it is best answered simply: "Because you keep trying too hard to be real, that's why."

On the other hand, as *Tonight's the Night* shows, sometimes fucking up isn't such a bad thing after all.

CHAPTER SEVEN

LOVE TO LOVE YOU BABY

Disco and the Mechanization of Music

Munich, September 1975

He made up the person he wanted to be
And changed into a new personality
KRAFTWERK, "Hall of Mirrors"

DONNA SUMMER TOOK AN unusual path to pop stardom. An American, she first found success in Germany as a stage actress in musicals such as *Hair* and *Godspell*. When she then started to record with Giorgio Moroder, she brought the skills of the musical theater along with her earlier singing experience. As she wrote in her autobiography, "I do not sing; I act. When I sing, I sing with the voice of the character in the song." And in her breakthrough hit "Love to Love You Baby," she took her acting to a new extreme.

Moroder was a talented Italian pop producer who had already had some minor success in both Germany and America. Now he was working with his long-term collaborator Pete Bellotte on demos for their songs, which they would pitch to established artists. When Summer heard he was looking for singers, she approached him, and they started working together regularly. Moroder knew her American voice would help make his songs more acceptable for the American market. Of his early 1970s work, he later said, "I would myself have liked to be able to make records like the classic Motown records, but I guess that . . . we weren't advanced enough. It's crazy trying to record soul-type music in Munich. There aren't—or I should say, weren't—the players available. We were very lucky to find Donna, the first really good black girl singer who was living here." Soon they were also working on solo material for Summer. "The Hostage," one of their early recordings together, was a minor hit in Europe; it was in the straightforward rock style with which Summer was most comfortable at that point. But it took a period of experimentation with different musical styles before they settled on the disco sound that would bring them both wider fame.

"Love to Love You Baby" grew out of a basic lyrical idea that Summer came up with. When she took it to Moroder, he liked it and overnight worked the hook around a repetitive funk groove. Summer returned the next day to put the first vocal down. They wanted to emulate the success of the dripping-with-sex "Je t'aime (moi non plus)," in which French songwriter Serge Gainsbourg had married his sixties lounge music to English actress Jane Birkin's breathy performance to create a hit single that titillated and scandalized the European pop audience. With this in mind, Summer intentionally performed the role of a sultry sex symbol. She later recalled that "I came up with an image of Marilyn Monroe singing the song in that light and fluffy but highly sensual voice of hers, and hers was the image I used when I laid down the first vocal track for the song." The simulation would soon become more elaborate.

A three-minute version of the song was released with only modest success in Europe but the song came to the attention of Neil Bogart at Casablanca Records in the United States. He had previously run Buddah Records, a successful bubblegum label, and was now trying to build up his new label, for which disco would become the mainstay. He suggested making a longer version of the song. The story goes that either he came up with this idea after playing the original record repeatedly, back-to-back at a Los Angeles party, or perhaps while making love afterward. He apparently felt that the hypnotic nature of the song developed over a longer period, and that they should extend the original to exploit this quality.

There may be a degree of myth in this account. The idea of a longer mix for dance records certainly didn't come out of thin air; Bogart's suggestion would also undoubtedly have been influenced by developments in the early disco scene in New York. In December 1974 *Billboard* had run a front-page story with the headline "Discos demand five-minute singles." The club scene had been gradually changing, in a way that was feeding back into the kinds of records that could succeed. New York DJs such as Nicky Siano, Tom Moulton, and Francis Grasso had been trying to work out how to provide a constant unbroken stream of music. Seeing that the three-minute, periodic nature of pop singles wasn't ideally suited to the dance floor, they had been experimenting with crossfades, varispeed turntables, and slip-cueing to cut seamlessly from one record to another. They had also been using two versions of the same record so that they could cut repeatedly from one to the other to repeat their favorite moments, and some had been experimenting with reel-to-reel edits of records—remixes, in other words. Finally they were also using songs that weren't often heard on the dance floor—from obscure African instrumentals to album tracks—to complement their other tricks. Before there was disco music, there were already discos, and many of the early club hits were records by obscure performers which DJs seized on as fitting with the mood they were aiming for. This was one reason why DJs became elevated over the performers, whose names would often not even be known by the disco audience.

Using these techniques, DJs were learning to provide an unbroken flow of music that was increasingly created on the hoof, and identifiably remixed from the original recordings. The first twelve-inch singles were created in 1975, reinforcing the idea that songs could be deconstructed and lengthened to improve their dance floor success. Bogart would have been aware of the growing importance of extended mixes and this knowledge probably influenced his suggestion of a longer version of "Love to Love You Baby."

At first Summer and Moroder weren't sure how their three-minute record could be lengthened. Moroder looped and extended the backing track, adding some embellishments to give the song more texture. But the vocal needed to be extended considerably if the music wasn't to be a mostly instrumental mix.

Their solution was for Summer to improvise an additional fourteen minutes of vocal. She was so embarrassed by this process that she could only perform in the dark, with everyone absent from the studio. Moroder dimmed the lights and lit some candles and Summer took it from there. As she later said, "Giorgio left all those oohs and aahs in because the song didn't have any more words!" The original vocal was already highly sexual, using rhythmic moans and sighs as an integral part. Now Summer created a tour de force of sexual simulation, extending the original version into a quasi-pornographic vocal performance in which she was literally "faking it" on tape. The moans and shouts of soul, and of rock'n'roll beforehand, had always carried an air of sexual spontaneity, but such an exact representation of female orgasm had rarely been heard in popular music.

The result was an extraordinary worldwide hit, and a record that helped establish the idea of the extended mix, leading to the ubiquity of twelve-inch records over subsequent years. Early disco had been influenced by positive hippie-ish vibes and had stressed the idea of coming together in dance as a collective, cathartic process. But in the gay clubs of New York, the scene was becoming increasingly hedonistic and sexualized. "Love to Love You Baby" captured this transitional moment precisely by combining the hypnotic drone of the dance floor with an outrageous sexuality. As Alan Jones and Jussi Kantonen note in *Saturday Night Forever: The Story of Disco*, "there are two disco time zones"—before and after "Love to Love You Baby." Disco had never been innocent:

Chakacha's 1971 "Jungle Fever" was nothing but semiporno-graphic moans, Sylvia's salacious "Pillow Talk" even made it into the Top 40, and there had been plenty of sex talk in funk songs. But "Love to Love You Baby" was the recording that really opened a Pandora's box: Diana Ross's "Love Hangover," the Andrea True Connection's "More More More" (Andrea True was a porn star before she turned to disco), Barry White's "It's Ecstasy When You Lay Down Next to Me," and Salsoul Orchestra's "Just the Right Size, among others."

After her sojourn in Europe, Summer was now an overnight success back in the United States. To her discom-fort, she was marketed and perceived as the sex goddess she had portrayed. As a committed Christian, she found it prob-lematic that, having acted out her most sensuous side for one specific song, the public now perceived that to be the whole truth about her. She said that "the most difficult thing ... was to remain my own person within the machine, to hold on to my real identity, to the me nobody knows." Even for someone who consciously acted out many of her best songs, the gap between who she felt she was and who she was perceived to be could cause friction.

As Summer's career developed, Moroder and Bogart found it harder to persuade her to perform the role of sex symbol, which was one of the reasons they eventually ceased working together. Moroder said that "having her biggest hit with a sexy song, she was suddenly saying that she wouldn't sing that type of song any more, and then she insisted on having a song about Jesus on her album." Increasingly she wanted to say something that felt true to herself—the Cinderella symbolism of the *Once Upon a Time* album, with several songs about a girl who lived in the "Land of Never Never" where "everything real is unreal" reflected the way she viewed her own life. She saw her progress from a difficult childhood as a fairy tale in which her faith and spirituality had helped her to survive. Now she wanted her songs to reflect her real life.

Later hits such as "Bad Girls" and "She Works Hard for the Money" showcased her songwriting and her enduring ability to perform a song in character. They also explored a wide range of possible female stereotypes, from princess to bitch, from working girl to whore. In "Bad Girls," the narrator wonders who the hookers on the strip really are, concluding that "like everybody else, they wanna be a star," and going on to admit that "now you and me we're both the same, but you call yourself by different names."

Summer had learned the hard way what it meant to have her femininity co-opted for the purposes of male gratification. Her sympathy for those trapped in the sex industry, her identification with any woman who has to work hard for her money, even her confusion about her own roles—all of these show how she was also exorcising the demons of her earlier work and reclaiming her portrayal of female sexuality as just one part of a fully rounded understanding of women's lives.

AT THE SAME TIME as it was becoming hugely successful, disco remained one of the most widely reviled musical genres of the postwar period. Even its passing could not go quietly. During the hate- and violence-filled "Disco Demolition Derby" at the Comiskey Park baseball stadium in Chicago in 1979, thousands of disco records were smashed and burned in public, with the event degenerating into a riot. Although disco had reached its zenith in terms of exposure and sales, signs of this hostility were everywhere, from "I Hate Disco" car stickers to radio jocks' antidisco rants.

Why was there such a virulent response against what was basically just good-time music? Homophobia was a major factor. But a more explicit and more widespread criticism was that disco had reduced the dance beat to its most mechanical basics. Anyone could dance to disco because it was so simple and predictable—it pandered to the lowest common denominator and lacked a genuine groove, according to its critics.

Another standard criticism of disco was that it was shallow or insubstantial—fake, in other words. But the genre had deliberately avoided the aesthetics of authenticity. A typical disco record made no attempt to tell us about the performer or about reality. Instead, it created a world of glitter and celebration, ecstasy and escape.

In any case, disco had strong reasons for evading authenticity. Against the backdrop of Watergate, Vietnam, and the general sense of bitterness and anxiety that marked the end of the sixties, the economy was in serious recession. New York City in particular was in a state of seemingly terminal decline. Disco was an escapist music that grew out of the friction between several subcultures fusing together in difficult times. The most obvious collision was between the gay scene and black music, although Italian Americans, ex-hippies, working-class clubbers, and other social or ethnic groups all had their own influence on the mix.

Black culture and gay culture each had their own reasons for treating authenticity with suspicion. There were huge differences between growing up black and growing up gay, but in either case you were more likely to be in an ongoing state of self-reinvention—to simply be yourself was to invite prejudice and hostility.

Different individuals had different remedies for this. Some presented a hyper-real version of their gayness or black identity, as in the Gay Pride and Black Power movements. Camp culture tends to celebrate manufactured poses and knowingly absurd pretenses as a deliberate response to the complexities of gay identity.

Others from black or gay backgrounds chose to try fitting in with normal society instead. But conforming was not a simple option and often involved simulations and contortions of one sort or another. Either path involved a keen appreciation of the gap between your self-identity and how you were perceived. As a result both these subcultures had a healthy skepticism about the complexities of simply "being yourself." In Peter Shapiro's excellent history of disco, *Turn the Beat Around*, he writes about Sylvester, a disco singer who was both black and gay, saying of his classic song "You Make Me Feel (Mighty Real)" that it "interrogated the African-American musical tradition and asked what 'realness' is supposed to mean to gay black men who, alienated from almost all of society, were forced to hide their true identities for most of their lives."

In any case, disco simply wasn't about everyday real life. If anything, it was about escape from everyday life, and for many gays and blacks, escape from prejudice through music in their local disco was pure relief. It was also about seduction and sex. As a result it attracted and scandalized people in the same way as Elvis's early music had. "Love to Love You Baby" was a defining recording, but disco was saturated with sexuality, from Labelle's "Lady Marmalade" to Cerrone's "Love in C Minor." And it was an ambiguous sexuality: disco crossed and blurred sexual boundaries, as well as racial ones. Throughout disco there was an aura of sexuality that could be confusing to an outsider. But there was an obvious appeal in the dance floor as sexual arena, or pick-up scene—this was clearly a place for dressing up and sexual display as opposed to the sweaty indeterminacy of rock gigs.

When the group Sister Sledge sang "He's the Greatest Dancer," it could be taken at face value as a song about sexual attraction, with the female narrators of the band flattering the subject of the song. But behind that, there are faint hints of mocking the dancer's vanity, and to the ears of gay clubbers there was the suggestion that this song was really about the self-absorption of dancers too busy admiring their own performance to think about anyone else. Part of the song's ambiguity also comes from the fact that the religious Sister Sledge were uncomfortable with the most blatantly sexual lines of the lyrics that Bernard Edwards and Nile Rodgers of Chic had written for them and preferred to tone down the song as far as they could. The result is a hint of repressed desire that also hit a chord with the gay audience. The song is far more layered than it first seems, a common trait in the songs of disco.

In the music, there was at times a masculine element to the relentless beat. For instance Donna Summer's "I Feel Love" sounds very dark and metallic, at least until the vocals come in, and the funk workout of Chic's "Le Freak" would have a completely different feel without the deadpan vocals. In the strand of disco that would eventually mutate into the high-tempo Hi-NRG, the macho drive of the beat was parodied in the muscular postures of the gay scene. But above these mechanical beats, the music was clearly feminine. The instrumentation is ethereal, with string flourishes and smooth harmonies. The vocals tend to be effeminate, featuring the voices of disco divas or men singing in falsetto and wearing glitter. Disco often elided feminine and gay desire, but both were presented in a way that could be threatening to the straight male listener. (Even the simulations of a song like "Love to Love You Baby," which on the surface pandered to a male point of view, expressed female sexuality in a frank and upfront way that was somehow more adult and real than previous representations of female sexuality in pop.) The mass audience that disco had attained by 1979 certainly included at least a few who took John Travolta's macho strut in the movie *Saturday Night Fever* at face value: witness how John Leguizamo took it one step further in his riveting portrayal of a disco- and sex-addicted Italian American in Spike Lee's *Summer of Sam*. But the backlash was to a large degree homophobic, as it became clear that this was a music that gave a strong voice to homosexuality. Of course, in the dying days of disco, the Village People would become hugely popular with the mainstream audience with an outrageously gay image, but as a rule the ambiguous yet genuine sexuality of disco was not tolerated as well as the Village People's cartoonish representation.

Disco was a curious mixture of democracy and exclusivity. The early discos were mainly for members only, and as the movement spread, doormen usually ensured that only the right crowd was allowed in. Like the hippies before them, the clubbers wanted to undermine the existing order while simultaneously creating a new heterogeneity. They wanted to be able to go to a place where everyone was in on their scene, to create their own community from a mixture of hipsters and outsiders.

But this scene was based around music that was capable of becoming resolutely mainstream, which meant that it appealed to a mass audience. The exclusivity simply couldn't survive once disco passed a certain critical point of popularity. On the other hand, a music that was tailored so precisely to the sensibilities of sexual and racial minorities was always going to repel or embarrass some listeners in the wider society, as the irony and sexual ambiguity of disco were far less capable of translation to the mainstream than the music. So even as it exploded into mass exposure, the seeds of its rapid decline were being planted.

MEANWHILE, GERMANY had its own problems in the 1970s. The country was still in a strange psychological state after the rebuilding that followed the Nazi period—part denial, part self-abnegation. The younger generation was uncertain of the future, feeling that the national consensus that had been built around pacifism and the pursuit of affluence was starting to unravel. The massacre of Israelis at the Munich Olympics and the bloody kidnappings and murders carried out by the home-grown revolutionary Baader-Meinhof gang created a disturbing undercurrent of violence. Although many responded to this state of affairs with serious political engagement, there was also a parallel to the escapism of American disco.

Apart from the creations of Moroder and Bellotte, Silver Convention was one of the most successful groups to come out of the Munich disco scene. They were a manufactured band, put together to front recordings that had been made by local producer Michael Kunze. One of the earliest exponents of Europop, Silver Convention used virtually meaningless lyrics to cross the language divide. The success in the United States of their rather frivolous confections probably didn't do a lot for German-American relations in this period. Fortunately a more bizarre and fascinating development was taking place in the industrial town of Düsseldorf.

Kraftwerk were disengaged, but in a very different way from the giddiness of Europop. They had started out as an experimental rock group, playing real instruments and improvising dense overlaid pieces that were close in spirit to the drones of their compatriots Can and Neu. But as they started to use synthesizers and electronic noises, founding members Florian Schneider and Ralf Hütter became increasingly fascinated by a new concept—music "made by computers and performed by robots." They recorded a series of albums that relied on internal structure and texture and avoided personal expression altogether. They incorporated noises that reflected the urban, mechanized environment that surrounded them. Their subject matter, when they used words at all, was determinedly mundane, dealing with the interface between man and machine in a detached, ironic tone of voice. "We are playing the machines, the machines play us, it is really the exchange and the friendship we have with the musical machines which make us build a new music," said Hütter in his typically cryptic fashion. Whereas Schneider had once played flute in a style closer to Jethro Tull's than to Stockhausen's, they now stood motionless on stage, doing nothing but twiddling knobs on their machines.

As a result, the Kraftwerk material released from 1970 onward was entirely at odds with the quest for authenticity so common in rock music of the period. While rock tended to be admired for being serious, skillful, and sincere, Kraftwerk made music that could (apparently) be played simply by pressing buttons, music that didn't address any personal, human concerns. And they did all this with a sly, deadpan humor that only emphasized the increasing distance between their music and that of their contemporaries. At the time, they sounded completely alien.

Their new approach achieved its first summation in "Autobahn" (1974), in which the rhythms and cadences of a motorway journey became the driving force of an extended musical journey. With clipped, monotonous vocals that deliberately and perversely recalled the Beach Boys ("wir fahr'n, fahr'n, fahr'n auf der Autobahn" is basically derived from "Fun, Fun, Fun") while creating a sense of electronic displacement, the song was absorbed with mundane detail while glorying in its own pop absurdity. The later song "Trans-Europe Express" takes the same approach to a rail journey, conjuring pan-European images of travel as passive consumption. On the same album, the band reacted to a journalist's gibe that their stage presence was like that of showroom dummies. The song "Showroom Dummies" depicted the group as a set of automatons, dummies with no self-consciousness, experiencing the world as a strange and alien place.

Hütter said, "Sometimes we play the music, sometimes it plays us, sometimes . . . it plays." He spoke often of the idea that the band would ideally be replaced by robots. While the pseudorobots they had constructed were used on stage for occasional songs, Hütter was now fantasizing about having the robots alone on stage for the entire show. He also talked about a tour in which the robots would be on stage while the band could stay at home in Düsseldorf controlling everything from their studio. Apart from revealing an understandable dislike of touring, these comments show how Kraftwerk emphasized and exaggerated the automation of their music.

There have always been debates about how much, if any, of the music at a Kraftwerk concert is actually performed and how much is prerecorded. But it has always seemed irrelevant, given that the band would be happy for us to believe that it is all automated. On another occasion Hütter said "We always found that many people are robots without knowing it. The interpreters of classical music, Horowitz for example, they are like robots, making a reproduction of the music which is always the same. It's automatic, and they do it as if it were natural, which is not true." To drive this message home, for the later song "Pocket Calculator" they constructed calculators, connected to the mixing desk, that could be used to "play" the music while they would stand on stage very seriously tapping the tiny buttons throughout the song.

Kraftwerk completely bypassed ideas of authenticity. Less commercial than disco, their music formed an interesting counterpart to it. Both would come to be reevaluated and recycled by future generations, their joint influence on the dance music of the 1980s and '90s being particularly notable. But Kraftwerk's approach to music was interesting for one more reason.

BEHIND QUESTIONS of authenticity in music we can often discern the shadow of a different question. This is the problem of how self-consciousness affects performers. The process of becoming a well-known musician almost always involves thinking about how you project yourself to others. There is a gap between the person you think you are and the persona that others perceive. As a musician in the public view, you are forced to contemplate how big a gap this is, and to think about how you want to be perceived. Donna Summer was not alone in feeling that her public wasn't really seeing "the me nobody knows."

There are two main responses to this gap. The first is to glorify the degree to which you are faking it—to theatrically celebrate your ability to perform a role and to take on a persona (or a series of personas) that is clearly not meant to reflect the real you. This highly theatrical approach is, for instance, typical of camp music and of extravagant performers in the Broadway style, such as Bette Midler. For performers as diverse as Little Richard, Divine, Freddie Mercury, Labelle, and Barry Manilow, accusations of faking it are simply irrelevant. Going further and adopting a series of personas helped performers such as David Bowie and Madonna sidestep questions of "real or fake" for much of their careers.

Authenticity is rarely an issue with music for which the performer intentionally adopts a theatrical approach. There are of course gray areas: hip-hop performers commonly combine a theatrical projection of bling and gangster personas with the credo of street credibility and keeping it real. Being streetwise in hip-hop terms often involves a degree of performance and projection of a tough exterior, so performing a role can in itself be seen as authentic. On the one hand, rappers have played knowingly exaggerated versions of gangsters and hustlers, while on the other they emphasize their street credibility and trophy bullet wounds. But this is an exception rather than a rule; theatricality and authenticity tend to remain at opposite musical poles.

The second approach to this problem is for the performer to try to minimize the gap between person and persona. To do this you must try to project the authentic person and also live up to the persona that you project. These are two slightly different tasks: the first involves simple honesty about who you are, the second can involve trying to avoid dishonesty by becoming the person that you are perceived to be. Sometimes it is extremely difficult to tell the difference, as the lives of John Lennon and Kurt Cobain show. But either way, this is the path that leads to the quest for personal authenticity, integrity, and sincerity in music.

Trying to close the gap between person and persona inevitably tends to involve you in bad faith, for two reasons. First, no matter how hard you try, the gap remains unclosable. Any human personality is too complex to be projected in full, in a way that will survive transmission by the simplifying lens of the mass media. Second, as soon as you try to live up to your persona, you become aware of the gap between the person you used to be and the person you have become. The perception of self is highly complex, and a high level of self-contemplation often changes who you are.

The self is a fractured, ever-changing entity. It is ironic that trying to be authentic by closing the gap between person and persona forces the performer into contemplating the impossibility of absolute authenticity, which is one reason why personal authenticity must always remain a holy grail, just out of reach of the performer. The harder you try to "be yourself," the more you discover that it simply can't be done.

■ ■ ■ ■

SELF-CONSCIOUSNESS IS an old philosophical problem. In "On the Marionette Theater," the nineteenth-century German writer Heinrich von Kleist gave the peculiar grace of marionettes as an example of a broader idea, that the most graceful performers are those who are the least self-conscious. He talked of the relative grace of innocent children in contrast to adult dancers, whose performance is marred by their self-awareness. Thus he saw self-consciousness as a root cause of awkwardness and bad faith. He went on to talk about this as a spectrum in which the only beings who have perfect grace have either no self-knowledge, such as the puppets, or perfect self-knowledge—and perfect self-knowledge, in Kleist's opinion, belongs only to God.

In this book we have focused on two main kinds of authenticity, cultural and personal. Kleist's spectrum gives us an interesting new way to talk about these. The quest for cultural authenticity has traditionally been a search for innocence, for the doll-like grace of musicians with little or no self-consciousness. Advocates of cultural authenticity tend to see the original folk, blues, or third-world musicians as representing a guileless way of making music, unsullied by experience. They tend to be disturbed by any suggestion that these musicians are actually more experienced or complex than they appear and that they have absorbed influences from, say, earlier pop junk or from contact with other cultures.

For those who look for personal authenticity, it often seems that people perceive authentic performers as being completely without self-consciousness, as though they simply open up their inner beings and their art pours out. When Lennon screams out his therapy songs; when Neil Young is venerated for channeling his soul into his music; in Kurt Cobain's admiration for Daniel Johnston, whose music clearly expresses a tortured inner life—here the artists' work is being seen as a window directly into their soul, with no intervention by self-consciousness, whose crucial role is denied.

Of course, real performers never completely lack self-consciousness. They are self-aware enough to understand the difference between who they are and who they are seen to be. Some performers use this inevitable dissonance to fuel their music, but others find it problematic.

Kraftwerk found a different way of dealing with it. By portraying themselves as robots, as unconscious showroom dummies, they transferred the innocence onto the actual machines. The machines became the puppets, the automatons that produce pure, graceful music. Their music purposely expresses almost nothing about the people who created it, and they distance themselves by claiming that the machines play them as much as the other way round. Insofar as they were present as human beings, they were there merely to facilitate the grace and fascination of the machines rather than the other way round.

WE'VE OUTLINED a few of the reasons why ideas of authenticity developed in pop music, but technology itself has an interesting part in the story. As soon as technology was used to record music, some aspects of artificiality were introduced. The use of recording horns and microphones to record music was a pretty artificial affair. But the development of more complex recording techniques and electronic effects and instruments allowed record producers a greater freedom to create sounds that went beyond anything a group of musicians could create live. This fed a growing feeling that the music one heard on a record might not have been authentically performed by the musicians. While this kind of straightforward representational inauthenticity was not particularly significant in itself, it was a background feature in the developing idea that music could be fake, which could in turn feed back into the demand for music that was personally or culturally authentic.

Kraftwerk were perhaps the first pop band to completely get beyond the dislocation caused by modern recording technology. Fifty years after the first big expansion of the recording industry, twenty years after the spread of the electric guitar, many musicians treated studio technology with suspicion, seeing it, at best, as something to be conquered and, at worst, as a distorting barrier that lay between them and the listener. Throughout most of the history of recorded popular music, the machinery had been seen as a necessary tool, but not something to be celebrated in itself.

During the sixties, a few artists had started to embrace technology and to place musical skill in a different sphere— that of being able to exploit and control the technology in an interesting way rather than being able to create the best "real sounds." For instance, Joe Meek's bizarre productions (including the Tornado's 1962 UK hit "Telstar") elevated his homemade version of studio technology over the artist, while Phil Spector's experiments with the Wall of Sound were also part of a process by which the use of studio technology came to be seen as a good thing in itself. But like later recordings such as the Beatles' *Sergeant Pepper* and the Beach Boys' *Pet*

Sounds, which continued to stretch the art of recording in new directions, these were essentially attempts to translate the artists' personal visions into sound. The machines were important, but so were the people using them. In Kraftwerk's music the whole idea of human agency became irrelevant. It didn't seem to matter whether they had performed this music, or simply discovered it by using their machines.

There were precedents for this approach. The avant-garde composers John Cage and Karlheinz Stockhausen had introduced similar ideas to classical music, although the results were often unlistenable. And there had also been previous attempts to create synthesized pop music, such as the odd novelty (like Hot Butter's 1972 "Popcorn") or art pieces that used synthesized sound. Wendy Carlos's 1968 *Switched-on Bach* had successfully married synthesizers with classical composition, thereby demonstrating the capabilities of the new technology to a mass audience.

However Kraftwerk's use of technology opened up a very different range of possibilities. They contemplated the serious rock music of their time and juxtaposed this with the idea of music played by machines. They used the noises of manufacturing and the city, both by synthesizing such sounds and by using recorded urban noise. Previously the avant-garde had used such noises for the purpose of disorientation. And rock bands had often glorified machines—for instance, Iggy Pop had sung "Look out honey, 'cause I'm using technology," in the Stooges' "Search and Destroy." But Kraftwerk managed to make machine noise into a thing of beauty rather than using it as a metaphor for dehumanization or dystopian menace.

Like the futurists of the 1920s, they saw machines as

important in themselves, and worshipped them as machines rather than as transmitting devices. The futurists' love of the sound of urban noise was reflected in Kraftwerk's "Autobahn." Their use of random overlays and dense collages of noise that mimicked the sound of urban life had an enduring influence. They also undermined the rock music of their contemporaries in one other crucial way: by doing all this with a dry humor that undercut the potential arty pomposity of their theoretical influences.

Kraftwerk was also articulating notions that were fully present in disco. The producers of disco had realized that machinery could be used unashamedly and with a sense of humor. For instance, the cover of the first Gregg Diamond and Bionic Boogie album featured a disco dancer as a machine, Phreek had mechanized dancers on their album covers, and the Universal Robot Band described their synthesized disco music as being played by robots, who were depicted on the record covers as cartoon automatons. The monotony of the disco beat was sometimes produced by machines, sometimes by real drummers playing a relentless rhythm, but either way, the result was intended purely as a mechanical beat to dance to. There was little attempt in disco to make the musicians' performances individually distinctive or expressive of their personality—the performers were simply cogs in a machine. The increased use of overt technological flourishes such as up-front syn drums helped to drive home the notion that the producers of this music knew that it was artificial but didn't care.

The vocal performances were of course more human, but were often knowingly contrived or overacted, rather than earnest or self-revelatory. Critics of disco liked to accuse the singers of performing in a style that owed more to Broadway than to funk or gospel, but as we've seen, this knowing simulation was part of disco's identity from the start. Disco was in this respect a subversive style, using simple dance music as a vessel for complex messages about identity and automation.

Disco also challenged the traditional focus on the personality of the musician. DJs were privileged over performers, while the real music makers often hid behind the label "producer" and issued songs and albums under a variety of names. It was less explicit than Kraftwerk's attack on personality, but it was still significant.

How deliberate was disco's subversion of the rules of rock music? For some it was entirely so. Niles Rodgers of Chic came from a highly politicized background. He had been a Black Panther as well as a successful rock session musician. But when he formed Chic with Bernard Edwards, they made a pact to create only celebratory music. They deliberately turned away from the kinds of music they had previously been involved in. The dark, political, personal mood of early seventies rock no longer satisfied them, so instead they chose to create music that was universal and joyous. Their songs were often subtly barbed. The "Halston, Gucci, Fiorucci" reference they slipped into "He's the Greatest Dancer" (which they wrote and produced) can be heard as a simple homage to those labels or as a passing dig at the consumerism of the times. "Dance, Dance, Dance" referenced the movie about the 1930s dance marathons *They Shoot Horses, Don't They?* to parody the club scene, but the audience either didn't get this reference or didn't care—it was still a great record to dance to. But in all this, Chic were fully aware that they were doing something entirely at odds with traditional rock music, and there were many in the disco movement who shared their outlook.

For others, the reaction against traditional rock was a more instinctive process. For instance, Giorgio Moroder saw himself as simply making pop music; he has said, "The disco sound, you must see, is not art or anything so serious. Disco is music for dancing, and I know that the people will always want to dance." The wider disco movement coalesced around a diverse group of musicians and clubbers, many of whom simply wanted a different kind of music to play and to dance to. But what was collectively created stood in very clear opposition to contemporary rock music. Where mainstream rock aspired to be authentic, personal, creative, and earnest, disco was theatrical, universal, manufactured, and tongue in cheek. Rock was built around rural, working-class values and around the white working-class male, while disco was urban, aspirational, and multicultural, and expressed gay and female sexuality. Rock emphasized traditional song structures and live instruments; disco was repetitive (often to the point of endlessness) and used machines. Whether or not intended by its practitioners, disco came to challenge and undermine ideas of authenticity in contemporary rock music on every possible front.

IN 1977, Donna Summer continued her success with the massive hit single "I Feel Love." The sound of disco had been evolving over the previous couple of years, becoming in many ways more regimented and less fluid. Where "Love to Love You Baby" had had a relatively traditional funk backing reminiscent of soul singer Isaac Hayes, "I Feel Love" was an alien, robotic, repetitive groove, made completely without acoustic instruments. It is passionate, yet cold, devotional but disturbing. It still sounds completely artificial, bizarre, and brilliant. In *Turn the Beat Around*, Peter Shapiro comments that "never before . . . had a record so reveled in its own artifice."

The song is built around a three-note keyboard hook that, because of the programming and delays, runs too fast to have been played by human hand. The seemingly random key shifts only move this hook up and down the keys without too much regard for standard harmonic arrangements, a procedure emphasized by the way the long minor note introducing the song shifts unexpectedly up a semitone to the major. This disregard for standard musical niceties would become more widespread with the advent of samplers in the 1980s, but at the time it was jarring.

Summer sang the song in a falsetto because the song was recorded slightly too high for her natural register. It was a happy accident because the resulting tremulous vocal has an oddly tentative feel that contrasts sharply with the industrial drive of the song's hook. In public appearances she performed a robotic dance, moving her arms but keeping her body motionless and staring fixedly forward as she sang. If she was still acting, she seemed to be impersonating a female alien or android.

Apparently, soon after its release Brian Eno gave "I Feel Love" to David Bowie, saying, "I've heard the future of music"; a similar quote has been attributed to John Lennon.

Whoever said it, they were right. In Kraftwerk's "Trans-Europe Express" and in "I Feel Love" you can hear the roots of house, techno, trance, drum and bass, and much of contemporary dance music.

So what happened to authenticity in music in the subversive wake of Kraftwerk and disco? There are two notable strands to briefly comment on here: the development of house and hip-hop, and, on the other side of the Atlantic, the rise of Europop.

Kraftwerk's influence on early house was clear. Afrika Bambaataa's "Planet Rock" was created around a sample from "Trans–Europe Express," and in many of the early house records one can hear echoes of their robotic style. In spite of their Teutonic efficiency, Kraftwerk was taken to heart by American dance-music producers. And the band's fascination with mechanization and industrial sound has influenced dance and pop music to the current day. One need only hear the classic track "Can't Get You Out of My Head" by Australian pop star Kylie Minogue to hear how both Kraftwerk and disco still influence twenty-first-century sounds.

In early house and hip-hop, the erosion of the cult of the performer's personality continued apace. House records were often recorded under fleeting pseudonyms, adopted and discarded at will by producers and teams. Singers were recruited to perform on a track with which they might have had little else to do, and stage performances were partly displaced by DJ sessions. Remixing other people's records came to be seen as a skill in itself, and as a result, the connection between artist and product was partly broken. Hearing a snatch of "Apache" emerging through a Led Zeppelin break beat, you admired the DJ or producer for the juxtaposition of samples rather than thinking of the original players of these sounds. But house music moved this process forward a step as the technology needed to create a record became ever cheaper, and sampling allowed even those without access to musicians to create their own backing tracks.

In the 1980s and early '90s, the music business struggled to come to terms with this process, as they partially lost control of their ability to build artists. The record companies were forced to understand how music was changing in ways that emphasized the performer less than the groove. But it turned out to be a transitory period. The wild freedom that allowed records made in bedrooms to be released under random names, the preponderance of white labels (records without normal identifying information) for tracks that traditional companies would have regarded as unreleasable—all this gradually subsided as the music business slowly realized how to integrate and absorb this music and as sampling became a more legal process. Individual rappers started to stand out from the crowd, and as hip-hop became a dominant style, new labels sprang up with a sharper understanding of how to build an artist in this new, fluid age of recording.

Record companies aren't the only ones who want performers to build careers. Most performers want to be (and to be seen to be) successful, and the relative anonymity of early house music was not of great value to some of the performers and producers involved. Early house and hip-hop gave musicians possible routes to circumvent the cult of personality, but these routes are now fully exploited only occasionally.

In the end, most musicians want the prestige and money that comes with being recognized.

Meanwhile, European pop musicians reacted differently to the decline of original disco; the road that had led from bubblegum to disco moved on inexorably as disco beats merged with Europop. Absorbing disco's monotonous beats and adding anodyne transnational lyrics, amid further layers of plastic production, the producers of Europop were as focused on sales and as uninterested in personal expression as the earlier bubblegum artists.

Europop had a few highs and many lows. In the years following Moroder's best recordings, it would be widely scapegoated for taking the groove out of dance music by making records that relied almost entirely on machines for the rhythm sections. Even American disco aficionados looked down on Eurodisco as being the most plastic version of the sound.

Swedish supergroup ABBA lay somewhere between Eurodisco and pure Europop. Classic-rock fans hated ABBA almost as virulently as they hated disco. They disdained their precisely manufactured sound, flawless harmonies, glittery image, and tacky presentation. Over the decades following ABBA's period of success, their music has gradually been reassessed. Of course, even some of their most enjoyable songs can seem deeply silly. The English-as-a-foreign-language lyrics combine awkwardly with a sense of kitsch that was intentional in their image, if not in their music. Nonetheless, from the unbeatable disco drama of "Dancing Queen" to the pure, undisguised heartbreak of "The Winner Takes It All," many of their hits are classics. But it is still common for those who listen to ABBA to make the excuse that they like this music for "ironic" or retro reasons, which is simply a cop-out that protects the listener from accusations of bad taste. ABBA was a great band, performing songs by one of the best songwriting teams of the period—songs that often showed the raw pain of the breakup of the two marriages involved. It's unfortunate that their music should so often be condescended to as mere kitsch.

New York Times critic Kelefa Sanneh has written well about the ways that this kind of attitude persists today, pointing out that "over the past decades, these [rockist] tendencies have congealed into an ugly sort of common sense. Rock bands record classic albums, while pop stars create 'guilty pleasure' singles. It's supposed to be self-evident: U2's entire oeuvre deserves respectful consideration, while a spookily seductive song by an R&B singer named Tweet can only be, in the smug words of a recent VH1 special, 'awesomely bad.'" Sanneh is commenting on the way that rockist attitudes straitjacket our responses to music, making it hard for us to enjoy styles that spurn the trappings of authenticity. But even if ABBA is underrated, that's not to say that all of Europop should be reassessed so generously. It may be irrelevant to criticize it for being fake or manufactured, but not much Europop has passed the test of time. The later example of Milli Vanilli is perhaps more representative.

Frank Farian, a German producer, had been behind the inexplicable success of Boney M., a group he created. Farian combined straightforward Euro beats with absurd but catchy lyrics about anything from Rasputin to Ma Baker, recruiting a group of session singers and dancers to perform the records. He later tried to follow up by using the same strategy again, but the results were less fortunate.

In 1989, the Farian-produced Milli Vanilli won a Grammy

for Best New Artist after hits like "Blame It on the Rain," "Girl You Know It's True," and "All or Nothing." The next year they were stripped of this award after it was revealed that the two frontmen of the band, Fabrice Morvan and Rob Pilatus, had not actually sung on the records.

Milli Vanilli were marketed in the United States as a rock group, which was a large part of the problem as this created expectations of authenticity in the audience that selling them more honestly (as Europop) wouldn't have done. Frank Farian had created the records with session musicians and hired break-dancers Pilatus and Morvan for their image. They had a dreadlocked, bare-chested look that seems risible in retrospect, but it was not out of place in the fashion hell of the late 1980s. The resulting records were huge hits, and the two "singers" received extensive media attention. Given their lack of involvement on the musical side, one can see that Pilatus was only helping to dig a bigger hole for the band with comments such as "Musically, we are more talented than any Bob Dylan. We are more talented than Paul McCartney, Mick Jagger . . . I'm the new Elvis."

Rumors started to spread, and after an awkward period of claim and counterclaim, Farian revealed the deception. He hoped that by doing this he could still salvage a future for the band, but without Morvan and Pilatus. Arista, their record company, quickly announced that they had been unaware of the pretense, an implausible, self-serving claim. Arista paid a high price, as sales for the band collapsed and a judge ordered them to give partial refunds to anybody who bought Milli Vanilli records or attended gigs believing that Morvan and Pilatus were actually singing. Thereafter the two tried to resurrect their career under the name Rob and Fab, but to no avail. They had become figures of ridicule after the initial scandal broke, and they were never to regain their lost fame and success. On April 2, 1998, Rob Pilatus was found dead after consuming quantities of pills and alcohol. Fabrice Morvan released a statement blaming their rapid rise and fall for his partner's death.

The sad but faintly ridiculous story of Milli Vanilli's exposure shows that twenty years after the Monkees gave us *Head*, faking it in the music business could still be a crime punishable with ridicule and worse. It highlights a few differences between European and American expectations of musical authenticity. And finally it is also a reminder of the sheer derision with which genres such as Europop and disco were treated.

DISCO'S LEGACY is a mixed one. In many ways it was moldbreaking music, and after its demise it continued to influence pop and dance music in myriad ways. But its influence is often disregarded, and many of its most successful performers and producers remain underrated.

Donna Summer has had a successful career, but it has been hard for her to escape from the perception that, because she was a disco performer, she is inauthentic, and this has always frustrated her. She felt undervalued and pigeonholed in disco, and she saw herself as capable of a broader range. In later years she has tried to project herself in a different light by performing in different styles, including traditional standards, rock and pop classics, and even country tunes. But within the standard critical canon even her most impressive work is not accorded the same respect as that of a soul diva or rock singer.

Summer's ambivalence about personal authenticity can sometimes be distracting. She acknowledges that her great skill was acting out a song—faking it, if you must. But at the same time she eulogizes artists who draw on their own personal pain to create songs. In her autobiography she compares herself unfavorably to artists such as Joni Mitchell and Carole King, saying that as singer-songwriters they were able to "open a very private part of their inner lives and let you in." Admitting that she would it find too painful, she once again emphasizes that she prefers to sing through the intermediary of a character. As a result, she doesn't seem able to fully celebrate her glittering pop persona or to take sufficient credit for her fine series of songs portraying the lives of ordinary women through the characters she adopted.

As a singer she was at her best as an actress, but she became ashamed of the roles she had played. Someone with less regard for personal integrity might have felt more able to play up to the plastic sex goddess she once portrayed and thereby disarm her critics more effectively. But Summer internalized much of the criticism that she received for her disco work and spent at least part of her subsequent career trying to prove that there was more to her than that. She was in a bind. She couldn't ham up to her theatrical heritage, nor was she ever going to be accepted as authentic.

Women have not always found it easy to project an "authentic voice" in the male-dominated music industry, but artists as varied as Nina Simone, Kristen Hersh, Liz Phair, Lucinda Williams, and P J Harvey have found ways of doing so. As a strong female performer who made her own success and wrote key songs in the process, one might expect Donna Summer to be held in the same regard. But the idea of authenticity has worked against her all the way: every bit as inventive a musician as her female peers, she has been perceived as only faking it the whole time.

PUBLIC
IMAGE

first issue

RELIGION
ATTACK
public image
THEME
Annalisa

CHAPTER EIGHT

PUBLIC IMAGE

Punk's Paradoxes of Authenticity

London, October 1978

No gimmicks, no theatre, just us. Take it or leave it.

JOHN LYDON, onstage, early PiL gig

IT IS HARD NOW to remember the strong sense of anticipation and uncertainty with which Public Image Ltd. (PiL) were awaited. By late 1978, the conflicts and compromises of the first wave of punk were fairly evident. The original Sex Pistols had disintegrated and the intense excitement they had generated seemed to be dissipating. But John Lydon, formerly Johnny Rotten, was still a figure of intense fascination, and everyone wanted to know about his next musical move. Until then he had been seen only through the prism of the Sex

Pistols. Now he was going to show the world who he really was—or so he said.

The period surrounding the release of his first post-Pistols single was somewhat overshadowed by the unpleasant news from New York where, on October 12, ex-Pistol Sid Vicious was arrested for the murder of his girlfriend Nancy Spungen. It was a few more months before Vicious died of an overdose, but he was clearly already on an inescapable downward spiral. As much as anything else, this emphasized that, in spite of ongoing activity and releases, the Sex Pistols really were finished.

Accounts of what had "gone wrong" with punk varied according to the teller—Malcolm McLaren and John Lydon each blamed the other for the Sex Pistols' demise. Politically aware members of the punk movement, including the Clash, were trying to move on from the Pistols' original disengaged nihilism by molding it into a more righteous anger through the Rock Against Racism organization. The artistic, fashion-oriented end of the movement (for instance the clique that centered on the King's Road boutique SEX, run by McLaren and his then-girlfriend Vivienne Westwood) felt that as punk had spread beyond the original elite it had been coarsened and destroyed. Whichever of the various accounts you believed, the huge burst of energy created by the heyday of punk was still spreading in all sorts of ways and, as a prime mover, Lydon was bound to be watched closely.

The release of Public Image Ltd.'s debut single, "Public Image," would finally give Lydon an opportunity to make a statement without interference. In the Sex Pistols, his nihilistic voice had been filtered through the showmanship of McLaren and interpreted in the light of Sid Vicious's violence and the band's destructive notoriety. The authorship of the lyrics of the Sex Pistols' songs is still disputed. The most plausible account is that McLaren, Vivienne Westwood, and their associates fed some of their ideas to Lydon, who added his own viewpoint and transformed these suggestions into his own powerful words. But McLaren and Lydon ended up with different views of the meaning, direction, and purpose of the Sex Pistols, and this was the major schism on which the original band fell apart. Lydon had given an eloquent account of his own views in interviews, often stressing that the most important thing to him now was keeping his self-respect—"It's all about being yourself," he wrote later in his book *No Irish, No Blacks, No Dogs*. But saying this is easier than putting it into practice: now his music would have to live up to his rhetoric.

THIS WASN'T, however, the only problem that Lydon faced. It was widely believed that punk's message was one of being authentic, of cutting through the bollocks and simply telling it how you saw it. But the reality was far more confused. Punk was riddled with a series of paradoxes: it hymned authenticity but relied heavily on simulation in its performance; it aspired to success on its own terms but glamorized failure; its do-it-yourself aspect raised the issue of how to take and keep control in a genre that glorified the individual against the corporate machine; and it presented itself both as a simple negation and as something far more knowing.

In the last verse of "EMI," Rotten affected a moronic monotone that transmogrified over a few lines into the derisive lines of the final chorus and the knowing pay-off ("Hallo

EMI, goodbye A&M"). Within a few seconds he had gone from dumb aggression to cutting sarcasm. This moment epitomizes the combination that bewildered and panicked the music business. Music journalist Caroline Coon has contrasted Rotten with Mick Jagger, pointing out that Jagger faked a working-class accent to gain credibility, but that "his view of what it was to be working-class was that you should be thick and stupid, yet another conceit about the English class system." Rotten was genuinely working class, and his parody of a stupid voice came as part of a package where he was clearly smart and confident—his dumb insolence was far more threatening to the establishment.

Earlier in the same song, he challenged "and you thought that we were faking?" as if even he wasn't entirely sure. Because it still was unclear if punk's real message was one of annihilation or a more constructive blend of free expression and mocking antagonism. Was this satire, insurgency, or a mixture of the two? And had the Pistols' chaotic progress through three record companies been a series of absurd accidents or the result of a master plan? By 1978, no one had any clear idea of how to solve these paradoxes, and they were all obstacles that Lydon had to negotiate if he were to progress and survive.

Attitudes toward authenticity were from the start a deeply confused part of punk, as Lydon and McLaren certainly both knew. McLaren was influenced by a variety of artistic and political movements including Dadaism and anarchism, and he was especially interested in the situationists. This political movement had little direct influence on the punk musicians but fascinated the older generation of McLaren and his friends, especially those who regarded hippie idealism with suspicion. Situationism was essentially a strand of anarchism, which had commented on, and to some degree influenced, the Parisian uprising of 1968, at which McLaren would sometimes falsely claim to have been present. Echoing the ideas of situationist gurus Raoul Vaneigem and Guy Debord, which became more widely known in the years after 1968, he saw punk as essentially a posture, a consciously assumed style and pose that created friction and revealed the simulations in bourgeois society.

Vaneigem, in particular, had seen authentic artistic expression as the route to the revolutionary transformation of society. He once wrote: "In a gloomy bar where everyone is bored to death, a drunken young man breaks his glass, then picks up a bottle and smashes it against the wall. . . . Yet everyone there could have done exactly the same thing . . . a gesture of liberation, however weak and clumsy it may be, always bears an authentic communication." This kind of rhetoric can be used to glorify rebellious gestures of any sort, no matter how irrelevant or risky. McLaren and Westwood were happy to play with such ideas and, in some instances, to instigate or encourage violence simply for the notoriety and publicity it brought. But for them punk's violence could always be seen as a game, or even as a piece of social experimentation they were carrying out on a younger group of people. At the Nashville club in London in April 1976, Westwood deliberately started a fight because she thought the Pistols' set was boring. Subsequently the Vaneigem quote above had an uncomfortable mirror in reality at a "punk festival" at the 100 Club in September of that year. Following the Sex Pistols' performance the previous day, the Damned headlined the second night. Their set was disrupted when Sid Vicious, who hadn't yet joined the Pistols but was already a fan, expressed his hostility to their set by throwing a beer glass at the stage. It smashed on a pillar, and the resulting debris hurt several people, including a girl whose eye was supposedly cut by a shard of broken glass. The girl's injury may in fact have been a journalist's embellishment of the incident, but the danger was clear in any case.

It is easy to see Malcolm McLaren as the embodiment of inauthenticity in the story of punk, and his later accounts of the period certainly emphasized the mocking pretenses rather than anything more fundamental. Musicologist Greg Wahl, for instance, has said that McLaren's "role in the 'creation' of punk as inherently artificial probably cannot be overestimated." But to McLaren, the music was subsidiary to a kind of political direct action, a form of self-expression for which the music and style was no more than a convenient conduit. Like so many vanguardists, including the situationists themselves, he felt let down by the masses who failed to enact his vision in the exact way he wanted them to. His ideal of a politically focused movement undermining conventional society, in a direct inverse of the sixties hippies he had despised, never materialized. As the punk scene started to expand and get out of control, he became emotionally detached from it and from the band. He started to feel that the music had never been the point, and tried to move into film and other projects to carry on the momentum. This was one of the reasons that he drifted apart from Lydon, who was still on the front line of the chaos that had been created.

The violence surrounding the group inevitably snowballed as they became more notorious. When John Lydon was attacked and stabbed by a group of youths who were hostile to punk following the release of "God Save the Queen," he saw one side of the violence that was increasingly being let loose. He was in an exposed position, out on the streets of London, where this game was for real. In any case, he rejected McLaren's belief that the members of the Sex Pistols were simply pawns in a political game. For Lydon the band was an opportunity to express a genuine, deeply held disgust with society. He felt that he had the ability to occasionally hit the nail on the head in putting across the feelings of alienation and boredom of many youths. Nonetheless, he understood that in doing so he was to some degree playing a part—the character of Johnny Rotten was a cathartic, extreme version of his personality from whom he could take a step backward when it became necessary. As Rotten, he hated traditional rock'n'roll and wanted nothing more than to destroy it. As Lydon, he liked all sorts of music—for a Capital Radio show in the summer of 1977 he chose records as widely varied as Captain Beefheart, Peter Hamill, and Neil Young, displaying a more complex side of his personality than he generally chose to reveal at that stage. It was an interview that infuriated McLaren for two reasons: it revealed Rotten to be more than the cartoon demon that suited McLaren's purposes and it was also a sign that McLaren could no longer control the star that he liked to regard as his creation.

So Lydon did not entirely identify himself with Rotten—he could take a step away from the "filth and the fury" when he needed to, as could many of his contemporaries. Ray Burns, Marion Eliot, and Susan Ballion, ordinary youths from London's suburbs, suddenly became Captain Sensible, Poly Styrene, and Siouxsie Sioux. The masks adopted by performers such as these allowed them to behave outrageously and to express themselves in ways that they couldn't otherwise have done. Different performers used punk as a vehicle to convey their own distinct styles and ideas. The Damned were frequently hilarious, X-Ray Spex skewered the absurdities of the disposable society, while the Banshees moved quickly from punk toward their own brand of gothic cacophony. For these and many others, extreme personas and stage names allowed a spectrum of self-expression that ranged far beyond the Pistols' nihilism. One of the most exhilarating aspects of punk was that feeling of complete liberation from yesterday's normality.

But for some of the youths who took up the punk ideas in this early period, the irony—the distance between persona and real person—was lost. For them the only way to become a true punk was to take on the full identity and costume and to become as reviled as possible. While swastikas or rapist hoods might have first been worn in an ironic or challenging way, others simply mimicked this style in a way that could be seen as offensive and dangerous. There were elements of actual fascism creeping in at the fringes of the poorly defined politics of the movement. Riots at Sham 69 concerts and elsewhere were providing an ugly counterpoint to the music, and the far-right National Front was increasingly interested in hijacking part of the energy and disruption that punk created. While much of the initial violence had been more simulated than real, it became increasingly hard to get the released demons back into their caves.

SID VICIOUS was the prime example of the kind of punk rocker who forgot, or never realized, that the punk attitude could be simulated and ironic. He took it to an extreme, making the idealization of spitting, hatred, bloodletting, and violence into a manifesto for life, leaving behind a large part of his genuine sense of humor on the way. The definition of the hardcore or authentic punk was being drawn either along the lines of who had been there first or who was prepared to be the most extreme in re-creating the original postures. In both respects Sid excelled. He had been one of the crowd of youths hanging around McLaren and Westwood's shop, and a close friend of John Lydon's from their teenage years in North and East London. Once Lydon became Rotten, Sid played in other transient punk bands and became the Pistols' überfan, being involved in several of the moments of violence that helped establish their notoriety.

One interesting aspect of punk's attitude to authenticity is the way it involved simulation. When someone's persona is as close as possible to the individual's actual personality, the persona is commonly seen as real, or authentic. In this way, Will Rogers or Woody Guthrie had been early exemplars of authenticity—what you saw was pretty much what there was. By contrast a very theatrical performer who adopted mannerisms to project a persona would be seen as relatively fake.

But punk actually turned this calculation on its head. Most of its protagonists adopted self-evident personas, indicated by their assumed names and absurd behavior. Paradoxically, this pretense allowed the performer a liberating degree of honesty: singing about a teenager's life of boredom and masturbation was easier to do through the guise of a fictional alter ego. Many punk performers used their masks as a fundamental way of channeling their self-expression.

However, since it was still seen as fake to be a different person from your persona, authenticity for the punks often became defined by how well you could turn yourself into your persona. John Beverly (or Simon Ritchie as he was sometimes called) had been a relatively polite, withdrawn teenager, a fashion victim who idolized David Bowie and Roxy Music. But once he entered the punk circle and became Sid Vicious, it was incumbent on him to turn himself into a real-life golem of derision and aggression. A lot of his persona was undoubtedly an exaggeration of parts of his real personality, but in order to be the hardcore punk he wanted to be, he eliminated all other aspects of his identity. In his autobiography, Lydon commented that Vicious "tried his very best to out-Rotten Rotten, but he didn't understand Rotten was my alter ego. He would think that made me a fake." The real John Beverly was still there, but it was rare that anyone was allowed to catch a glimpse.

When Sid finally joined the Pistols, after Glen Matlock's departure in early 1977, he found himself in a band under siege. They played rarely, and every gig was subject to uncertainty and confusion. But when he got the chance to perform or appear in public, Sid took his chance eagerly and played out his fantasies of the uncontrollable rock star to the fullest extent. By doing this he quickly became emblematic of the band, in spite of his lack of musical competence or input. His personal life started to get out of control as he and girlfriend Nancy became more heavily involved with heroin. By the time the Pistols reached America for their first, and ultimately final, tour, his behavior was so erratic that Rotten, his oldest friend in the Pistols clique, was barely speaking to him. Unable to comprehend how jaded his bandmates were, Sid complained that he was the only one who really entered into the Pistols' spirit on that tour. In San Antonio he used his bass to club a stage invader over the head. In Dallas he was headbutted and bled heavily over his instrument. "Look at that—a living circus," was Rotten's acid comment onstage. At one point Sid made his oft-repeated boast—that he would die a rock'n'roll death—to photographer Roberta Bayley, saying that he wanted to die before he was thirty, "like Iggy Pop." Bayley broke the news that Iggy was still alive, but even that didn't seem to dent his romantic aspirations. Not only was Sid living out other people's fantasies, he was even following in imaginary footsteps.

At the final show at San Francisco's Winterland, Sid pulled rock'n'roll poses with abandon while Rotten's contorted body language revealed his withdrawal and disdain. Rotten's famed parting words—"Ever get the feeling you've been cheated?"—referred to himself as much as to the audience that night, and to the punks in general. He had had enough of the circus and wanted out.

McLaren had high hopes that Vicious might replace Rotten as the face of the Pistols, but by this stage Sid hated McLaren almost as much as John did. Nonetheless McLaren managed to persuade Sid to participate in the later recording sessions and the filming of *The Great Rock and Roll Swindle*. This led to one of Sid's defining moments, the film's absurd parody of "My Way."

A CHAOTIC MIXTURE of fact and fiction, *The Great Rock and Roll Swindle* was partly a vehicle for McLaren to give his own version of the Sex Pistols' story (with himself as antihero and prime mover) and partly a piece of conscious mythologizing.

Jean Fernandez of Barclay Records, the band's French record company, suggested "My Way" for Sid, initially because his company owned the publishing rights to the song—yet the idea stuck, and the filming was arranged in an empty Parisian theater. Sid had been reluctant to make the journey to France, but in the end he was coaxed into giving an entertaining performance. Dressed in a trashed dinner suit, he part crooned, part brutalized his way through the song and, as the final touch, enthusiastically opened fire with a fake gun on his audience. The song was released as a double A-side, with the preposterous "A Punk Prayer" on the reverse, and was one of the best-selling Pistols singles, comfortably outselling "God Save the Queen."

Earlier, after the glass-throwing incident at the 100 Club, Sid had spent a few weeks locked up in Ashford Remand Centre. While he was there he wrote a letter in which he mentioned that Vivienne Westwood had lent him a book about Charles Manson, and that "one of the things I believe in since being slung in here is total personal freedom." The problem with half-baked ideas of anarchism is that the idea of freedom tends to become detached from more arduous concepts of how to live responsibly in a society without rules. By contrast, the anarchist Pierre-Joseph Proudhon once wrote that "it is our right to maintain our freedom. It is our duty to respect that of others." Vicious, in his eagerness to please and be accepted as a real punk, had aspired to an ideal of irresponsible freedom. He felt genuine pride in his notoriety. But for a young junkie to boast, even in parody, of doing it "My Way" was a bathetic reflection on his eventual self-destruction.

His use of the song also tangentially illustrates some of the ways that the cult of personal authenticity had affected music over the previous decade. The original, "Comme d'Habitude" written by Claude François, was adapted, very loosely, by Paul Anka in 1967. In the postwar period there had been a much stronger tradition of songs adapted from foreign sources— "It's Now or Never," "Strangers in the Night," "You Don't Have to Say You Love Me," and "I Can't Help Falling in Love with You" are all examples. This tradition, which had enriched and broadened popular music, was largely curtailed by the era of singer-songwriters.

"My Way" was a late flowering of this very different era of popular music. For all the inanities and simplicities of postwar pop, its songwriters did periodically manage to take on broader themes. One aspect of this was a fascinating tradition of songs that looked back over the narrator's experiences from the end of life. It's no surprise that the greatest of these songs were written by skilled songwriters capable of the emotional detachment needed to enter into a third-person state of mind, and were best executed by performers who were able to "act" out a song. Leiber and Stoller wrote "Is That All There Is?" an elegant survey of life's disappointments, performed with cheerful abandon by Peggy Lee. Charles Aznavour's "Yesterday When I Was Young" is equally elegant, but far more melancholy. In Randy Newman's "Old Man," the narrator dispassionately observes his dying father and comments that "everybody dies." French songwriter Jacques Brel's morbid and hilarious takes on mortality included "Le moribund" in which the dying narrator forgives his wife for her many infidelities and invites his friends to dance and sing with abandon as he is lowered into his grave.

("Le moribund" was [mis]translated into English as

"Seasons in the Sun," and the song's fortunes reflected the shift of perspective in pop music. With bland lyrics that removed the sharpest stings from Brel's original, it was performed with modest success by the squeaky clean Kingston Trio in 1964. But ten years later, the personal had become inescapable, and Terry Jacks's 1974 version became a massive hit on the back of mawkish publicity stressing that the song was recorded as a tribute to a recently deceased friend.)

Within this tradition, "My Way" represents a certain summit. Maybe it's not a great song—it is a relatively mundane narrative, although it has an inescapable grandeur in its pacing and cadences. Frank Sinatra's definitive version, recorded late in his career in 1969, precisely conveyed the feeling that here was a singer who had lived through the ups and downs that the song demands. Brash, boastful, yet reflective, his spirited performance made it into a classic, a ready-made cliché that anyone could join in with after a few drinks, a generation before the rise of karaoke. It was also an example of how songs could become identified with a singer who wasn't a songwriter. People identified this song as Sinatra's own, even though it was written neither by nor about him.

When Sid Vicious sang "My Way," he was also near the end of his career, but he couldn't know that yet. "My Way" was seen by those around him as a holy cow, an idol overdue for desecration. Sid's version made a thorough job of disemboweling it. He swore, boasted of killing a cat, and twisted lines of the song so that they referred to drugs and apathy—"There were times, I'm sure you knew, when there was fuck fuck fuck else to do."

It was a grimly effective comedy performance. In Vicious's hands, the song became self-referential but empty. By this stage Sid was a junkie, pure and simple, and it's unwise to read too much into his state of mind when he sang the song. And, of course, it was by no means a representative punk song—there were many punk moments that were more interesting or worthwhile. But it does serve as an example of the dead end that Sid's version of punk had driven into. This was a private joust against conformity and normality—what else could it be for a twenty-one-year-old with no real knowledge of life outside the strange world he inhabited?

THE IMPULSES BEHIND the wider punk movement had been varied—there was in the mid-seventies a real feeling in Great Britain, the United States, and elsewhere that something new was needed. Seeing the blandness of pop and overblown verbiage of rock, the young bands that would end up as punk were looking for their own kind of music, one that really meant something to them. But for many, meaning had become identified with personal, solipsistic issues, darkness and negativity, while honesty was often signified by brutal simplicity and lack of musical skill. Punk may have declared a year zero, but it was nonetheless drawing on a wide variety of antecedents that ranged from the Velvet Underground and the Stooges to the garage bands of the sixties. Iggy Pop had started out as a blues drummer but with the Stooges had consciously set out to create music for "suburban white trash." John Lydon was one of many in his generation of London musicians who saw Iggy, post-Stooges, playing a seminal gig at the Scala in Kings Cross, a dilapidated cinema that doubled as a seedy but memorable concert venue. When the punks tried to re-create music, they were at first drawing almost entirely on white rock antecedents, and they took the quest for personal authenticity, as it was expressed in rock music, largely for granted.

In the United States, the initial wave of what would become known as punk or new wave was extremely varied. Patti Smith used stripped-down instrumentation as backing for her poetic visions on a wide range of subjects. Pere Ubu created a manic collage of disturbing art noise and absurd ideas. Television used guitars in a rigorous, direct way that negated rock's overblown tendencies while creating new directions for the guitar band. Talking Heads took this further, using guitars in a rhythmic chatter to underpin David Byrne's dislocated lyrics. Richard Hell introduced the subject matters of nihilism and sexual dysfunction that would become commonplace as punk developed.

But it was two other bands that most directly influenced the UK punk scene. The Ramones played rock songs with a minimum of musical complexity but the most extreme amphetamine speed possible. In their regulation leather, uniform dork haircuts, and adoption of the same last name, they were more cartoon than reality, and used their mixture of assumed idiocy and cunning to play around with controversial and brutal ideas, from "Blitzkrieg Bop" to "Beat on the Brat." A large part of the London punk scene developed in complete isolation from the scene in New York, but the Ramones' first album was one of the few American punk albums that was widely listened to in the UK in 1976–77. The New York Dolls were less well known in the UK and had less direct influence on the musicians, but their disinterred rock'n'roll style was the direct source for Malcolm McLaren's search for confrontation, transgression and twisted glamour in a London band.

The influence of these two bands, filtered through the Sex Pistols, meant that English punk took only a restricted range of possible influences from across the Atlantic. Three-chord drones and breathless speed were favored over any sign of musical complexity. The poetic and doomed romantic influences of Rimbaud and Verlaine via Patti Smith and Television and the industrialized cutups of Pere Ubu had little impact. The first wave of British punk concentrated on two lyrical possibilities: a basic focus on the here and now (whether nihilistic in the case of the Pistols, or wryly humorous as with the Buzzcocks or Alternative TV) and the espousal of outrageous and controversial thoughts and ideas ("White Riot," "Holidays in the Sun," "Oh Bondage, Up Yours"). These options were preferably expressed in a voice that echoed the anger and incoherence of youth, rather than in any more sophisticated style.

This restriction partially fed back into the American punk scene, which absorbed some of the simplifications of the British equivalent. Black Flag, the Dead Kennedys, the Circle Jerks, Minor Threat, and other bands across the country showed the influence of British punk in their lyrical approach, aggression, and simplicity. Prior to this, most American punk bands could be identified as art-rock—even bands like the Ramones, the Dictators and the Stooges saw themselves this way. In this respect they were all following in the footsteps of the Velvet Underground. But now the complete contempt for "art" shown by the British punks started to be the dominant attitude in the American punk scene as well.

David Thomas of Pere Ubu has complained that the new-wave movement "wiped out a generation of musicians," lamenting that the interesting bands of the period, such as Devo and Talking Heads, had developed in isolation. In his view, punk created a template for young musicians to aspire to, but one without substance, a straitjacket that limited their aspirations. "All these people suddenly had something to copy, and at that point, it doesn't matter what you're copying—you're still copying."

IN TRYING TO CREATE meaningful songs for adolescent minds, punk had the virtue of using simple ideas based in everyday life. In this respect, it was a refreshing and liberating influence. Belfast's Undertones are just one example of a band that took punk's limited style and applied it in a fresh way, focusing on teen concerns and everyday scenes to create basic music that was joyous and exciting. Many other bands of the period based their approach on punk's ideals but found ways to take a step forward. But for John Lydon, it was hard to see a way out of punk. He had been defined by the negation and anger of the Pistols, and this severely restricted his options. The huge task facing him in his solo career was how to expand to something meaningful and worthwhile.

He had watched Sid's decline and had experienced first-hand the problems created by punk's cartoonish glorification of violence. He had observed with disdain McLaren's attempts to depict himself as the antihero of punk, and his attempts to film the story of the Sex Pistols as nothing more than a giant situationist con. Now he had to decide how to react.

Having declared what he was against, what he regarded as being fake and worthless, in great detail, the specific question Lydon now had to answer was what he saw as being real and worthwhile. "Public Image" was his first statement of intent. He wanted to debunk the image he had created; he would refuse to be a star, refuse to play out the pantomime of punk, and go his own way. Using his real name (he had to do so because of McLaren's claim to legal ownership of his alter ego, though he may have wanted to in any case), Lydon would be true to his real self, not to the idiotic expectations of the press or the punk faithful. To do this, he needed to redefine his public persona.

"Public Image" was stunning in its achievement of these limited aims. It blew away McLaren's assertions that Rotten was a mere tool in his literary creation. Keith Levene's chiming guitars cut remorselessly across Jah Wobble's driving bassline as Lydon's lyrics attacked the shallowness of those who saw nothing but surface image and ambiguously claimed his own public image as his own creation. In dismissing the fakery of McLaren, he set himself up by default as a genuine artist, one who simply spoke his mind and told the truth as he saw it.

There's never been a voice that comes within spitting distance of Lydon's for its intense, scabrous assault on the ears. Listening to his early recordings now, it's no surprise that he frightened people. The first two lines of "Anarchy in the UK" with their threatening declamation and harsh dissonance still sound like the purest distillation of malevolent rage conceivable. In "Public Image," from the sinister opening "Hello"s that descend into derisive laughter to the final howls, Lydon was at his magnetic, repulsive best. Musically the song went significantly beyond mere punk. Listening to it now, it seems to weirdly prefigure a lot of disparate later music from U2 to Radiohead to the Prodigy in its driving guitars, oblique rhythms, and concentrated fury. But at the time it was simply a fascinating, pure assertion of escape and individuality. It showed that Lydon was someone to be reckoned with, not a puppet who would fade away once the original band disintegrated.

The grim determination that drove Lydon to make this record should perhaps have been a warning to McLaren that he wouldn't be easy to beat. More than a decade of legal battles over the Sex Pistols' finances ensued; Lydon was the ultimate victor, together with band members Steve Jones and Paul Cook, who became late defectors to his cause, having initially supported McLaren's case.

Public Image Ltd.'s second album, recorded in 1979, was a three-record 45-rpm limited edition packaged in a steel case and labeled *Metal Box*. Here the band tried to create a kind of antimusic, bringing in some of the reggae influence that had become a strong part of the punk scene. Lydon had visited Jamaica in 1978 with the DJ and filmmaker Don Letts, looking for bands to sign to Virgin Records. Virgin's owner Richard Branson, unsure how to deal with the Sex Pistols' break-up, had suggested the trip as an interim measure, knowing that Lydon had been interested in reggae since his youth in Finsbury Park. *Metal Box* was a clearer glimpse of Lydon's intended direction, absorbing influences from dub (reggae's stripped-down, remixed cousin) and from more dissonant sources—such as the krautrock of Can and the exuberant weirdness of Captain Beefheart—to create a twisted backdrop for Lydon's disturbing vocals.

However, it is questionable whether even at this stage of his career, Lydon consistently achieved the degree of personal authenticity he tended to claim in his interviews. He always stressed that his targets were hypocrisy and fakery. But throughout his career, his actual lyrics showed the strain of trying to express himself without fakery, and in this respect there was a mismatch between his professed goals and the resulting music. He often wrote in poetic fragments that were hard to interpret. And rather than speaking directly about himself, he wrote about the sheer complexity of self-expression. Lines such as "There are no easy answers to elongated questions" ("Open and Revolving") or "I can only feel and think in the language of cliches" ("God") suggest a writer confronting the difficulty of making a genuine statement. Lydon certainly didn't want to lie, but he couldn't always find something true that he wanted to say.

The stand-out track of *Metal Box*, "Swan Lake" (also known as "Death Disco"), took on the intensely personal subject matter of the cancer suffered by Lydon's mother. It is an oblique but emotionally affecting song. However, the refrain of "words cannot express" acknowledges the impossibility of truly recording the experience, even as Lydon confronts the pain and confusion caused by his mother's death. It makes a fascinating counterpoint to Lennon's "Mother" (discussed earlier). Lennon's attempt at personal authenticity led him to a bald statement of his pain, whereas Lydon took a more nuanced and indirect path, partly reflecting his different personality. One could even argue that Lydon's is the more honest approach because he clearly understands the impossibility of trying to communicate something so personal.

Over the years following this album, Lydon led his band

through a variety of innovative and dislocated musical styles, always maintaining his derisive attitude toward image and fakes. His message remained somewhat blank and opaque at times, but to the surprise of many, he found a way forward from the staged outrage and aggression of punk while continuing to make a living in a business he had scorned. The band suffered from persistent financial, personal, and organizational problems, and their musical output was irregular. Guitarist Keith Levene departed after their third album, *The Flowers of Romance;* thereafter the band became little more than a backing group for Lydon, with no settled lineup. As a result, the later material was of very uneven quality and style. Yet no one should underestimate the difficulties Lydon faced, or his achievement in finding any kind of route out of the situation he was in after the Pistols' breakup. His long-term musical career may not have been entirely satisfying, but for him to have survived and prospered at all under the circumstances is remarkable.

WHILE JOHN LYDON found his own way of dealing with its aftermath, the first wave of punk was still spreading slowly across the globe. The message that survived the transition of place and time was in many cases less cynical than Lydon's worldview. The idea that anyone could start a band, given a few rudimentary instruments and the right attitude, was empowering and liberating for tens of thousands of adolescents. An unprecedented explosion of new music occurred (seeing punk as being only about the Kings Road in 1975–77, as some of the original British participants do, is a bit like saying you weren't involved in the War of Independence if you weren't at the Boston Tea Party). The London punk scene rose up and imploded over a very short time, as did parallel scenes in the United States. With punk and new wave on both sides of the Atlantic, early participants have tended to deride those who followed in their wake as imitators. But some of the most interesting consequences of the punk ideals developed only during subsequent years.

Punk had been based on a radical posture that hit a chord with youths because of their genuine feelings of alienation. At first it was defined mainly by opposition: to hippies, disco, the music business, the status quo—well, to almost everything. The Ramones succinctly parodied this negativity in "I'm Against It," following a list of dislikes by singing "I don't like anything."

The Sex Pistols in particular had been a largely nihilistic force, with Johnny Rotten remembered for declaring "no future" and wanting to "destroy passers-by." As he wrote in his book about the period: "Sometimes the absolute most positive thing you can be in a boring society is completely negative." But punk was also about simple apathy and boredom that was transformed into energy when it was given a voice. The challenge for punk was how to use that energy and whether or not it could be transformed into anything more positive than early punk's postures of boredom and anger. By 1978, the Clash and others were attempting to channel the spirit of punk into positive politics—at home through the antiracist movement and abroad by interacting with other musical cultures and political movements. The two-tone scene (a British-based ska revival) would subsequently take this baton by creating the first genuinely multicultural music scene England had seen. Meanwhile, bands like Crass and

Chumbawumba fostered a more politically literate approach to music, combining agitprop with performance. In these ways, punk's influence was very positive, as it demonstrated to a generation the power that such a basic and direct form of music could generate.

One strong impact the British scene had on American music came in the idea that anyone could start a band, and many bands developed the do-it-yourself, or DIY, philosophy into a way of life. The Replacements were a good example of the new "postpunk" bands. Starting up in Minneapolis in 1979 as a straightforward punk band, their songs were autobiographical in an adolescent but drily humorous way that avoided the petulance of the angrier bands of the era. In this way they were perhaps closer in spirit to the Buzzcocks than to the Sex Pistols. In songs like "I Hate Music," they demonstrated their punk nihilism while simultaneously undercutting the message with sly comedy ("It's got too many notes").

As the band progressed, they embodied the transformation of punk from a music that was frequently negative into one that celebrated misfits and losers of all kinds. They also took the original punk influences—the garage bands, Iggy's suburban slacker blues, and the less nihilistic New York punk of Television and Patti Smith—and reinterpreted them in a more down-to-earth way. From punk roots, they developed an ironic eclecticism in their music, taking them close to pop success in the mid-1980s with songs like "I Will Dare." But their celebration of failure carried through into their major-label years, and they tended to deliberately sabotage themselves, performing drunk on TV and, in the early years of MTV, issuing a video for "Bastards of Young" that consisted of nothing but a static shot of a record being put on a turntable and then rotating through to the close of the song. The idea behind it, a refusal to conform to the rule that says you should perform for your audience, was strongly reminiscent of Public Image Ltd.'s first concerts, in which the band played their entire set behind an opaque curtain. It also embodied a rejection of fakery—rather than lip-synch, or pretend to perform in any way, the band put up a metaphorical blank wall. Seeing performance itself as a kind of fakery led Public Image to an ethic of antiperformance, which affected their approach to all aspects of their music.

The Replacements embodied the contradictions that were bequeathed to this generation of bands. Both attracted and repelled by success, they strongly wanted in their early years to avoid selling out. Their chaotic *Saturday Night Live* performances were exact mirrors of many of their drunken live shows (like the Sex Pistols, they swore on air), and to change their style just for the cameras would perhaps have felt untrue. But there is a big difference between the comic bonhomie of watching a chaotic live gig and seeing the same disarray through the cold light of television.

Having started out with a credible punk manifesto, the band's refusenik attitude won them admirers but also handicapped them when it came to winning new fans beyond their original constituency. Singer Paul Westerberg was an important player in punk's slow journey toward the grunge bands of the nineties, casting himself as the champion slacker, a role he found hard to cast aside. Prior to their 1987 album *Pleased to Meet Me*, the band threw out their most reckless member, guitarist Bob Stinson. The title and cover image (a handshake between a "suit" and a punk who were actually the same person) clearly flagged this album as a self-conscious "sellout."

And there was a noticeable move toward the mainstream in the greater ambition and musical complexity of the songs: for the first time, this sounded like a band that actually knew how to play their instruments. However, the quality of Westerberg's songwriting was disguised by rough production, giving it a vibrant urgency but at the same time guaranteeing that it wouldn't be too successful. Even as they were making a song and dance about how they were selling out, they couldn't entirely bring themselves to let go of their roots and really go the whole hog. Commenting on one of the best tracks, music writer Stephen Thomas Erlewine said that "the fan love letter 'Alex Chilton' reveals more than necessary—even though Westerberg is shooting for stardom, he has more affinity for the self-styled loser, which means he never wants to make the full leap to the mainstream."

The Replacements did have one more attempt at commercial success, the album *Don't Tell a Soul* in 1989, for which they even made MTV-friendly videos. After ten years they were finally playing by standard music business rules, but by then their best chances of broader success were gone. The single "I'll Be You" was a minor hit, but there was no major breakthrough. The album alienated many of their hardcore fans, who hated its highly produced sound, and the band subsequently disintegrated.

In the career of the Replacements, we see the problems caused by glorifying a lack of musical competence and the difficulty of turning a cult of failure into success. These troubles persisted in American underground music. They came closest to being solved by Nirvana, who actually managed to turn slackerdom into mainstream success but who nonetheless succumbed to the friction contained within this paradox.

In any case, the aversion to competence and success was largely an irrelevant fetishization. Punk's do-it-yourself philosophy was partly expressed through a dislike of overproduction. Musical proficiency had certainly been overrated in the earlier part of the decade, leading to the musical excesses of progressive rock and to pompous absurdities such as Deep Purple's *Concerto for Rock Band and Orchestra*. So for a while, the punks' refusal to admire proficiency was refreshing. The raw sounds of unskilled players had long signified passion and meaning in some quarters. Punk was following in the footsteps of earlier artists such as Neil Young and the sixties garage bands, and even some country music, although it was perhaps the first time that an entire movement had taken this attitude as a commandment. And because some apparently meaningful music was created by musicians of limited skill, two non sequiturs came to be accepted as fact by the punks. First, anyone who was musically incompetent could create something more meaningful than a skillful musician. Second, and more unreasonably, it became an unwritten law that it was impossible to do anything meaningful in a more skilled way.

Of course, excessive slickness can be a dull trait in any kind of music—a degree of looseness or rawness carries passion, even with skilled performers. Punk's search for energy mirrored attitudes among fans of other styles—including jazz and standard rock—who often preferred a "live," spontaneous feel in music. One of the great things about punk was the vibrancy that resulted from this attitude.

However, do-it-yourself at this stage was recognized as such only if the rough edges were visible enough to imply that the music was being played incompetently. Bad playing became a signifier of DIY and therefore a guarantee of authenticity, which helps to explain the hostile reaction of many of the Replacements' fans to their increasing level of skill and production. In the immediate postpunk period, those influenced by punk ideals tended to treat any sign of slickness with disdain. A decade later, the advent of samplers and home studios would mean that the potential quality to be achieved by do-it-yourself recording was completely transformed, and it became normal for dance records with slick production values to be made in musicians' living rooms. However, the original DIY ethos survived in the tradition that exalts the lo-fi production values of, for instance, Liz Phair's first album, the first three Sebadoh records, Daniel Johnston's cassettes, the four-track recordings of Guided by Voices, and the peculiar mumblings of Jandek.

Some odd examples of faking it sprang up in response to the DIY aesthetic. In the immediate aftermath of the Sex Pistols, musical skill was looked down on, so many musicians pretended to be far more incompetent than they really were, for the sake of their credibility. The Stranglers, for instance, a UK band that predated the punk movement but immediately adopted its ethos, suppressed their prog-rock instincts and musical skill, playing in a thuggish, basic style on songs like "Peaches."

One irony is that the Sex Pistols were far from incompetent themselves. Steve Jones played his guitar in a way that sounded simple because of its brutality but that actually took a great deal of musical understanding and competence to execute. The wall of sound he built on the Pistols recordings was quite an elaborate achievement, which in some respects owed more to Phil Spector than to Iggy Pop—the skill involved is demonstrated by how feeble many attempts to imitate him sounded.

While the Replacements were badly afflicted by the wish to seem incompetent, on a wider scale they were probably fatally hamstrung by their conflicted approach to music business success. One can interpret their career as a journey from heroic resistance to sellout wannabes or just as a missed opportunity. But as punk moved into the past, many bands still retained the purist diktats of those who had interpreted it as being fundamentally about authenticity and self-expression. Loserdom, musical brutalism, and rage would be the touchstones of rock played by white youths for decades to come, from postpunk to straight edge and from thrash to grunge.

PUNK, IN ITS CONFUSED regard for authenticity and its rejections of fakery, created a series of traps. For all its confusion, it was an exciting, revitalizing music. But it was also a simulation that came to be seen as authentic, a failure cult that wanted to reinvent music, and a progressive genre in which incompetence and emotional immaturity were badges of honor. These traps were inescapable, even though many of those caught in them created fascinating music—Nirvana would eventually get stuck in the most unbearable trap (as discussed earlier), but in their own ways, Public Image Ltd. and the Replacements demonstrated the problems well.

John Lydon avoided the cartoon tendencies of punk better than many others of his generation, but in the end it has been hard for him to break free from the restrictions of authenticity—restrictions he was forced to adopt as his means of escape from punk. He has been as haunted by the ghosts of punk as Donna Summer has been by those of disco. He first acknowledged this in 1981, when he started to perform

"Anarchy in the UK" on stage again, playing with the idea that selling out by pretending to be Johnny Rotten was a suitably cynical act. In 1996, he eventually took this line of thought to a logical conclusion when he consented to re-form the Sex Pistols for their Filthy Lucre tour, something he had frequently claimed he would never do. In many ways it turned out to be a celebratory moment: finally free of their legal battles, the band was able to show a new generation that behind all the outrage they were a brilliant rock band that deserved their place in history. But it was also an implicit admission that whatever Lydon achieved, he has never truly been able to get away from the Pistols.

In trying to escape the original paradoxes of punk, Lydon had walked into a new one. Part of his means of escape was to attach himself to ideas such as self-expression, individuality, and authenticity. This was only one segment of the punk idea, but it was the element furthest removed from McLaren's game playing and detachment. By defining McLaren as inauthentic and himself as authentic, Lydon was able to create a role for himself, though one that became a straitjacket in spite of his valiant attempts to escape from it. His audience has been suspicious of any attempt to do something merely entertaining or overly experimental and has been most satisfied when Lydon works in the sphere of personal expression and truth telling. While he is sufficiently cynical and emotionally secure to disregard this suspicion (his humor and ability to distance himself has always been his saving grace), it has certainly made it hard for him to depart from the idea of authenticity by more than a few degrees. When PiL made a different kind of record—*Happy?*—in which the experimentation was based around relatively standard pop structures, a large part of Lydon's audience reacted with incomprehension. Anytime he appeared to drift off the road of personal authenticity in his music, those who carry the "true faith" have accused him of selling out. This has happened even when he has been honestly expressing his own confusion, as he did in "Rise," singing "I could be right, I could be wrong."

There is a degree of built-in friction in Lydon's attitude to authenticity. Above all, he always wanted to express his individuality, but at the same time he rejected the self-absorption of grunge and other white rock, saying that music was worthless if it didn't relate to other people. Surveying the music scene around him, he later commented, "People were changing and moving on. Why couldn't I?" But it was difficult for audiences to perceive Lydon as anything other than the punk icon he had once been. In the same vein, he also wrote, "Audiences are far too fucking demanding on the people they like and dislike. The truth always lets them down because it destroys their fantasies." One can see the frustration he must sometimes have felt at the way he was treated, and that his emphasis on personal authenticity was not as clear-cut as it might sometimes have seemed.

He understood that the self he was trying to convey to the world was not a simple, unchanging entity. "I always hoped I made it completely clear that I was as deeply confused as the next person." His message was in fact far more complex than simple authenticity; he wanted to express himself, partially by showing the true confusion, the multidimensional aspects of splintered thought that underlie personal identity. While he has often been judged on the grounds of whether he is being a fake or the real thing, he has in fact been projecting ideas that defy analysis in these terms. His ideas of complex and fractured selves and of the incoherence of personal communication might have been easier to convey if he were not saddled with the obligation to continually demonstrate his honesty and authenticity. This perhaps explains why his musical career feels not quite to have achieved all it could, even though he has been an influential artist who was fascinating to observe.

Since the Pistols re-formed, he has continued to play around with public expectations, threatening to take the Pistols to play a gig in Baghdad in the run-up to the invasion of Iraq and constantly challenging the way in which the press tend to typecast him. More recently, his career has taken some odd turns. His fascination with the medium of television was demonstrated by his involvement in the Rotten TV project, a loosely defined experimental program he worked on for the station VH1 in 1999–2000. Even so, it came as a surprise when he agreed to appear in the UK reality show "I'm a Celebrity, Get Me Out of Here!" a show that regularly requires its celebrities to participate in ludicrous games to win food and privileges. Seeing Lydon play a game in which he had to pick up plastic stars in an ostrich pen to win meals while the birds pecked at him unmercifully was one of the more surreal television moments of recent history. But it was his acerbic performance there and an unexpected communion with the Australian jungle that led to his next gig: presenting wildlife shows for the UK's Channel Five.

Incongruous as it may seem, Lydon appeared at his happiest and most unaffected in this role. Perhaps because the weight of his musical past was not an issue, he finally seemed able to focus his considerable personality on something beyond the solipsistic ideas of celebrity and self-expression. Playing with apes in the jungle or watching sharks from a metal cage under the ocean, John Lydon at last seemed free to actually be himself, without endlessly having to prove that he was being himself.

CHAPTER NINE

¿Y TÚ, QUÉ HAS HECHO?

The Re-creation of Cultural Authenticity

Havana, March 1996

[The 1999 movie *Buena Vista Social Club*] was a
German fairy tale in which the good wizard
flies in from California and rescues the humble
bootblack who was really the greatest singer in
the land and they all live happily ever after.

Music historian NED SUBLETTE,
author of *Cuba and Its Music*,
when interviewed for this book

RECORDED IN JUST SIX DAYS with a stellar cast of Cuban
musicians, the album *Buena Vista Social Club* was a musical
phenomenon. Awarded a Grammy in 1997, it has sold well

over five million copies to date and might be said to have reintroduced the world to Cuban *son*. But why was it Ry Cooder, a musician from remote Los Angeles, who achieved this breakthrough?

Cooder used to be best known as a hired studio musician who played atmospheric slide guitar with everyone from Captain Beefheart to Randy Newman. He also worked successfully in film soundtracks—for instance, his guitar underpinned the sweeping, somber atmosphere of *Paris, Texas*. His solo recording career was a mixed affair, although he made some memorable records in the 1970s. In albums such as *Chicken Skin Music* and *Paradise and Lunch* he roamed restlessly around different "roots" styles: blues (including several Leadbelly songs), gospel, early rock'n'roll, and folk music of America and of other cultures such as Hawaii, Africa, and the Caribbean. Cooder had a particular fascination with the songs of the pre–World War II era. But he seemed sometimes to struggle to find the right way to express himself, whichever style he played in. His unusual musical eclecticism made it hard for him to forge a distinct identity for himself as a performer. It was as though, living in Los Angeles, the world's final melting pot, he was never sure where he belonged. Or perhaps, like an actor, he just felt most comfortable speaking in a variety of voices.

He had little patience with the personal approach to music exemplified by singer-songwriters such as Joni Mitchell and James Taylor. He went out of his way to denigrate "this white, middle-class introspective stuff—people elevating their neuroses to mythic heights." His aims were quite different from those who sought personal authenticity in music.

Cooder frequently collaborated with other musicians,

including many from an older generation who performed in the styles that fascinated him. The jazz pianist Earl Hines, the Chicano accordionist Flaco Jiminez, the Malian singer and guitarist Ali Farka Toure—Cooder has worked with an extraordinary array of talented people in his career. His musicological enthusiasm for the styles he adopts reflects a genuine willingness to learn from the players he admires, a diffidence about his own personal importance, and a belief that he can make better music by playing with others. In spite of (or perhaps because of) his broad and skillful approach to music, Cooder found it hard to project himself into the limelight, and his records were less successful than they deserved to be. He also disliked the grind of publicity tours, and by the late eighties he had mostly withdrawn from solo work, concentrating on film music and working on other people's projects.

A collaborative plan led to the *Buena Vista* project. Cooder went to Cuba in 1996 to record with a group of musicians from Mali; when that fell through, he tried to find the oldest and best group of Cuban musicians around and form a "supergroup" to make an album. Local producer Juan de Marcos González helped him track down performers such as Rubén González, Ibrahim Ferrer, and Compay Segundo. The resulting sessions produced a hybrid of Cuban and American styles. Rather than simply capture these musicians playing the styles of music they had originally created, "authentic" Cuban *son*, *guajira,* and *bolero*, Cooder largely removed the *bongó* drums—the archetypal Cuban percussion instrument—from the standard lineup and replaced or overlaid them with his son Joachim on African drums. He then added his own slide guitar (a Hawaiian guitar method picked up by country and blues musicians in the 1930s), at times using volume control to produce a pseudo-violin sound. He recorded the percussion sounds off-mike and distant, deliberately replicating one of the worst flaws of the Cuban records of the 1940s. All of these sounds had a nostalgic air, reminiscent of a film soundtrack's idea of retro music. He had thus managed to create a facsimile of authenticity—a distant echo of the sound he had glimpsed at the Havana Film Institute in the tantalizing film reels of Cuban musicians of the 1940s and '50s.

In spite of everything, it was a beautiful record in its way. And because of that faded beauty, it was also one of the most successful examples of "faking it" in the past ten years—this knowingly inauthentic, hybrid music ended up being marketed as "the real thing." The huge success of the record is emphasized by the Web site *All Music Guide*'s opinion that "Cooder brought just the right amount of reverence to this material, and it shows in his production, playing and detailed liner notes. If you get one album of Cuban music, this should be the one."

Cooder's bowdlerization was driven partly by necessity. He wasn't reassembling an original band or trying to exactly re-create a musical scene. The aging musicians' natural styles came from various stages of the island's past, and Cuban music had long since moved on to new styles. He was thus gathering together a group of talented musicians who would not necessarily have played together in other contexts. He recalled that "Compay (Segundo) and Rubén González had never been in the same room, probably on the same block. Stylistically, this was pretty clearly defined. If you were Rubén González you were in cha-cha-cha bands with Enrique Jorrín, playing cha-cha-cha rhythms and chord progressions like he did. If you're Compay, you're doing the old song period, not cha-cha-cha music." So faced with a group of musicians who knew more about what they were doing than he did but who would not necessarily cohere, Cooder consciously reshaped elements of their approach. He tried to create a record that derived from their shared background but that would nonetheless be distinct from the original musical forms on which it drew.

He also faced the problem that it is all but impossible to replicate a big band style with limited resources. Even if he had had access to enough musicians and skilled orchestrations, the big band sound depends on a group of regular players who have played together long enough for their sound to become tight and coherent, something extremely hard to achieve in a few short weeks. So instead Cooder pictured the *Buena Vista Social Club* as an idealized version of the real (long-gone) Havana club—a kind of 1960s gathering of Cuban musicians jamming together in a looser style. This imaginary reference point led him to the final sound.

Modern Cuban music is available in many forms, but is not as popular outside Cuba as Cooder's rather dusty representation of a golden age. And it is important to remember that the golden age Cooder is trying to represent is not real—there was of course a great period for Cuban music in the 1940s and '50s but it was not the music that appears on the *Buena Vista* recordings.

Should we chastise Cooder for making an inauthentic record? From his point of view, it was a sincere attempt to preserve the remnants of a fading culture, even if those remnants had to first be adulterated to sell them to the world. He never claimed any more than this. And it is not entirely his fault that the record has come to be treated with such reverence in spite of its shortcomings as an authentic Cuban record. However, in this respect, it is entirely characteristic of the most successful world music of the last few decades. Rather than importing the music that Cubans were listening to at the time (most Cubans have never heard the record, and would probably not care for it if they did), Cooder attempted to re-create something that sounds (but isn't) more authentic, less "commodified."

ONE OF THE successes of the *Buena Vista* project was the rediscovery of the vocalist Ibrahim Ferrer. In the 1940s and '50s, Ferrer had performed in legendary Cuban bands such as the Orquesta de Chepín and those led by Pacho Alonso and Beny Moré. But he had a gentle voice that matched his laid-back demeanor and he was rarely credited on records. He lacked the star quality of a performer like Beny Moré (or even of the more obvious showmen in the *Buena Vista* setup such as Compay Segundo). As a result, the relatively introverted Ferrer drifted out of the spotlight as the big band era of Cuban music passed.

Ferrer was living on a pension and shining shoes for spare cash when he was tracked down for the *Buena Vista Social Club* project. At first he was reluctant to go back to singing but he came to be a central figure in the project, and Cooder returned to Havana in 1998 to record an album devoted to his singing, one of several follow-ups to the original record.

(Ironically, one of the best things Ferrer did was a collaboration with the British cartoon band Gorillaz on a song called "Latin Simone (Que pasa contigo)," which never tried to sound the least bit "authentic." "Latin Simone" was most likely heard by just as many people as *Buena Vista Social Club*, since the Gorillaz' debut album also sold five million copies.) Ferrer loved to sing *bolero*, but had often been denied the chance in the bands of the 1940's and 50's, when the preference was for a stronger voice. But in the quieter context of the *Buena Vista Social Club*'s impression of backyard spontaneity, his voice shone. Cooder said that it was "the last chance in the world to work with such a voice," a view that emphasizes Cooder's ethnographic (and slightly patronizing) approach.

Ibrahim Ferrer became a star around the world in the wake of the Buena Vista Social Club, and no one could wish otherwise or deny such a gentle man his time in the spotlight. He was unthreatening, charming, and mild. He represented a kind of musical innocence and apparent lack of self-consciousness that hit all the right buttons for those who look for cultural authenticity in music. He unintentionally projected an image of Cuba as a ramshackle idyll, island home to centuries-old traditions of music. In the *Buena Vista Social Club* film he spoke passionately of how strong the Cubans are, saying that "if we cared about possessions, we'd have disappeared years ago." But he spoke joyfully, celebrating Cuban life and survival, rather than with any sense of bitterness. Someone younger or feistier, someone who stressed the origins of Cuba's political state, might have been more off-putting for the target audience.

Ferrer's late acclaim is reminiscent of the way Mississippi John Hurt was perceived by the 1960s blues audience. Like Hurt, he was unsuccessful in his own time but lionized by a future generation. And like Hurt, Ferrer was to some degree

fortunate in that his attributes and mild manners were a perfect fit for the romantic aspirations of the audience that took
the *Buena Vista Social Club* to heart.

The world-music audience has shown traits similar to those
of the blues audience: both have at times emphasized gentler,
rural forms and both have been guilty at times of patronizing
or misunderstanding the music they sought out. And in the
case of Cuban music, Cooder was looking back to a golden
age while disregarding more modern developments, an
approach in which he might be compared to John Lomax and
blues fans who preferred a fictionalized past to the realities of
the modern day.

RY COODER is not the only one to find the problem of how
to interact with the music of other cultures a vexed one.
Western approaches to world music have always tended to
distort their source material: witness the exotica of the 1950s
or Peter Gabriel's addition of synthesizer washes to the world
music of the 1980s. Those who sought authenticity relied on
ethnographic recordings, which emphasized the sounds of
the most remote areas rather than the cities in which cross-
pollination had occurred.

This raises the problem of what present-day world music
really is. It is essentially a marketing term rather than a genuine category. There has been a lot of debate about whether
or not the term is a good one to use. Some have suggested
alternatives such as "roots music," although this doesn't really
address the problems inherent in the term. World music is
now broadly taken to mean the music of isolated, undevel-
oped cultures. Forms such as Finnish techno or Israeli pop

music do not really qualify because they originate from afflu-ent countries and because they are too sophisticated. Bulgarian choral singing qualifies because of its undoubted antiquity, while Bulgarian punk clearly doesn't. So "world music" as a label aims to group together music that is cultur-ally specific, that seems unadulterated over time, and that expresses the soul of relatively unadvanced cultures. Anything that smacks too much of professionalism or sophistication tends to disqualify a music from being described as "world."

Given this, what is it about Western musicians dabbling in world music that makes us uncomfortable? Paul Simon had to defend himself against accusations of exploitation after his work with South African musicians on *Graceland*, and similar criticisms have been made of David Byrne's post–Talking Heads solo work, Damon Albarn's post-Blur solo work, and others. But the criticism tends to be confused. Is the real problem that the Western musicians are gaining reflected glory from the third-world musicians with whom they per-form, or is it that they are not doing enough to help those musicians (or their countries)? If you benefit from a musical culture, it does seem fair to give something in return, although you could argue that any exposure to the Western music mar-ket creates an opportunity for local musicians to sell more records and is therefore helpful in itself. Also, any self-conscious attempt to help the local culture can look even more patronizing than simply collaborating with local musi-cians on as equal a basis as possible. It's probably a no-win sit-uation for any Western musicians who get involved in such collaborations—they can be damned for trying too hard and seeming worthy yet condescending or they can be damned for not trying hard enough.

Musicians such as Simon and Cooder are essentially tourists. They valorize the most non-Western aspects of the cultures they encounter simply because those aspects seem most exotic to them. We've encountered similar figures throughout this book, ranging from the Lomaxes to Harry Smith. These vaunted collaborations make many of us uncomfortable because they do exactly the same thing in musical terms as what so many Hollywood films do—they send in a white hero to rescue the disadvantaged dark-skinned native from suffering and oblivion, thus perpetuating the myth of the noble white imperialist. In these Hollywood tales, just as in these "collaborative" records, it's never the black native who initiates the successful project, it's always the white European or American who has to come riding in to save the day and make all the glory possible. It is absolutely impossible to imagine someone like Compay Segundo having asked Ry Cooder to play on one of his records, and it is equally impossible to imagine Mahlathini having asked Paul Simon to play on one of his.

However, there is a further line of attack that betrays odd assumptions. In a recent article in the *Independent*, the critic Michael Church criticized the BBC's world music policy for favoring a "degenerate tendency," featuring bands such as Tinariwen, whose masses of electric guitars borrow equally from Malian music and the blues, rather than more "authentic" groups. He suggests that if you "go to the mountains of Georgia . . . you'll find the same rugged harmonies that Tamerlane encountered six centuries earlier." Church seems to see any kind of musical hybridization as problematic, or even imperialist. He criticizes "music filched from other cultures, and filtered for consumption by the West." He goes on to complain about world music performers who play too loudly, using amplifiers in mainstream venues.

Church's fear is that the "real music" of these cultures is disappearing as artists around the world grow in confidence, seeking markets, audiences, and collaborations in other countries. He dislikes the fact that more and more world music artists are aiming to sell their music abroad, as though the only authentic way to make music is in amateur isolation. In this view, the real music of a culture is local, acoustic, uncommercial, and pure, whereas the degenerate form is hybrid, commercial, loud, and Westernized. This conservationist viewpoint tends to downgrade styles such as highlife, a loud, vigorous African music built around the needs of local dance floors. Like other strands of African music, highlife is influenced by a wide variety of other cultures, especially Cuban, rather than being an unadulterated form. Even small towns and isolated areas of Africa have had radios and recorded music for at least the last fifty years, and it is natural that the music of these areas incorporates external influences.

Again there is an echo here of the 1960s blues fans who often preferred acoustic, country musicians to those who had moved on to electrified, hybrid styles. And like an earlier generation of blues musicians, players such as Salif Keita have taken a more acoustic approach only in response to the demand for such "authentic" music from the West.

British composer Michael Nyman has described those who hold views such as Church's as the "world music police," which catches well the tendency to dictate from afar what is permissible for world musicians. And behind the political or moral criticisms of some Western collaborations with world musicians, one often catches a hint that the real problem is the whole idea of hybridization—that as soon as a Westerner plays with local musicians or as soon as those local musicians incorporate any Western styles or instruments into their music, the original music becomes tainted and debased.

There may in fact be other good reasons for criticizing musicians, such as Paul Simon, who utilize the music of other cultures. For instance, his attitude toward the political implications of his actions—he was working within the apartheid system—was discomfiting at times. Other musicians have been guilty of borrowing credibility from world music by adding ethnic instruments or mannerisms to their music, thus conveying an empty idea of integrity and purity.

In the case of Ry Cooder, it may be irrelevant to criticize the hybrid nature of the music he makes. The worrying aspect of the *Buena Vista Social Club* is not, in fact, that it is hybrid music but that Cooder's re-creations of ethnic styles have come to be seen as more real than the originals.

In general, disapproving of collaborations or hybridization per se, on the ground that Western influence is corrupting, seems misguided. And to insist that all world music should fit our preconceptions prevents us from listening with open ears. The conservationist approach to world music often distorts and ossifies the original culture it aims to preserve. It is also an echo of the earlier attitudes of musicologists such as John Lomax and Cecil Sharp. Both had very specific views on what kind of music they wanted to gather from the cultures they were observing. As Sharp cycled on English country lanes, or traveled through the Appalachians, he was searching for unadulterated folk material to back up his protofascist theories of a pan-European Aryan race.

The modern world-music movement is not openly imperialist or racist but it has a very clear idea of the kinds of simple local, sustainable cultures it is looking for. In this respect the world music police are more like condescending missionaries, or anthropologists of the nineteenth century, always willing to believe the best of the natives as long as they play along with our naïve ideas of their simple life.

The result of this attitude is that world music becomes a ghetto. The only way for a third-world musician to move beyond the local scene is to collaborate, or to travel and perform to foreign audiences, but both of these options are frowned on by those who prefer their world music to remain pure and isolated. This desire for cultural authenticity can easily become a kind of disdain, or paternal tolerance, for third-world musicians who aspire to improve their situations.

The world-music boom was built on the perception that the music of other cultures was innocent, that it had grown in isolation, that it was culturally authentic in a way that Western music could no longer be. But real world music has always been highly syncretic, combining traditional elements with the latest technologies and related sounds from across the world. And, particularly in today's climate of dictatorships and brutal wars, its messages have often been urgent and highly political. Our approach to world music has often diluted or banished the "edginess" of the music and clothed it in trappings of authenticity instead. In this way, world music can sometimes be more of an obstacle to than a conduit for genuine cultural communication.

With the increase in globalization, the musical cultures of the world have become increasingly interdependent. Ry Cooder mentioned being haunted by the idea that "somewhere on some little island in the Pacific, there's [a musician] who's great, but I'm probably never going to hear him." But as fast as new kinds of world music are "discovered" and marketed, they are absorbed into the mainstream via sampling, imitation, and advertising. The ever-widening search for pure musical cultures overlooks the fact that music is universal, and universally hybrid.

IN THE SAME WAY that we look to the early days of country and blues as golden ages, we have come to see world music as an uncorrupt fountain. Like folk, country, and blues, it has also become prime source material for renewing and energizing other popular musical styles. And, as with those earlier styles, certain aspects of world music have become signifiers of authenticity in themselves. Rural, simple, and acoustic sounds are generally regarded as more authentic than urban, complex, or electronic ones. This aesthetic influences the world music we hear in two ways. First, it affects the selection of existing music that is marketed to the West. And second, it affects the kind of music that is recorded, both by world musicians with access to the Western market and also in collaborations between Western and third-world musicians.

The record company Putumayo has been hugely successful in issuing well-annotated and beautifully packaged compilations of music from all over the world. These are marketed primarily through unusual trade channels such as the café market. The company also produces a widely syndicated radio show, the "Putumayo World Music Hour," which influences current attitudes toward world music. The Putumayo slogan is that they sell music "guaranteed to make you feel good."

Perhaps because of this aim, rather than fairly representing the music of the cultures they choose (as do the *Rough Guide* CDs) Putumayo celebrates acoustic and decidedly "mellow" sounds, using the same approach to world music as *MTV Unplugged* did with rock. For example, their *República Dominicana* CD almost completely avoids the most characteristic Dominican rhythm, merengue, in favor of *bachata* and *son*, in which the rhythms are derived from Cuban music. The emphasis here, on guitars over drums, partly reflects the market they are targeting, in which the CD is often used as background music in retail outlets—the owner Dan Storper based the label's sound on the music he chose for his earlier chain of clothes shops.

Putumayo describes itself as "the place where the traditional and contemporary meet," which at least recognizes that this is a very specific take on tradition. Its compilations emphasize the generic aspects of a culture rather than individual artists. This allows the label to dip into a wide variety of cultures without committing to long-term deals with any of the artists. But it also means that the compilations are selected in a way that reduces the culture of regions of the world to simple formulas, excluding anything that would be too challenging or idiosyncratic for their market.

With *Buena Vista Social Club*, the success of Putumayo, and dozens of other projects, world-music marketers have hit on the perfect combination: make it sound familiar (i.e., emphasize acoustic guitars rather than African drums) yet overlay it with a patina of authenticity (i.e., focus on older or more rural musicians; add elements of other "roots" music; avoid synthesizers, drum machines, and samplers). Putumayo emphasizes these signifiers of authenticity in the music it chooses to distribute. But in other cases these signifiers have become the guiding principles behind the creation and production of music. And record companies that work in the area of world music have passed the demand for such signifiers back to the artists with whom they work, meaning that the signifiers are absorbed into their original creations.

Even long-established African musicians Baaba Maal and Salif Keita have been persuaded to record "unplugged" records in the last few years. For instance, Keita says of his album *Moffou* that "Universal wanted me to make an acoustic record, and I wanted that too." These recordings minimize the innovations that Maal and Keita have brought to West African music. That's not to say that they aren't good records. On the contrary, at least in the case of Baaba Maal (*Missing You*), the album has reinvigorated not only his career but his music. His work has always been marked by a variety of fusions, but the collaborations with Western sounds he had explored in albums such as *Nomad Soul* seemed to be increasingly diluting his originality. His return to the complexities of traditional Malian instruments and ensembles has had a positive effect. But the pressure that leads to such acoustic records also filters out other work and artists whose music is more hybrid, allowing through only those that fit the required mold.

THE SAME AESTHETIC of authenticity was influential in the creation of *Buena Vista Social Club*. Ry Cooder personified the Western attitude to world music in this affectionate, confused record that misrepresents "real" Cuban music at the same time as it demonstrates his fascination with it. He was aware of the pitfalls of recording with the local musicians, worrying that they would think, "Here come the carpetbaggers, let's just give them what they want and send them on their way"; but he went on to eulogize the Cubans—"They're a bunch of open-hearted people. . . . They share whatever they have. They don't drive on freeways, they don't talk on cellular phones, or go rent videos. They have nothing else that occupies their entire being. . . . And they love the music, and of course with total respect."

But the Cubans live in isolated poverty with a crumbling infrastructure for political reasons, not because they want to. Cooder's wistful preoccupation with this materially impoverished yet musically rich culture is reminiscent of John Lomax's appreciation of Leadbelly. Like the *Buena Vista Social Club* film he helped Wim Wenders to make, Cooder's words steer nervously around the question of why the Cubans live the way they do. The film avoids mentioning the international treatment of Cuba as pariah or tourist destination—a child condescended to and disciplined. Scenes of poverty and degradation are used merely as picturesque backdrops to interviews with the musicians. No matter how lovely the music may be, *Buena Vista Social Club* partakes fully of Cooder's naïve and occasionally patronizing attitude toward Cuban culture.

Of course, musical collaborations between rich and poor cultures look different depending on whose point of view you take. A Western musician like Cooder adding elements of his own style to Cuban music will inevitably be criticized for opportunism, whereas the local musicians who play with him can be depicted as innocents being exploited or as collaborators allowing their music to be exploited. But is this fair? Would the same be said of, for instance, an African musician incorporating Middle Eastern sounds into his music?

The film *Buena Vista Social Club* centers on a 1998 performance at Carnegie Hall. Ry and Joaquin Cooder's faces were the most serious on the stage, as they concentrated on their supporting roles in the band. Meanwhile the Cubans' faces showed exactly how much fun they were having. The sheer verve of eighty-year-old Rubén González's piano playing was astonishing, and there were extraordinary performances all around.

Old men often like to have fun. Looking back they sometimes like to simplify and parody their past, partly to remember what was best about it and partly to tease the younger generation. This was a generation of Cuban musicians who were proud of their pasts but who hadn't expected this last chance to enjoy the limelight, and they took their chance with glee. If they conspired with Cooder in misrepresenting the music of their past, they did it with relish and gusto, knowing that by doing so they had a chance to play the songs they loved. They appreciated the opportunity they had been given, but perhaps they sometimes also amused themselves a little at the expense of Cooder and the Americans. The film concludes with the old men (and woman in the case of Omara Portuondo) unfurling the lone-star Cuban flag on the stage at the end of their triumphant performance. One can't help but feel that they got the last laugh.

With *Buena Vista Social Club*, Cooder managed to entertain, and perhaps to inspire us to discover more Cuban music, while making use of that music for his own purposes. As a musician, he took great pleasure in playing with others. By recording at Egrem Studios in Havana, by playing himself with these musicians, by including his son, he was able to feel momentarily that he was part of this scene. He was only a tourist, but for a few days he could feel that he belonged. Curiously, it is, in the end, a record that tells us as much about the man who made it as it does about the culture it aims to represent.

It is to Cooder's credit that he seems to have partially realized this fact, recently saying that "this is the thing about music, as far as I can tell. You can go places, you can be somebody—all you have to do is just play and conjure up the sounds, and you're there. Of course, you're not *quite* there. That's the funny part. I found that out later. It didn't quite work. It was never enough. It was always over, or too far away, or I wasn't *that*, and it was kind of a sad thing to have to finally acknowledge."

Cooder was raised in Santa Monica, a city near Los Angeles, in an area he has described as "so flat and so dull." As a young man he was fascinated by the more exotic areas of L.A., like the remnants of downtown and older neighborhoods such as Bunker Hill and Angel's Flight. After the *Buena Vista* period, he returned to the subject of his hometown with *Chavez Ravine*. This 2005 album tells a stylized version of the story of the eponymous, largely Mexican neighborhood that was demolished in the 1950s to make way for the Dodgers' stadium.

Chavez Ravine basically follows the *Buena Vista* formula. Cooder, fascinated by the Mexican-American music of the 1950s, enlisted a cast of older local musicians, including both the pachuco boogie star Don Tosti and Lalo Guerrero, the "father of Chicano music." Once again Cooder created a simulation of music from a time and place that had long since disappeared, and once again he watered down the original music at the same time that he was popularizing it.

However, there is a hint of something more going on in this record. In a recent interview, journalist Derk Richardson refers to Cooder's frustration of never feeling that he belonged to the cultures he loved and describes *Chavez Ravine* as serving a dual compulsion: "to bring to light a social injustice that he took personally and to find a kind of cultural ground for himself." It seems that Cooder was trying to face the fact that part of his quest for the authenticity of other cultures had arisen from a sense of emptiness or confusion about his own background. The bland surfaces of modern Los Angeles conceal depths of fascinating hybrid cultures and the remnants of political machinations of decades past. Growing up there, Cooder was aware of the richness of the culture that had disappeared in the destruction of areas such as Chavez Ravine and Bunker Hill. At the same time he saw the homogeneity that had often been imposed in their wake.

In the end, perhaps Cooder is still just trying to find out where he belongs. If he is looking for roots in *Chavez Ravine*, at least he is looking in the right place—his own backyard. He has gone around the world without being entirely satisfied by what he found. Now he has come home to continue the search. However, he has once again idealized the past by failing to recognize that things weren't always so good in the good old days; and he has once again preferred to present a numbed version of that past instead of finally making contact with the reality of the present.

It may be that the quest for cultural authenticity in popular music is always a search for something that seems more profound than the reality of our own lives. In the exotic, the nostalgic, the foreign, or the primitive, we can hope to perceive eternal truths that seem lacking in the confusion of modern life. But hunting for authenticity in other cultures or past times is unlikely to cure a perceived lack of authenticity at home. Because wherever you go, you take your own self with you.

PLAY

Moby, the KLF,
and the Ongoing Quest
for Authenticity

New York, 1998

. . . rockroll as a system of thought. *A*
system!—the ultimate system—the one that eats
its own guts out.

RICHARD MELTZER, *A Whore Just Like the Rest*

I have nothing in common with myself.

FRANZ KAFKA, *Diary*

AS A YOUNG MUSICIAN, Richard Melville Hall played in
punk, reggae, new-wave, speedmetal, and industrial bands,
then became a hip-hop DJ. As Moby, he finally found success
as a techno artist with strong alternative rock tendencies. But

nothing could have prepared him for the worldwide success he found with his 1999 album *Play*. Essentially a pop dance record, it has snatches of punk rock, trip-hop, and even baroque piano fugues. But the most notable aspect of the album, and the one that helped it to achieve its great success, was its use of samples taken from the field recordings of John and Alan Lomax.

Moby weaved old cappella and voice-and-percussion samples into accessible pop grooves. As a result his songs gained a cachet of authenticity entirely borrowed from their source material. Before this, most techno artists who had sampled primitive recordings did so with a dose of irony, but here the music was presented straight. The strong emotions evoked by the original recordings partially survived translation into a new environment—thus the songs have an impact that far exceeds what we would normally expect from the clinical production and straightforward songwriting evidenced elsewhere in the album.

Moby represents the marriage of dance music to both punk and puritan ideals. The DIY sampling and production that had been so liberating in recent dance music became a moral imperative for Moby, just as it had for the punks. In interviews, Moby continually stressed both his vegan and Christian puritanism and his DIY credentials (the album was recorded entirely at Moby's New York home over a period of eighteen months; it consists of eighteen songs culled from over two hundred).

When *Play* was released it went to Number One in many countries, sold ten million copies and three million singles, and propelled Moby to the position of the world's best-selling dance musician. In turn, the tracks were sold as commercials for a wide range of luxury goods. Producers of commercials recognized that while the music was modern and unobtrusive, it had an emotional effect on the listener, which made it ideal for underpinning the selling moment.

Amusingly, Moby has defended his music's ubiquity in advertisements on the basis that it is a kind of guerrilla marketing, compensating for his underdog status: "The music I make doesn't get played on the radio, especially in the United States. If you've spent a year and a half working on a record and you've poured your sweat and your blood into it and you're really proud of it, you want people to hear it." There's nothing wrong with making music that is successful in a commercial context, but this justification reveals a degree of dissonance between his success and his purist ideals: prior to his first commercial license of a song in 1995, he had said, "I had been really opposed to the idea of letting my music be used in advertisements. I had been a punk rocker growing up, and I always avoided things that sort of reeked of selling out or compromise."

Moby also demonstrates a degree of doublethink about the way that he used the field recordings to add authenticity to his music, recognizing that some critics have made the negative comparison between his approach and Paul Simon's in *Graceland*. As ever, there is a touch of the patronizing missionary coming to rescue the humble natives in such collaborations even when, as with Moby, the collaboration is with artists from long ago. He disarmed one interviewer's questions on the subject by replying that "Maybe what I have done is wrong. And if someone can make a compelling argument as to why what I've done is wrong, I hope I am open-minded enough to listen to it. The only thing I would say in my defense is that I was quite genuine and naive in my approach and I am not being so presumptuous to lay claim to any aspect of the African American experience."

When Norman Cook (aka Fatboy Slim) married an affecting a cappella vocal to modern dance music on his track "Praise You," he was less tactful and made the mistake of giving an interview in which he claimed that he was taking old or forgotten songs and improving them. Camille Yarborough, whose soul/gospel song provided the main sample for "Praise You," was very much alive and hit back at Cook's slur, pointing out how heavily his song depended on her original creation. And comparing the two tracks, the Fatboy Slim one does seem like little more than larceny. Moby has the advantage of using the voices of a distant age. There is no one left to speak out for the original singers. But neither this fact, nor the fact that Moby understands the possible criticism, means that his use of these samples is not problematic.

Moby's success came about because he clothed dance music—which had been since the advent of disco the most transparently and gleefully "inauthentic" of musical genres— in the trappings of authenticity. He used a ragbag of the hallmarks of authenticity: old black roots music, slide and acoustic guitars, vegetarian diatribes in the liner notes, navel-gazing lyrics (as on "If Things Were Perfect" and "The Sky Is Broken"), even his emphasis on autobiography on his Web site, which includes a personal journal. But at the same time, he successfully diminished the unbridled passion that made blues and gospel seem so exotic for most of the twentieth century, and thus made the music more palatable. With *Play*, Moby managed to homogenize almost every significant "authentic" musical genre—blues, gospel, punk, hip-hop, even folk—into a melange perfect for mass consumption. No wonder the advertising executives loved him.

Play, like *Buena Vista Social Club* (not to mention the TV show *American Idol*), demonstrates the degree of homogenization of music in recent years. They all recycle music of the past into a bland product for the widest possible audience. And this tendency is ubiquitous. Even such an outrageous and once offensive punk anthem as the Ramones' "Blitzkrieg Bop" is now used in a TV commercial—just another sound to be sampled. One can't help but wonder whether the Sex Pistols' graphic abortion diatribe "Bodies" is next.

But unlike *American Idol*, both *Play* and *Buena Vista Social Club* derived their success from the quest for authenticity, because today, despite the many changes in the music business and recording processes, and despite all the apparent toleration of perceived inauthenticity that *American Idol* epitomizes, this quest still has enormous power.

WHEN WATCHING a show such as *American Idol* (or, in the UK, *Pop Idol*), we can feel as though authenticity doesn't matter any more. Reality television and pop music have melded together in a seamless blend of light entertainment. Like VH-1's *Behind the Music*, the show reveals and glorifies the manufacturing of music. The pop music business has momentarily succeeded in turning its darker arts into a central achievement to be celebrated as the creation of successful pop acts and records is seen as an end in itself. Celebrity is the ideal, and the struggle to attain success is treated as more important than the actual music.

But even *American Idol* is haunted by questions of authenticity: the constant cutting between the performances and the backstage "private" moments emphasizes the idea of the performance expressing the artist's true self in a way that *American Idol*'s many predecessors (going all the way back to *Arthur Godfrey's Talent Show* in the 1940s) wouldn't have. Nor would those earlier shows have had the judges urging the performers to be themselves, to show us their real selves.

A century ago, not many people were concerned with how authentic a piece of music was; now the concern seems, at times, overwhelming. Issues of authenticity have crept into every kind of music we listen to: they've been ubiquitous in country, rock, and hip-hop for decades, but with Moby they infiltrated dance music, and now pop singers such as Ashlee Simpson have to justify themselves with album titles like *Autobiography* and *I Am Me*.

Even at its most superficial, contemporary pop music embraces the idea of confession and therapy through music. Simpson, a lightweight pop star and reality TV graduate, was widely derided for a lip-synching debacle on *Saturday Night Live*. So on her second album, she recorded "Beautifully Broken," a fairly weak riposte to her critics. Of course, much of the controversy recalls the hypocrisy of previous attacks on the Monkees and the Backstreet Boys. Critics who are perfectly aware of all the reasons why Simpson was likely lip-synching reacted in mock-outrage and schadenfreude at her televized humiliation. In response, the songs recorded by Simpson show increasing self-absorption and a dependence on personal detail for their effect. And Simpson is far from alone in trying to reveal her life to the world, no matter how uninspiring it may be. While Avril Lavigne's first album of teen grunge lite was a success largely because of the quality of the songwriting—songs like "Complicated" and "Sk8er Boi" were supplied by the Matrix songwriting team—she was stung by criticisms that she was a manufactured star and insisted on co-writing the songs for her second album to prove that she was for real. Inevitably the result was a weaker album, with self-referential songs that continued Lavigne's angsty pose, but with less pop glitter and focus. Meanwhile the UK's pretend teen punksters Busted joined the long list of chart bands that have proclaimed their creative contribution to their (co-written) songs in an attempt to counter accusations that they were fake.

These are all minor examples, but they demonstrate the way that even the most transparently manufactured pop musicians look for fig leaves of authenticity. And this leads to a larger question: can pop music even exist without the idea of authenticity anymore? It seems to have played such a central role in the story of rock and pop that it's hard to imagine music without it.

ONE EXAMPLE of how peculiarly difficult it can be to escape from the effects of this quest for authenticity is the career of the KLF.

A hugely successful band in the early 1990s (they sold more singles worldwide than any other act in 1991), the KLF publicly quit the music business while they were still at the peak of their success and went on to demonstrate their contempt for the whole charade in the most extreme way they could imagine. They announced their departure with a derisive performance at the 1992 Brit Awards (the main British music business ceremony). A freshly slaughtered sheep (plus eight gallons of blood) was laid at the entrance to the post-awards party. Bill Drummond, the former A&R man and manager who cofounded the band with Jimmy Cauty, later claimed that his original plan had been to cut off his own hand and throw it into the audience while performing. Two years later, in July 1994, on a remote Scottish Island, the two band members deliberately set fire to one million pounds in cash (supposedly the largest cash withdrawal in UK history), filming the event for posterity. It was most of the money they had made from their music. What inspired this spectacular run of self-destruction?

In the early 1990s, the KLF had used samples from a bizarre variety of sources to create a series of clever but absurd hit records that contemptuously recycled the same themes and tunes with only minor variations. They were one of the most anarchic, perverse bands of the time. Perhaps only the experimental American group the Residents have matched their disdain for celebrity and personality within music. KLF's initial singles coincided with the explosion of sampling in pop, and they were gleefully unrestrained in their use of the new technology. Borrowing or stealing from any genre, artist, or sound that took their fancy, they created sardonic, absurd pieces of dance music that were nonetheless catchy and funny. After their first hit they released a book called *How to Have a Number One the Easy Way*, and it seemed that in their world-weary cynicism they had indeed found the formula for success.

They regularly changed names, flouting the idea of celebrity, and their music became more and more bizarre before they quit the business altogether. They married the theme from the TV show *Doctor Who* to a sample from seventies glam rocker Gary Glitter to create "Doctorin' the Tardis," a dadaist house tune fronted by two police cars. They resampled their own songs to create new variations, persistently reusing themes such as "What Time Is Love" and the "Mu Mu" chant of their absurdist alter egos, the Justified Ancients of Mu Mu. They even managed to persuade Tammy Wynette to sing on their hit "Justified and Ancient" ("They're justified and ancient, and they drive an ice cream van"). It's hard to imagine a band that so completely skewered the absurdity of pop music while simultaneously creating gloriously funny hits that actually seemed to be a part of the mainstream dance scene that they were parodying.

They didn't turn anticorporatism into a badge of honor, but their whole career displayed a radical disdain for the values that sustain music as a business. They also retained a large degree of control of their own music, at least in the UK, eventually deleting their entire back catalogue there and burning most of its profit. Why did they do it? Because they could. Having briefly embodied the forces that threatened the music business, the KLF departed, leaving behind a music scene in flux.

The great sci-fi writer Philip K. Dick once pondered what would happen if someone sneaked into Disneyland and replaced the fake animals with real ones. How would people react to the "fake fakes"? This is not a widespread problem in popular music, but U2 is one example that comes to mind: from *Zooropa* onward they strived to project a showbiz fakery that was far removed from their true earnestness in a self-conscious attempt to get away from their po'-faced image.

The KLF was a different kind of "fake fake." When they were at their peak, one always had the sneaking suspicion that behind the glitz, the sloganeering, the sheer absurdity of their image, there was something real going on, even if it wasn't always clear exactly what it was.

Bill Drummond spoke recently of the triumph he felt when, after a typically absurd and self-defeating comeback performance, he met a journalist who had once been his number-one fan and who had even written a book about the band. After the performance, the journalist stayed with them as they daubed the walls of London's National Theatre with one of their typical slogans ("1997: What the fuck's going on?"). Shaking hands at the end of the evening, Drummond realized that during the evening he had managed to disappoint even this great admirer. Looking into the fan's eyes, he caught a glint of "disillusionment, as real and pure as disillusionment can get." In his book *45*, he goes on to say that "that moment of disillusionment was maybe our greatest creation. Without that final state of disillusion, the power and glory of pop is nothing."

There is a kind of anger that musicians can feel toward their audience when they sense that the audience is either trapping them or perceiving only a cartoon version of what they want to project. Think of Kurt Cobain, at a huge Brazilian gig, refusing to play "Smells Like Teen Spirit," the hit that every audience demanded of him, and instead performing a cover of Queen's "We Will Rock You," with the words amended to "We Will Fuck You." Think of Sid Vicious walking those showbiz boards in *The Great Rock and Roll Swindle*, singing "My Way" in his Sinatra suit, then firing a gun indiscriminately on the audience—an act reprised by KLF, who fired blanks on the audience from an automatic rifle at the 1992 Brit Awards.

Disillusionment is the realization that something that seemed real is not. There is a paradox here: the KLF's number-one fan had looked up to Bill Drummond as a hero, as a prankster genius, as the scourge of the music business, and as a political idol. But when Drummond finally managed to disillusion him, the number-one fan belatedly realized that Drummond was none of these things.

He was only a real person after all.

THE KLF DID everything in their power to deconstruct conventional notions of celebrity, success, fan worship, and even authenticity itself, forcing their followers to confront their most cherished assumptions about the rules of popular music. Their self-destructive and perverse behavior and their spectacular sabotage of their own success seemed to be part of a master plan. On the other hand it may simply have been the gut reactions of two performers who stumbled into success at the exact moment when they despised the music business too much to behave any other way. In the end they took solace in their own demise. By setting themselves up as anti-establishment heroes and then failing to live up to their own hype, they had obliged their fans to realize that, by extension, all performers are only playing a part, "faking it." For the KLF, it seemed that only by disillusioning one's fans could one be truly real.

But somehow we refuse to be disillusioned. The quest for authenticity has always been our quest as listeners just as much as it has been that of musicians. It has informed and shaped our tastes, and it has placed requirements upon the performers we follow. And it seems unlikely that it will ever go away.

Our own tastes have changed from when we (the authors of this book) were younger. Large parts of our record collections we listen to only rarely, whereas other genres and artists that we might once have disdained have become staples of our everyday listening. And then there are other artists we loved when we were younger that we still love to hear, even if our perceptions of them have changed.

One of the axes along which our respective views on music have changed is authenticity. When we were younger, both of us mostly accepted the quest for authenticity in music as a fundamental way of judging artists. Honesty, self-expression, and cultural integrity were essential parts of our basic critical tools. In preferring Hank Williams to the Carpenters, the Velvet Underground to the Archies, or Nirvana to KISS, we were making judgments based on an idea of which artists were more real, less fake.

Over time, as our tastes changed, we found this distinction breaking down and becoming increasingly meaningless. Hugh rarely sits at home and listens to the Archies (well, maybe sometimes . . .), but he does listen to the Carpenters and ABBA; Yuval still listens to Neil Young, but often prefers Elvis and disco singles. Both of us realized that, no matter how gritty and real they are, we don't really enjoy listening to Hank Williams or Robert Johnson anymore, although Hugh still loves Johnny Cash and Yuval still loves Bob Dylan. These are personal prejudices, and everyone will have personal examples. But the key point is that over time the importance of authenticity to our judgments has to some degree faded.

Not that we always prefer inauthenticity to authenticity, it's just that we both see far more complications in making these judgments at all.

A late Johnny Cash recording happens to provide a good example of how complex it can be to judge authenticity. On *American Recordings*, Cash took a stripped-down acoustic approach that derived from the *MTV Unplugged* aesthetic of authenticity. With producer Rick Rubin he chose a range of songs that worked well to showcase his legendary voice in an emotional, mature setting. It was a very self-conscious attempt to create an "authentic" sound to match the audience's expectations of the elder statesman's status. Years of music being judged on the grounds of authenticity have taught producers how to use basic production tricks to accentuate authenticity—by using traditional-sounding effects and acoustic sounds, and by allowing rough edges to show. *American Recordings* used many of the same production values as *Buena Vista Social Club*. And it worked: the records in the series rejuvenated Cash's career. They carry a strong emotional charge, even though it is clear at times that one's emotions are being exploited by the choice of songs and arrangements. Interestingly, the records were all but disregarded by the country establishment; they were instead admired by a new generation of rock fans.

In "The Mercy Seat," Cash took on a Nick Cave song about incarceration and execution. The song vividly describes the dying moments of a convicted murderer who spends the song proclaiming his innocence, only to reveal the guilty truth in his final moment. Cave blatantly uses blues and country music as signifiers of emotion and authenticity. But his original of "The Mercy Seat" is a histrionic production that does little to disguise its bogus credentials. The song is, after all, by an Australian songwriter who specializes in facsimiles of Southern American music and accents, pretending to be a criminal with lunatic tendencies. It is comic in a very dark way, but it's not really convincing.

In Cash's hands, something strange happens to the song. Cash is much older than Cave and is known for his miserable childhood in the Southern cotton fields. In spite of his carefully cultivated outlaw image, he never served a jail sentence, although he had a few overnight stays in the cells in his youth. But he was known for "Folsom Prison Blues" and for his electrifying San Quentin performance that helped to cement his reputation. Cash was also religious, something else that stayed with him from his childhood, especially after the horrific death of his brother in an accident.

When Cash sings "The Mercy Seat," there are no histrionics. The biblical references, the reluctant recognition of death approaching, and the song's bitter details of prison life all suddenly ring true. The song is convincing in a way that Cave's version could never be.

Is it authentic? Of course not. It's not an honest personal account, and it's a secondhand rendition of a distant cultural facsimile. But our knowledge of Cash and his performance of the song give it an emotional charge that rides through the inauthenticity, creating an affecting drama, even if it is not an authentic document.

When one hears this song, judgments of "real" and "fake" become all but meaningless. Because realness has so often been seen as a morally superior quality in music, it feels uncomfortable, like a kind of apostasy, to point out the inauthenticity in a song like this. It is probably possible to really appreciate the song only if one lays aside all notions of authenticity and hears it as a performance, pure and simple.

BUT ONE CAN'T always put authenticity to one side. Tastes formed on a base of authenticity change only slowly, and many old prejudices survive. Most rock fans still crave authenticity, and many have become increasingly extreme in their quests. Some, disillusioned with the degree of fakery even in the most seemingly authentic performers (e.g., Kurt Cobain), have turned instead to idolizing those who couldn't fake it even if they tried—so-called outsider musicians.

Outsider musicians are by definition authentic: these hopeless aspirants to pop music fame have talents that are foreign to all conventional definitions of "good music," and their creations are sincere and occasionally inspired. These are artists with no conventional training in music—and often with no talent for it either—who buck the odds and make music despite their handicaps, which range from mental instability to tone-deafness to obsessions with creatures from other worlds. The results can be wildly entertaining by any standard, and their sweetness and naïveté can be hard to resist.

Daniel Johnston is one example of a performer who has gained a cult following based on his outsider status. Revered by Kurt Cobain among others, his background of mental instability gives his music a fractured feeling. The lo-fi, homemade productions for which he was first known seem absolutely direct and unrefined. As a result, his music seems to carry a charge of honesty and openness that fans of indie music were finding increasingly hard to perceive in more cultured performers. Johnston's high status in indie rock circles says much about that community's thirst for authenticity.

The search for authenticity in the rural performers recorded in the late 1920s, or in modern-day world music, has often been a search for the last musicians untouched by self-consciousness. And the adherents of outsider music, like the folk fans, are not immune to taking a patronizing attitude toward their largely primitive protégés. Yet these "talentless weirdos" may not be irrelevant: it could easily be argued that Thelonious Monk, Ornette Coleman, Captain Beefheart, and Syd Barrett of Pink Floyd were all outsider musicians to some degree. It may seem unlikely, but from where else but "outside" can true musical innovation come? Unfortunately, few of the outsiders praised by their fans can be called innovators; most of them are simply naïve. Outsider music is a fascinating alternative, but by definition it's unlikely to ever truly enter the mainstream. It does, however, illuminate to what lengths today's music fans will go in search of authenticity.

AS WE'VE NOTED, there are two sides to the problem of authenticity in music: how ideas about authenticity affect the listener, and how they affect the performers themselves. The two can't be completely disentangled, because part of most artists' motivation is based on the perceptions and approval of the audience. But one can at least consider the two sides of the issue separately.

In this book, we have considered the various snares that awaited artists as different as John Lydon and Donna Summer, John Lennon and Jimmie Rodgers. We could go on to write similar chapters about such artists as P J Harvey, Merle Haggard, and U2, all of whom have reacted to the quest for authenticity in unique ways. And a whole book could be written about authenticity in hip-hop, which has been based largely on a semi-autobiographical approach, harnessing the anger and energy of punk without going to its ideological extremes, yet complicating the question with its glorifications of violence and luxury.

But we have mostly avoided discussing the quest as it applies to us listeners; without some kind of sociological survey, it's hard to tell whether most of us tend to prize authenticity or whether it's simply those of us who grew up in specific times and places.

So for those of us who do still prize authenticity to one degree or another, is it possible to put authenticity to one side for a while? To refuse to accept that "authentic" is always morally better than "inauthentic"? If you get up, turn on the radio, and listen to some music you haven't liked before because it struck you as "fake," how do you feel now? Liberated? Bored? Scared? Maybe even entertained? Is it possible to just listen and react to it without worrying about why you do so? And if you are enjoying music that you would normally regard as fake, do you feel ashamed?

When we're young, a large part of our original motivation in discovering music comes from trying to find out about our identity—perhaps to fit in, or, in contrast, to differentiate ourselves from the rest. The musical morality we adopt at an early age often becomes enshrined, making it hard to change our views later on. From this comes the notion of "guilty pleasures"—any music that we regard as inauthentic but still enjoy becomes a shameful secret, rather than something we can honestly admit to liking. But labeling music in this way allows us to retain the simple identification of music as real and good or fake and bad (but occasionally secretly enjoyable), and thereby prevents us from analyzing more deeply the reasons why we like this music.

We're not trying to say that it's always wrong to like music on the basis of how authentic it seems. Often in talking about authenticity we are also talking about other attributes that can be important to us. Music can be great to listen to exactly because it is heartfelt, emotional, honest, personally or culturally revealing, and so on. It's just that when we aggregate all these into an ideal of authenticity we can lose sight of the fact that some of the things that make us judge music as inauthentic—such as theatricality, glamour, absurdity, pointlessness, and cultural cross-pollination—can also enrich our musical experience considerably.

WHICH BRINGS US back to Moby. One of the best songs on *Play* is "Run On," which essentially takes a track by the Landfordaires, a gospel group, and adds some drums, piano, turntable scratching, and a rather surprising slide guitar. Moby almost spoils the song when he adds synthesized strings at the end, but it's still far more fun than most of *Play*. There's nothing overly sanctimonious about this cut—it's truly *play*ful, and rather than homogenizing or deadening what it samples, it simply supplements it in an amusing way.

But it's a song about keeping it real: "Better tell that lonesome liar," Bill Landford sings, "tell them God Almighty gonna cut you down." It's about avoiding sin and God's retribution. Despite how much fun the song imparts, the singer is being dead serious, and so is Moby. This is a song about death and salvation, subjects that can't be more important. And in the middle of it, Moby interjects another gospel moment: a woman's voice singing "What is the real thing?"

All this is to say that perhaps there's yet a third way to listen to music. It's not only a choice between valuing authenticity or not. So many artists nowadays, from Moby to P J Harvey to the KLF, are consciously playing with ideas of authenticity. Why shouldn't we, as listeners, do the same? A good part of the pleasure we get from a song like "Run On"—or Johnny Cash's "The Mercy Seat," or that prototypical outsider music album the Shaggs' *Philosophy of the World*, or the next semiconfessional celebrity pop hit or gangsta rap single—is in figuring out what's authentic and what's not authentic about it. It's a new game we can play with the music we listen to. All it requires is that we keep our ears—and our minds—as open as we can.

SOURCES

Chapter 1: WHERE DID YOU SLEEP LAST NIGHT?

Azerrad, Michael. *Come as You Are: The Story of Nirvana*. New York: Main Street Books, 1993.

Cantwell, Robert. *When We Were Good: The Folk Revival*. Cambridge, MA: Harvard University Press, 1996.

Cobain, Kurt. *Journals*. New York: Riverhead Books, 2002.

Cross, Charles R. *Heavier than Heaven: A Biography of Kurt Cobain*. London: Hodder & Stoughton, 2001.

Filene, Benjamin. *Romancing the Folk: Public Memory and American Roots Music*. Chapel Hill: University of North Carolina Press, 2000.

Lindsay, Vachel. *The Congo and Other Poems*. New York: Macmillan, 1914.

Lomax, John A. *Adventures of a Ballad Hunter*. New York: Macmillan, 1947.

Lomax, John A., and Alan Lomax, eds. *Negro Folk Songs as Sung by Lead Belly*. New York: Macmillan, 1936.

Porterfield, Nolan. *Last Cavalier: The Life and Times of John A. Lomax, 1867–1948*. Urbana: University of Illinois Press, 1996.

Weisbard, Eric. "A Simple Song That Lives Beyond Time." *New York Times*, November 13, 1994, B36.

Wolfe, Charles, and Kip Lornell. *The Life and Legend of Leadbelly.* New York: HarperCollins, 1992.

Chapter 2: NOBODY'S DIRTY BUSINESS

Alger, Dean. Unpublished proposal for "Mr. Blues Walks In: The Legendary Lonnie Johnson, the Music of African Americans, and the Quest for Equality." 2005.

Brown, David. "From Avalon to Eternity." Liner notes to Mississippi John Hurt, *Worried Blues 1963.* Rounder, 1991.

Calt, Stephen. *I'd Rather Be the Devil: Skip James and the Blues.* New York: Da Capo Press, 1994.

————. Liner notes to Mississippi John Hurt, *The 1928 Sessions.* Yazoo, 1988.

————. Personal correspondence, 2005.

Cantwell, Robert. *Bluegrass Breakdown: The Making of the Old Southern Sound.* Urbana: University of Illinois Press, 1984.

————. *When We Were Good: The Folk Revival.* Cambridge: Harvard University Press, 1996.

Charters, Samuel. "Working on the Building: Roots and Influences." In *Nothing But the Blues: The Music and the Musicians,* edited by Lawrence Cohn. New York: Abbeville Press, 1993, 13–32.

Cohen, Andy. Correspondence to the Pre-War Blues Yahoo Group, 2005.

Cohen, John. Notes to *Harry Smith's Anthology of American Folk Music, Volume Four.* Austin, TX: Revenant, 2000.

Cohen, Ronald. *Rainbow Quest: The Folk Music Revival and American Society, 1940–1970.* Amherst: University of Massachusetts Press, 2002.

Cohn, Lawrence. "Mississippi John Hurt: The Dramatic Rediscovery of a Near-Legendary Blues Singer-Guitarist." *Down Beat,* July 16, 1965. Reprinted in the CD booklet for Mississippi John Hurt, *Avalon Blues: The Complete 1928 OKeh Recordings.* New York: Sony Music, 1996.

David, John Russell. *Tragedy in Ragtime: Black Folktales from St. Louis.* Dissertation, Saint Louis University, 1976.

Davis, Francis. *The History of the Blues: The Roots, the Music, the People.* New York: Hyperion, 1995.

Dixon, Robert M. W., and John Godrich. *Recording the Blues.* New York: Stein and Day, 1970. Reprinted in *Yonder Come the Blues*, edited by Paul Oliver. Cambridge: Cambridge University Press, 2001.

Dixon, Robert M. W., John Godrich, and Howard Rye. *Blues & Gospel Records, 1890–1943.* Fourth Edition. Oxford: Clarendon Press, 1997.

Filene, Benjamin. *Romancing the Folk: Public Memory and American Roots Music.* Chapel Hill: University of North Carolina Press, 2000.

Hentoff, Nat. "The Playboy Interview." In *Bob Dylan: A Retrospective*, edited by Craig McGregor. New York: William Morrow, 1972.

Heylin, Clinton. *Dylan's Daemon Lover: The Tangled Tale of a 450-Year-Old Pop Ballad.* London: Helter Skelter, 1999.

King, B. B. Foreword to *Moanin' at Midnight: The Life and Times of Howlin' Wolf*, by James Segrest and Mark Hoffman. New York: Pantheon, 2004.

Kingsbury, Paul, ed. *The Encyclopedia of Country Music.* New York: Oxford University Press, 1998.

Lomax, Alan. *The Land Where the Blues Began.* New York: Pantheon, 1993.

———. "Music in Your Own Back Yard." *The American Girl*, October 1940. Reprinted in *Alan Lomax: Selected Writings, 1934–1997*, edited by Ronald D. Cohen. New York: Routledge, 2003.

Lomax, John A., and Alan Lomax. *American Ballads and Folk Songs.* New York: Macmillan, 1934.

———, eds. *Negro Folk Songs as Sung by Lead Belly.* New York: Macmillan, 1936.

Malone, Bill C. *Country Music, U.S.A.* Rev. ed. Austin: University of Texas Press, 1985.

———. *Singing Cowboys and Musical Mountaineers: Southern Culture and the Roots of Country Music.* Athens: University of Georgia Press, 1993.

———. "The South and Country Music." In *The Encyclopedia of Country Music*, edited by Paul Kingsbury. New York: Oxford University Press, 1998, 529–31.

Mann, Woody. *The Anthology of Blues Guitar.* New York: Oak Publications, 1993.

Meade, Guthrie T., Jr., with Dick Spottswood and Douglas S. Meade. *Country Music Sources: A Biblio-Discography of Commercially Recorded Traditional Music.* Chapel Hill: Southern Folklife Collection, 2002.

Obrecht, Jas. "Mississippi John Hurt." www.mindspring.com/~dennist/mjhjas.htm.

O'Brien, Geoffrey. *Sonata for Jukebox: Pop Music, Memory, and the Imagined Life.* New York: Counterpoint, 2004.

Odum, Howard W., and Guy B. Johnson. *The Negro and His Songs: A Study of Typical Negro Songs in the South.* Chapel Hill: University of North Carolina Press, 1925.

"The Old American Dance" (unsigned editorial), *Dearborn Independent,* December 12, 1925, p. 11.

Oliver, Paul. *Songsters and Saints: Vocal Traditions on Race Records.* Cambridge: Cambridge University Press, 1984.

Orvell, Miles. *The Real Thing: Imitation and Authenticity in American Culture, 1880–1940.* Chapel Hill: University of North Carolina Press, 1989.

Place, Jeff, ed. *A Booklet of Essays, Appreciations, and Annotations Pertaining to the Anthology of American Folk Music Edited by Harry Smith.* Washington, DC: Smithsonian Folkways Recordings, 1997.

Porterfield, Nolan. *Jimmie Rodgers: The Life and Times of America's Blue Yodeler.* Urbana: University of Illinois Press, 1979.

———. *Last Cavalier: The Life and Times of John A. Lomax, 1867–1948.* Urbana: University of Illinois Press, 1996.

Russell, Tony. *Blacks, Whites, and Blues.* New York: Stein & Day, 1970. Reprinted in *Yonder Come the Blues,* edited by Paul Oliver. Cambridge: Cambridge University Press, 2001.

———. *Country Music Records: A Discography, 1921–1942.* New York: Oxford University Press, 2004.

Sante, Luc. "The Birth of the Blues." In *This Is Pop,* edited by Eric Weisbard. Boston: Harvard University Press, 2004, 68–74.

Smith, Harry. *Think of the Self Speaking: Harry Smith—Selected Interviews.* Ed. Rani Singh. Seattle: Elbow/Cityful Press, 1999.

Southern, Eileen. *The Music of Black Americans: A History.* Third Edition, New York: Norton, 1997.

Stewart, Mike. Personal correspondence, 2005.

Sublette, Ned. *Cuba and Its Music: From the First Drums to the Mambo.* Chicago: A Cappella, 2004.

"Those Good Old Songs" (unsigned editorial), *Dearborn Independent,* July 17, 1926, p. 11.

Titon, Jeff Todd. "Reconstructing the Blues: Reflections on the 1960s Blues Revival." In *Transforming Tradition: Folk Music Revivals Examined,* edited by Neil V. Rosenberg. Urbana: University of Illinois Press, 1993.

Tosches, Nick. *Country: The Twisted Roots of Rock 'n' Roll.* New York: Da Capo Press, 1996.

————. *Where Dead Voices Gather.* New York: Little, Brown, 2001.

Wald, Elijah. *Escaping the Delta: Robert Johnson and the Invention of the Blues.* New York: Amistad, 2004.

————. Personal correspondence, 2004.

Whisnant, David E. *All That Is Native and Fine: The Politics of Culture in an American Region.* Chapel Hill: University of North Carolina Press, 1983.

Wolfe, Charles. *The Devil's Box: Masters of Southern Fiddling.* Nashville: Country Music Foundation Press, 1997.

————. "A Lighter Shade of Blue: White Country Blues." In *Nothing But the Blues: The Music and the Musicians,* edited by Lawrence Cohn. New York: Abbeville Press, 1993, 233–64.

Wondrich, David. *Stomp and Swerve: American Music Gets Hot, 1843–1924.* Chicago: A Cappella, 2003.

Chapter 3: T.B. BLUES

Calt, Stephen. Personal correspondence, 2005.

Davis, Francis. *The History of the Blues: The Roots, the Music, the People.* New York: Hyperion, 1995.

Dixon, Robert M. W., John Godrich, and Howard Rye. *Blues & Gospel Records, 1890–1943.* Fourth Edition. Oxford: Clarendon Press, 1997.

Garon, Paul, and Beth Garon. *Woman with Guitar: Memphis Minnie's Blues.* New York: Da Capo Press, 1992.

Guthrie, Woody. *Bound for Glory.* New York: Dutton, 1943.

Klein, Joe. *Woody Guthrie: A Life.* New York: Knopf, 1980.

Malone, Bill C. *Country Music, U.S.A.* Rev. ed. Austin: University of Texas Press, 1985.

Monge, Luigi. "Blindness Blues: Visual References in the Lyrics of Blind Pre-war Blues and Gospel Musicians." In *The Lyrics in African American Popular Music,* edited by Robert Springer. Bern: Peter Lang, 2001.

Oliver, Paul. *Blues Fell This Morning: The Meaning of the Blues.* London: Cassell, 1960.

Peer, Ralph. "Ralph Peer Remembers Jimmie Rodgers." *Meridian Star,* May 26, 1953.

Porterfield, Nolan. *Jimmie Rodgers: The Life and Times of America's Blue Yodeler.* Urbana: University of Illinois Press, 1979.

Russell, Tony. *Country Music Records: A Discography, 1921–1942.* New York: Oxford University Press, 2004.

———. Personal correspondence, 2004.

Smith, Chris. Correspondence to the Pre-War Blues Yahoo Group, 2005.

Wald, Elijah. Personal correspondence, 2004.

Yagoda, Ben. *Will Rogers: A Biography.* New York: Alfred A. Knopf, 1993.

Yronwode, Catherine. Correspondence to the Pre-War Blues Yahoo Group, 2004.

Chapter 4: HEARTBREAK HOTEL

Boussiron, Richard. *Elvis: A Musical Inventory, 1939–55.* York, U.K.: Music Mentor, 2004.

Burke, Ken, and Dan Griffin. *The Blue Moon Boys: The Story of Elvis Presley's Band.* Chicago: Chicago Review Press, 2006.

Charles, Ray, and David Ritz. *Brother Ray: Ray Charles' Own Story.* New York: Dial, 1978.

Dalton, David. *James Dean: The Mutant King.* Rev. ed. New York: St. Martin's, 1983.

Dewitt, Howard A. *Elvis, The Sun Years: The Story of Elvis Presley in the Fifties.* Ann Arbor, MI: Popular Culture, Ink, 1993.

Gillett, Charlie. *The Sound of the City: The Rise of Rock and Roll.* Revised and Expanded Edition. New York: Pantheon, 1984.

Guralnick, Peter. *Last Train to Memphis: The Rise of Elvis Presley.* Boston: Little, Brown, 1994.

————. *Lost Highway: Journeys and Arrivals of American Musicians.* Boston: David R. Godine, 1979.

Guralnick, Peter, and Ernst Jorgensen. *Elvis Day by Day.* New York: Ballantine Books, 1999.

Jorgensen, Ernst. *Elvis Presley, a Life in Music: The Complete Recording Sessions.* New York: St. Martin's Press, 1998.

Keogh, Pamela Clarke. *Elvis Presley: The Man, the Life, the Legend.* New York: Atria Books, 2004.

Marcus, Greil. *Mystery Train: Images of America in Rock 'n' Roll Music.* New York: Dutton, 1976.

Martin, Linda, and Kerry Seagrave. *Anti-Rock: The Opposition to Rock 'n' Roll.* Hamden, CT: Archon Books, 1988.

Mason, Bobbie Ann. *Elvis Presley.* New York: Viking, 2002.

McEwan, Ian. *The Innocent.* New York: Doubleday, 1990.

Meltzer, Richard. *A Whore Just Like the Rest: The Music Writings of Richard Meltzer.* Cambridge, MA: Da Capo Press, 2000.

Middleton, Richard. "All Shook Up: Innovation and Continuity in Elvis Presley's Vocal Style." *Southern Quarterly,* Fall 1979.

Pleasants, Henry. *The Great American Popular Singers: Their Lives, Careers and Art.* New York: Simon & Schuster, 1974.

"The Rock Is Solid," *Time,* November 4, 1957.

Shaw, Arnold. *The Rockin' '50s: The Decade That Transformed the Pop Music Scene.* New York: Hawthorn, 1974.

Titon, Jeff Todd. "Reconstructing the Blues: Reflections on the 1960s Blues Revival." In *Transforming Tradition: Folk Music Revivals Examined,* edited by Neil V. Rosenberg. Urbana: University of Illinois Press, 1993.

Tucker, Stephen. "Rethinking Elvis and the Rockabilly Moment." In *In Search of Elvis: Music, Race, Art, Religion,* edited by Vernon Chadwick. Boulder, CO: Westview Press, 1997.

Chapter 5: SUGAR SUGAR

Amburn, Ellis. *Dark Star: The Roy Orbison Story.* New York: Carol Pub. Group, 1990.

Baker, Glenn A. *Monkeemania: The True Story of the Monkees.* New York: St. Martin's, 1986.

Coleman, Ray. *Lennon: The Definitive Biography.* New York: Harper Paperbacks, 1992.

Hinton, Brian. *Country Roads: How Country Came to Nashville.* London: Sanctuary Publishing, 2000.

Lefcowitz, Eric. *The Monkees' Tale.* San Francisco: Last Gasp, 1985.

Lindgren, Hugo. "Cranking the Volume to 11, Just Like Their Heroes." *New York Times,* Sept. 7, 2003.

Marsh, Dave. *The Heart of Rock & Soul: The 1001 Greatest Singles Ever Made.* New York: Da Capo Press, 1999.

Schaffner, Nicholas. *The Beatles Forever.* New York: McGraw Hill, 1978.

Viglione, Joe. Interview with Victor "Moulty" Moulton, *Discoveries,* July 1998.

Wenner, Jann S. *Lennon Remembers.* New ed. New York: Da Capo Press, 2000.

Chapter 6: TONIGHT'S THE NIGHT

Bordowitz, Hank. *Billy Joel: The Life and Times of an Angry Young Man.* New York: Billboard Books, 2005.

Jarrett, Keith. Interview in *New York Times,* Sept. 18, 2005, B4.

McDonough, Jimmy. *Shakey: Neil Young's Biography.* New York: Random House, 2002.

Chapter 7: LOVE TO LOVE YOU BABY

Bussy, Pascal. *Kraftwerk: Man, Machine and Music.* London: SAF Publishing, 1993.

Jones, Alan, and Jussi Kantonen. *Saturday Night Forever: The Story of Disco.* Chicago: Chicago Review Press, 2000.

Mackinnon, Angus. Interview with Giorgio Moroder. *New Musical Express,* December 1978.

Sanneh, Kelefa. "The Rap Against Rockism." *New York Times,* October 31, 2004.

Shapiro, Peter. *Turn the Beat Around: The Secret History of Disco.* London: Faber & Faber, 2005.

Summer, Donna, with Marc Eliot. *Ordinary Girl: The Journey.* New York: Villard, 2003.

Chapter 8: PUBLIC IMAGE

Erlewine, Stephen Thomas. Entry on the Replacements' *Pleased to Meet Me.* www.allmusic.com.

Lydon, John, with Keith Zimmerman and Kent Zimmerman. *Rotten: No Irish, No Blacks, No Dogs: The Authorised Autobiography, Johnny Rotten of the Sex Pistols.* London: Hodder & Stoughton, 1994.

Public Image Web site: www.fodderstompf.com.

Savage, Jon. *England's Dreaming.* London: Faber & Faber, 1991.

Vaneigem, Raoul. *The Revolution of Everyday Life.* London: Rebel Press, 1983.

Wahl, Greg. "Punk Simulation and Parody: The Erasure of 'Generation X.' " Essay posted on Web, 1995 (no longer available).

Chapter 9: ¿Y TÚ, QUÉ HAS HECHO?

Arcos, Betto. Interview with Ry Cooder. Pacifica Radio, June 27, 2000.

Church, Michael. "The BBC's Growing Debasement of World Music." *Independent,* February 28, 2005.

Eyre, Banning, and Sean Barlow. Interview with Salif Keita. www.afropop.org, September 2002.

Hoskyns, Barney. *Hotel California.* London: Fourth Estate, 2005.

Richardson, Derk. Interview with Ry Cooder. *San Francisco Chronicle*, June 23, 2005.

Shorter, Matthew. Matthew's Blog. www.fly.co.uk/matthew, February 28, 2005.

Sublette, Ned. Personal correspondence, 2005.

Chapter 10: PLAY

Drummond, Bill. *45*. London: Abacus, 2001.

Nowinski, Amanda. "Play Time for Moby." *Metro Newspaper*, May 27, 1999.

Peisner, David. Interview with Moby. www.well-rounded.com.

Smith, L. C. Interview with Moby. *MBA Jungle Magazine*, May 15, 2003.

Smith, Tod. "Putumayo: The Place Where the Traditional and the Contemporary Meet." www.allaboutjazz.com, January 2005.

Weidenbaum, Marc. "Play Boy." *Disquiet: Ambient Electronica*, 1999.

INDEX

Page numbers in *italics* refer to illustrations.